JONATHAN ALLSOPP

THIS THING OF OURS

TWENTY YEARS ON

A YEAR IN THE LIFE OF FAN-OWNED FC UNITED

First published by Pitch Publishing, 2025

1

Pitch Publishing
9 Donnington Park,
85 Birdham Road,
Chichester, West Sussex,
PO20 7AJ
www.pitchpublishing.co.uk
info@pitchpublishing.co.uk

A CIP catalogue record is available for this book
from the British Library.

ISBN 978 1 83680 137 5

Typesetting and origination by Pitch Publishing

Printed and bound on FSC® certified paper in line with
our continuing commitment to ethical business practices,
sustainability and the environment.

Printed and bound in India by Thomson Press

THIS THING OF OURS

Contents

I thought love was standing on the Stretford End,

Thought no other love could ever be,

Glazers out to get me,

That's the way it seemed,

Disappointment haunted all my dreams,

Then I saw FC,

Now I'm a believer,

Not a trace of doubt in my mind,

I'm in love,

I'm at FC yeah,

I couldn't leave here if I tried ...

An FC United song sung to the tune of
'I'm a Believer'

Introduction

'SO WHEN it gets to the height of winter and you're standing in grounds without cover getting very wet watching mediocre football, will you regret this?'

'No, I'll just get a big coat.'

Sky reporter Gary Cotterill's enquiry to an FC United of Manchester supporter prior to the new club's second match, a summer 2005 friendly at AFC Wimbledon, the fellow fan-owned club who provided so much help and inspiration for FC in those early days, was typical of the scepticism, at the time, about the longevity of the 'punk' football club established by Manchester United fans following the hostile takeover of United by Malcolm Glazer in May 2005.

Many reckoned the protest would soon fizzle out and it would 'all be over by Christmas'. Why would glory-hunting 'Man U' fans leave Old Trafford to watch tenth-tier football? Two decades earlier a *Sunday Times* editorial had referred to football as 'a slum sport ... increasingly watched by slum people' and fans couldn't even be trusted to behave themselves inside grounds, so how on earth, a few years later, were they going to own and run a club?

But the succinct reply hinted that the hundreds of supporters who'd left to form our own football club were in it for the long haul. Imbued with the radical spirit of the city of Peterloo, Marx, Engels and the Suffragettes, there was defiance against the increasing commercialisation of the game we love that was being rammed down our throats. The formation of FC was a two-fingered salute to the excess and greed that culminated in the Glazer takeover. We didn't have to meekly accept it – there was a better way for football. Our club, our rules. In August 2024 that club began its 20th season.

FC United's founding manifesto was clear that it was here for the long haul, referring to 'ambitious and long-term plans', stating that 'above all we want to be seen as a good example of how a club can be run in the interests of its members and be of benefit to its local communities' and that 'we are a relatively new club and will require patience in order to reach our goals'. Ah, patience, that thing all football fans are renowned for.

The manifesto set out seven core principles that would frame how the club would operate: having a board democratically elected by the club's members; members taking decisions on a 'one member, one vote' basis; keeping admission prices as affordable as possible; developing strong links with the local community and trying 'to be accessible to all, discriminating against none'; striving, wherever possible 'to avoid outright commercialism'; encouraging young, local participation – playing and supporting – whenever possible; and being a non-profit organisation.

Over the last two decades it's been difficult to imagine a greater contrast between the owners of Manchester's two red-shirted football clubs who bear the name 'United': one a family who are distant, devoid of any emotional connection to the club they own and intent on squeezing every last pound from a huge global brand; the other the club's own supporters determined to preserve this thing of ours and ensure it strengthens its community. One a club where supporters are bottom of the pile versus the other where supporters' interests are its cornerstone.

While a red thread connects the two clubs – FC fans sing a song that refers to 'two Uniteds but the soul is one' – they occupy distant corners of the football universe. If a club's annual revenue was received in equal instalments across the calendar year, then by sunset on New Year's Day Manchester United would already have earned the amount of revenue that it takes FC United a full year to generate.

Much has been made of new Manchester United co-owner Jim Ratcliffe's Failsworth roots but in 2023/24 more than 800 people with a Manchester postcode co-owned a local football club and have been doing so for years – so Failsworth Jim's hardly a trendsetter. And more than 100 of those co-owners live in the north Manchester communities of Moston, Newton Heath, Collyhurst, Miles Platting, Harpurhey and Blackley, which contain some of the most deprived neighbourhoods in England – probably not typical of areas where you'd expect to find a cluster of football club owners.

Certainly not those in the world of television advertising anyway. For several weeks in the spring of 2024 the faces of the Hollywood actors Ryan Reynolds and Rob McElhenney gazed down from a billboard along the busy Queen's Road in north Manchester in an advert for the third season of the Disney+ *Welcome to Wrexham* documentary about Wrexham FC. The modern obsession with celebrity means that the Hollywood takeover of the formerly fan-owned Wrexham – whose fans viewed supporter ownership as a handicap rather than a strength and voted to relinquish control of their club – is tailor-made to generate interest.

But only a couple of miles away in Moston the underdog story of FC United slips quietly under the radar. Only nine years ago a crowd of more than 2,000 had watched FC

United and Wrexham draw 1-1 at Broadhurst Park in the Supporters Direct Cup, an annual competition that celebrates supporter ownership. The two clubs are now poles apart, not only in terms of their ownership and league position but also in the attention lavished upon them (or not) by the media.

There was a time when it looked like FC United might make it into the Football League after winning promotion in each of its first three seasons – but it took us seven seasons to make the next step up to the National League. For some this was viewed as a period of stagnation but, if nothing else, it proved that the club was here to stay. Its focus shifted from being an anti-Glazer protest vehicle to securing a home of our own in Manchester which culminated in the opening of our own ground at Broadhurst Park in Moston in 2015 – the first new ground in England to be built by a supporter-owned club – and its £6.5m cost was financed by more than £2m of community shares purchased by FC United members.

But the arrival of a ten-year-old semi-professional club in a working-class community in north Manchester felt strangely out of kilter with how football clubs usually develop. Many English clubs were formed in the late 19th and early 20th centuries to provide a form of recreation – playing or watching – for their local communities, and grew organically. FC United, in contrast, had been conceived in a Manchester curry house but had spent a decade growing elsewhere and had arrived in Moston as an almost fully formed club looking to put down roots in north Manchester.

Not everyone was happy. Some residents claimed that building a football stadium in Moston would bring traffic chaos, destroy valuable green space and lower house prices, and when the council invited feedback from locals on the plans for the ground it received around 1,000 letters of objection. But more than 5,600 people sent letters of support.

Promotion to National League North eventually came in 2015 and it looked like it might be a springboard for further success on the pitch. But the reality of managing a multimillion-pound community asset and a £1m turnover business together with the debt incurred in the building of the ground (and, yes, the irony of being the supporters who had protested against the Glazers' debt-laden takeover of Manchester United was not lost on us) meant that we could no longer 'wing it' as we had tended to do in our early years as tenants at Gigg Lane.

We were now in charge of something that had to be run professionally and this led to a tumultuous struggle for the soul of the club in 2016 – well documented by John-Paul O'Neill in his 2017 book *Red Rebels: The Glazers and the FC Revolution* – which eventually led to the election of a new board committed to openness and transparency and greater participation by co-owners in the running of their club.

FC United found it difficult to compete in our four seasons in National League North and were relegated back to the Northern Premier League in 2019 where we've remained. With fan ownership comes a caution that prioritises the long-term sustainability of the club over boom-or-bust bids for promotion. There is no wealthy backer ready to pump money into the club to chase promotion or avoid relegation – it's reliant instead on the collective strength of more than 2,000 co-owners.

The misconception that FC United are minted is a common one and you can understand why – we are the biggest football club of its kind in England with co-owners from 45 countries across the world, average crowds that are more than double those of most clubs in the same league and a social media following that rivals that of many clubs in the EFL. Yet we've perennially struggled to find sponsors and are firmly in the bottom half of the league when it comes to how much we're able to pay our players.

With this financial caution, some have questioned whether, stripped of our 'punk football' rebelliousness, FC United has become 'just another football club'. I guess the answer to this question partly depends on how you define a football club in the first place. If you're chiefly interested in what happens on the pitch, then, aside from not having a sponsor's name plastered on the front of our shirts and regularly attracting crowds that wouldn't look out of place in the EFL, there's probably little to distinguish us from most other clubs in the seventh tier of English football. And our mid-table berth in the Northern Premier League hardly screams success. But off the pitch, whether in the stands, the boardroom, the bar or in its day-to-day operation, the club is a remarkably different beast to most other football clubs.

There are more than 1,000 football clubs in the top ten tiers of the English football pyramid and, according to the Football Supporters' Association (FSA), in August 2024 only 37 of them (less than four per cent) are supporter-owned. Within those clubs the extent of supporter ownership varies – Exeter City and AFC Wimbledon, the only two in the EFL, are both majority owned by their supporters' trust – but some are 100 per cent supporter-owned like FC United which is the largest fully fan-owned club in the country by number of co-owners.

Being a democratically run football club wholly owned by more than 2,000 fans means that, as one former board member put it, 'Every mistake or misjudgement is scrutinised by supporters on the terraces, in the bars and on the internet and while this can be uncomfortable at times it's in learning from these mistakes that the club grows and continues to demonstrate its founding principles as a community-owned football club.' With the democratic one member, one vote structure, each co-owner gets an opportunity to have their say on how the club is run and ensure that it remains true to its founding principles.

But how does this work in practice? How does a football club wholly owned by its supporters survive and flourish in an age when footballing success is increasingly dependent on money? Since 2016 I've attended and reported on more than 80 monthly board meetings at FC United in my capacity as volunteer board reporter – a role that exists at very few football clubs – and gained a unique insight into how the club works.

This book therefore offers a boardroom and terrace perspective on the day-to-day life of FC United through the 2023/24 year – from July 2023 to June 2024 – and gets under the skin of what it's like for a group of supporters to own and run their very own club in the midst of a cost of living crisis and at a time when its continued existence was being questioned as the Glazer family began to loosen its grip on Manchester United. From the shock departure of the club's CEO right at the beginning of the year, a power cut in Poland, the loss of a major sponsor after a *Panorama* investigation, a new signing who left the club within minutes of being announced, a points deduction to a European trophy on the shores of Lake Garda and another one in Rochdale, it's all here.

Jonathan Allsopp

Please note that whilst most of this book was written contemporaneously through the 2023/24 year there are occasional passages that reflect on the club's history so the text sometimes switches between present and past tense. I hope it doesn't spoil your enjoyment.

1

From Milan to Nuneaton

IN THE club's early days, having swapped flights to glamorous European ties with Manchester United for bus rides to the mill towns of the North West Counties League, some FC United fans jokingly referred to our temporary home at Gigg Lane in Bury as the 'Stadio del Gigg', complete with its very own Curva Sud. At the time we had no idea that this football club we'd assembled from scratch might one day be playing in a European competition in one of the world's great stadiums. But, incredibly, the 2022/23 season had ended in June with FC playing in the San Siro in Milan in the third-place play-off in the second edition of the Fenix Trophy, a European tournament for non-league clubs whereby FENIX is also an acronym for Friendly, European, Non-professional, Innovative, Xenial. The tournament's aim is to provide a friendly environment for clubs, players and supporters from different countries to come together.

FC, roared on by more than 400 travelling fans, beat Brera 1-0 with a late goal from Matt Van Wyk, who had originally been due to sit a college exam on the day of the match but had decided to postpone it so he didn't miss this once-in-a-lifetime opportunity to play in the San Siro.

For part-time footballers and supporters to get the chance to play and watch their team in one of the world's great stadiums – providing memories to cherish for ever – was something special.

There were some gripes about the state of the toilets, some killjoy stewarding and waiting nearly an hour in the midday sun to get into the ground for an early kick-off – dictated by the need to get the stadium ready for a screening of Inter's Champions League Final against another team from Manchester a few days later – but none of this diminished the sheer joy of seeing the football club you own play at this most iconic of venues.

And the feel-good factor continued throughout the early summer although we weren't quite reaching for the giddy-o-meter just yet. The men's first-team manager Neil Reynolds told the board at its June meeting that he was 'excited for the season ahead' and felt that we had recruited well during the summer and he was grateful for a significantly higher playing budget this year on the back of the increase in commercial revenue last season. We'd finished the previous season in eighth, only five points outside the play-off places, after being deducted three points for fielding too many loan players in a win against Warrington Town, so a tilt at the play-offs wasn't out of the question.

Meanwhile, the women's team manager James Mulvihill had spoken well at the club's general meeting in May at the end of a season in which he had led the women's team to promotion to the National League Division One North in the fourth tier of the women's game. So it was a double shock when, in the last week of June, James resigned and then, a week later the club's chief executive officer, Natalie Atkinson, also announced she was leaving. The timing, as both men's and women's teams began their pre-season preparations, couldn't have been worse.

'It's a decision that I have made for me and my family,' said Natalie, who added she was 'happy and proud' with what she had achieved since joining the club in February 2022 – in particular in 'driving the vision and business plan, reviewing the club's structure with the introduction of revenue-raising roles, and building a cohesive community programme'.

Natalie had overseen a threefold increase in income from sponsorship and advertising in 2022/23, which had allowed the club to increase its playing budget for the coming season, but the review of the club's structure and the introduction of revenue generating roles wasn't to everyone's liking.

In August 2022, six months into her time at the club and shortly after Frances Fielding and Rachel Hughes had also joined FC as commercial manager and events and hospitality manager respectively, an FC fan had tweeted that 'punk football is what we signed up for but all I can see is poundshop corporate football' with 'highly paid twats in "leadership" roles'.

Meanwhile, around the same time, a co-owner emailed Natalie to point out that 'with the salaries of yourself, the manager, commercial manager, events and hospitality manager, health and safety officer … it's no wonder the club is haemorrhaging money … We are trying to be a Premier League club on NPL money. It's an absolute disgrace. This is not what my club is about.' All this at a football club that proudly speaks of 'making friends not millionaires' and that many of its fans refer to as an 'FC family'.

You could see why one former board member had wondered if FC United is actually ungovernable given the volatile mix of sport, business and politics at play – the need to marry the raw, unfiltered emotion that comes with being a football supporter with the often hard-headed approach required to run a successful business while still maintaining that all-important link back to the club's founding ideology.

Board chair Dave Ashurst thanked Natalie, on behalf of the board, for leaving the club in 'a better place than it was when she joined us'. But the statement stopped short of offering the usual 'welcome back at the club any time' message that had accompanied the resignations of senior staff members in the past. Meanwhile, an interim leadership team consisting of commercial manager Danny Davis, financial controller Steve Durrands and first-team manager Neil Reynolds took over while the club looked for a new CEO.

Although one of the early responses by fans to the news of Natalie's departure referred to it as 'catastrophic news', overall it received a measured response and a general recognition that, while her departure was disappointing, Natalie's hard work, together with that of senior staff and committee members, had given the club a solid platform from which to move forward.

The committee structure had been launched in 2022 to encourage co-owners with particular skills and experience to support the club across six key areas – commercial, communications, community, co-ownership, football, finance and risk – with delegated authority from the board. The committees mostly meet online – and most work can be done remotely – so it gave everyone a chance to get involved, even those who live miles away from Manchester.

With the support of the committees and the likes of Danny, Steve and Neil, all experienced managers, able to step in while the club looked for a replacement CEO, there was acknowledgement too that the club was better able to cope with a high-profile departure such as this than it would have been a year ago.

Natalie's tenure as CEO at FC United was similar to her previous senior roles at other clubs having left her first CEO role at Curzon Ashton after 18 months to join Southport where she was CEO for little over a year before leaving to 'pursue a fresh challenge', which turned out to be as managing director at Oldham Athletic where she worked from June 2019 to September 2020. There's something of a pattern of only staying at clubs for a year to 18 months.

But FC United was meant to be different wasn't it? When she joined in February 2022 Natalie described it as 'like coming home' and, shortly after, at a Q&A session with supporters she remarked that in joining FC she had found a football club that matched her own values. Natalie had been involved in the building of FC's Broadhurst Park ground during her time at the Manchester Football Association so the club was, she said, 'close to my heart'.

James Mulvihill's resignation a week earlier was announced unexpectedly on the club's women's team's official Twitter account with a quote from James which said, 'I have loved every minute I have spent at FC. The girls have been a pleasure to coach and the fans have been amazing,' but he added, 'It has become impossible to continue without the proper support needed to carry out my role effectively.' As one of the early responses to this news on the members' forum put it, 'That's quite a quote from an official FC account.'

The board, like everyone else, were taken by surprise by this announcement and Warren Heppolette said that he was 'extremely disappointed in today's events and incredibly sorry to see James go' and offered some background to

James's decision. Warren explained that James had been seeking several changes to ensure the women's team and staff were supported to succeed in a higher division next season – including the reimbursement of expenses and allocation of any cup prize money – and the board had agreed to these changes at its latest board meeting the night before his resignation.

Two weeks later Mulvihill was named as the new manager of Wythenshawe FC's women's team, who had recently announced that, along with their newly promoted men's team, they were set to become semi-professional for the 2023/24 season – a huge step forward for a club competing in the women's North West Regional League, two levels below FC United.

It followed the appointment of Sacha Lord, then Greater Manchester's night-time economy adviser, as the club's chair in April, and his new investment and the subsequent dropping of the word 'amateurs' from the club's name (they were previously known as Wythenshawe Amateurs) signalled their ambition.

Shortly after, several of FC's women's team chose to follow Mulvihill to Wythenshawe including our longest-serving player and club legend Kirsty Chambers. It's not unusual for this to happen in the women's game but the departure of the manager and a substantial number of players at this stage of the summer inevitably had a serious impact on the women's team's pre-season preparations, resulting in the postponement of some pre-season games.

FC struggled to field a women's team at Clapton CFC on 15 July in the Supporters Direct Shield, an annual celebration of supporter-owned football which also involved a men's game between the two clubs. A depleted FC side lost 3-1 in east London – quite a contrast to the women's team's 9-0 victory over Clapton in another double header at Broadhurst Park two years before. There was also some reputational damage to the club which initially made it difficult for us to recruit a new manager and new players.

In unrelated news, while James Mulvihill had spoken of being a 'successful businessman', it emerged, after he'd left FC, that he had, in fact, been disqualified from being a company director for seven years from July 2020 for conduct during his time as the director of a company which went into liquidation in 2018. And later on, Mulvihill's new boss, Sacha Lord, was also under investigation as the *Manchester Mill* published a story in May 2024 which revealed that Primary Events Solutions, a company owned by Lord, grossly misled Arts Council England in obtaining more than £400,000 of public money during the pandemic.

* * *

The men's team's pre-season campaign was described as 'the most enjoyable in years' by FCUM Radio and included an impressive 4-1 win against Altrincham, from the National League. Afterwards Neil Reynolds mentioned how a significantly bigger football budget for the coming season had enabled him and assistant manager Brian Richardson to strengthen the squad with an exciting crop of young players – a squad of 22 players with an average age of less than 23. Although only one of those players, Jan Palinkas, comes from the club's academy and, sadly, another academy graduate, Sandro Da Costa, who lit up the San Siro in June with his exciting wing play, was signed by Salford City over the summer.

Neil's outlook, and the mood around the club, was considerably more upbeat than this time last year when there was some uncertainty around the playing budget which resulted in us appealing to supporters to 'Boost the Budget' through a crowdfunder which ultimately, and unsurprisingly in the midst of a cost of greed crisis, failed to hit its target by some distance.

It demonstrates that all-important connection between what we're doing off the pitch to drive revenue from sponsorship, advertising, events and hospitality and what happens on it. It might sound like a tired old cliche when we read that 'football is the engine that drives everything we do' in the business plan – but it's true. This increase in the football budget has not come about through a fabulously wealthy owner pumping tens of thousands of pounds more into their club to 'buy' a promotion push but is the carefully planned product of weeks of graft by dozens of staff and volunteers – and by the club's owners, who outlined our priorities for the club over the next few years in a members' survey in 2021.

Arguably, the highlight of pre-season came in the penultimate friendly with a 5-0 thrashing of Nuneaton Borough, although the game was also notable for a mass brawl, just before half-time, after a Nuneaton player thumped an FC player and should have been sent off. Adrian Seddon, a former board member and chair and now FC's volunteer matchday secretary, went to see the referee at half-time and the Nuneaton manager agreed to withdraw the offending player in the second half but refused to voluntarily go down to ten men as he reckoned that FC had played so well in the first half that a depleted team would have 'no chance' of getting back into the match. This was a team that had narrowly missed out on promotion to National League North only a few months earlier.

* * *

Ahead of the 2023/24 year, two new non-executives – Bhavna Mistry and Gemma Avery – joined the board and, arguably, they were as important as any new additions to the men's and women's squads. It stemmed from a recognition that, with the club's business plan built on driving commercial revenue, the board lacked commercial expertise, so it had sought to remedy that by seeking to recruit a non-executive director with a strong commercial background. The club's rules, which allow for up to seven board members, permit the board to fill 'casual vacancies' arising from the retirement or removal of board members.

Both Bhavna and Gemma applied and the board decided that they would both make excellent additions as Bhavna has a strong commercial background and was an executive director for a multinational company until shortly before joining FC while Gemma is a specialist in communications and marketing who has previously worked in football-based marketing roles. So they were both offered non-executive roles and joined the board in June, with Bhavna becoming the board lead for commercial activities and Gemma leading on communications and marketing.

* * *

At July's meeting the board learned that a local company, brought in to review the club's usage of gas and electricity, discovered that, unbeknown to anyone at the club, there are solar panels on the roof of our Broadhurst Park ground and it appears that we have been making a significant contribution to the national grid over the last eight years – not to mention Manchester's bid to become a zero carbon city by 2038 – without receiving a penny or using any of this power for the club's own purposes. It appeared that the solar panels were originally installed to power the club's boilers but this had not happened. Although with all the hot air generated at FC you'd question whether solar panels would be needed at all.

There is a possibility of us being able to use the power generated by the solar panels and thus make a significant saving on our future energy bills but the board and management team were keen to avoid making any assumptions until we know more. We're not quite ready to go full-on Forest Green Rovers just yet.

2

We've not got millions of pounds to throw at it

FC UNITED'S seasons in the Northern Premier League have generally begun sluggishly and with the fixture computer generating early visits from recently promoted Worksop Town and Macclesfield, two sides who won their leagues at a canter last season, it appeared unlikely that this season was going to be any different. While Macclesfield were the bookies' favourites to win another title this season, it was expected that Worksop would also be in the mix having won last season's Northern Premier League Division One East title with seven games to go.

But, remarkably, FC won their opening match of the season for the first time since 2012, beating Worksop Town 3-0 in the Moston sunshine with an impressive performance.

This was also the first time we'd ever won at home on the opening day of the season. Goals from Michael Donohue and Max Cane gave FC a 2-0 lead in a first half in which they were the better side and although Worksop came back strongly in the second half, a goal from substitute Nic Bollado, beating the offside trap in the 90th minute, wrapped up a comfortable victory.

It was our first match against the Nottinghamshire side since 2014 when, like FC, they were beaten in the play-off semi-finals and missed out on promotion to Conference North. They'd spent heavily on players' wages that season in an attempt to win promotion but ultimately were unsuccessful, and when owner Jason Clark declared that he would no longer carry on funding the club it precipitated a financial crisis that led to Worksop's resignation from the Northern Premier League and saw them join the Northern Counties East League, at the ninth level of the pyramid, for the start of the 2014/15 season.

In 2018 a group including local businessman Paul Tomkins took over the club and in an interview with the *Worksop Guardian* the new owners described themselves as 'not like sugar daddy football owners, we've not got millions of pounds to throw at it', stating their intention to make Worksop self-sustaining.

The FC United players wore the new home shirt which incorporates the names of more than 1,000 co-owners into its design to show the club's appreciation for their ongoing support, particularly through the pandemic and the cost of living crisis.

It was the idea of one of the co-owners and was chosen as the preferred design for the 2023/24 home shirt – from a shortlist of four designs – at last November's annual general meeting.

Although, not everyone was happy with the new design. One supporter, detecting a whiff of commercialism, wrote simply, 'putting names on shirts to flog a few more … ummm'. We're a democratically run football club and everyone's entitled to their own opinion about how the club is run but, sadly, comments like these serve little purpose other than shit-stirring.

After the match a delighted Neil Reynolds, who had been like a kid on Christmas Eve the day before, remarked on the feeling of togetherness across the club right now – not only apparent on the pitch but off it too with the interim leadership team, supported by the volunteer-run committees, stepping up to keep FC ticking over at a difficult time following the departure of the CEO.

Little did we know, however, that this would turn out to be the high point of our men's team's league campaign – our highest league position and the only time all season that we ended a match with a positive goal difference.

This fixture also saw the introduction of red recyclable paper cups – bearing FC's badge and the Joseph Holt's brewery logo – at the bars around the ground. Members had voted in favour of a motion at the general meeting in June 2022 that the club should stop using single-use plastic glasses and the club had originally planned to do this during the 2022/23 season. It's part of the club's commitment to reduce its carbon footprint 'where possible' including travel and food and drink provision and a reduction in the use of plastic. Although, given the number of flights to Europe in the Fenix Trophy over the past few seasons, it's likely that FC's carbon footprint is larger than most clubs at this level of football.

* * *

The Worksop match also marked the start of another season for FC's regular pre-match 'Course You Can Malcolm' event. The club's long-standing mantra that it's 'doing things differently' often feels like a done-to-death Mancunian cliche but CYCM is something that's unique in British, if not European, football and is one of the most unusual cultural events in a music-mad city.

It began in 2007 when co-owner Robert Brady, recognising the need to re-energise matchdays, submitted a proposal to the board – written in the rambling style, familiar to readers of his 'Manchester is sausage-shaped' column in the Manchester United fanzine *United We Stand* – for a pre-match event 'combining football, beer and not-so-popular music' that was to be run by supporters and would take place in Starkey's Bar, a function room in a corner of Bury FC's Gigg Lane ground where FC played most of its home matches up until 2014. He called the event 'Course You Can Malcolm', a line borrowed from a 1970s television advert for Vicks nasal spray but also a nod to the Glazer takeover. 'So you thought we couldn't form a football club? Course you can Malcolm.'

The idea was that a local band or solo artist (typically unsigned by a record label) or comedian, poet or other act would perform for free in front of a very different audience and at a different time of day from what they were used to.

And this would be accompanied by local beers and food with all the money raised going to the club. It quickly became a much-loved part of many supporters' matchdays at a time when many of us were beginning to tire of trekking to Bury on a Saturday afternoon. CYCM gave us a reason to get there early and bag a seat in Starkey's which had a capacity of 80 and was invariably full.

But it wasn't everyone's cup of Bovril. Some fans baulked at the idea of bands and poets in a football ground, as it wasn't 'football', but Brady had anticipated this in his proposal to the board in which he memorably wrote, 'Anyone who knows anything about football knows that football is not about football. Anyone who does not know that knows nothing about football.'

There was also a ragged trousered-ish notion that culture wasn't for 'the likes of us' working-class football supporters – that it was all a bit 'arty-farty' – but Brady, who was a bricklayer, and other CYCM volunteers, including railway workers and an electrician, recognised the power of arts and culture to warm hearts and broaden horizons. CYCM was born of a recognition that there are some of us who prefer our weekly football fix accompanied by something more substantial than cheap lager, saturated fat, fixed-odds coupons and gawping at a big screen.

Over several seasons at Gigg Lane there were highlights galore with appearances by the likes of Slow Readers Club, the Eccentronic Research Council (featuring actor Maxine Peake) and Josephine Oniyama – all musicians I later paid to watch at much bigger venues. One of Manchester's most mysterious bands, WU LYF, appeared on David Letterman's show in the US not long after two members of the band had played an acoustic set at CYCM. The brilliant Gideon Conn, described in one CYCM preview as 'without doubt the most eccentric Mancunian performing on the Manchester circuit', made several appearances and came back to play at Broadhurst Park in 2023. And you could have heard a pin drop in Starkey's as Rebecca Joy Sharp played the harp in possibly the most un-football-like build-up to a football match ever. Yes, a female harpist at a football match.

And we were spellbound as Aziz Ibrahim, formerly of the Stone Roses, played not only before the match but again during a lengthy half-time set that resulted in dozens of us missing the first 15 minutes of the second half. But we didn't care that we'd missed two FC United goals as we'd just seen and heard one of the finest guitarists of his generation in action. There's a lovely photo of Aziz post-gig in front of the 'Manchester – We Are All Immigrants' banner, which is one of many flags regularly on display at CYCM.

Poetry has long been a part of CYCM too. Many years ago Attila the Stockbroker came all the way from Brighton to rant about asylum-seeking Daleks and there was barely a dry eye in Starkey's as Mike Duff read his poem. 'And John Terry Cried', about caring for his terminally ill brother in his final hours while the penalty shoot-out in the 2008 Champions League Final played out on television in the background.

Prestwich poet and FC fan John Darwin told of how CYCM had changed his life: 'I was in a pub near Gigg Lane before a midweek FC United match in 2008 when someone mentioned that CYCM was short of an act for the coming Saturday, so I volunteered to do some of my poetry. Truth was that although I really wanted to be a poet I hadn't written anything for years but I managed to write four poems before Saturday, read them at CYCM and loved it. After that I did other local poetry nights and just carried on from there.' John is now a regular on the northern spoken word circuit and won the award for Best Spoken Word Performance at the Greater Manchester Fringe Festival in 2021.

Later at Gigg Lane, FC United's board, keen to move the club on to a more commercial footing, asked CYCM to raise its beer prices – which had remained unchanged since its inception – but this was resisted by the volunteers who pointed out that there had been no increase in the costs of buying in the beer. And it led to a standoff that became known as 'beergate', and although CYCM continued for the remainder of FC's time at Gigg Lane it wasn't clear if it would still have a place at the new ground in Moston and some volunteers drifted away. The Space Monkeys, the last band to sign for Factory Records, were also the last band to play at CYCM in Bury.

After a two-year hiatus CYCM eventually returned in the summer of 2016 and made its first appearance in the function room at Broadhurst Park. One memorable early edition in Moston featured a pulsating set by the young Mossley post-punk band Cabbage who were hotly tipped by the music press at the time. 'Playing at FC United has galvanised inspiration in me richer than the thousands of records I've sat in awe at in my bedroom growing up,' posted a band member on Facebook after the gig.

Prior to Cabbage's set, the scriptwriter Charlotte Delaney spoke about growing up in Manchester and Salford as the daughter of the groundbreaking Salfordian playwright Shelagh Delaney. Meanwhile, a refugee charity from Buxton collected clothes and other items for Syrian refugees surviving a freezing European winter and a cabbage was raffled off as a prize in a 'guess the weight of the cabbage' competition.

CYCM eventually found a comfier home in the refurbished space under the St Mary's Road End terrace at Broadhurst Park which was officially reopened by ex-United skipper Martin Buchan, who famously led his team to victory in the 1977 FA Cup Final against Liverpool which denied the Scousers a crack at the treble. Off the pitch he developed a reputation as something of an outsider with his preference for reading books and disdain for laddish banter – he was perfect for CYCM.

Not even the Covid lockdown of spring 2020 could deter Malcolmses as it adapted to a strange football-less period by shifting online. Sets of video clips of old and new performances – introduced by compere Simon King – were broadcast on YouTube at the times that FC

United would usually have been kicking off matches, and supporters generously chipped in what they would usually have spent on a matchday to keep the club ticking over at a time when, like most non-league clubs, FC had barely any income coming in.

Simon said that his involvement in these online shows had been 'life-changing' for him as 'filming the skits and links led to me getting back into acting and performing, something I'd not done for over ten years'. He's since gone on to appear on stage at the Hope Mill Theatre in Manchester and is part of an improv troupe that's performed at the Edinburgh Fringe.

So what's the secret of CYCM's success? Andy Davies, who has booked bands and acts for CYCM for many years, reckons that it very much taps into the club's DIY ethos as it's 'created by the fans, for the fans' – we're not passive consumers of a matchday experience created by someone with a spreadsheet, we do it ourselves. 'Bands love it,' says Andy, 'as there's a ready-made audience here, they don't have to worry about selling tickets.' And word gets round from other bands and performers that playing at CYCM is fun. With temporary blackout curtains and stage lighting it feels like a proper gig venue – similar in size to the Castle Hotel in town – and a few musicians have been known to forget it's still the middle of the afternoon and refer to a 'good night'.

CYCM has generally been well received by locals in Moston with many of the bands coming from north Manchester – the likes of Scuttlers from Middleton, the Battery Farm from Moston and Dirty Laces from Failsworth – and Andy recalled that when Dirty Laces played for the first time in 2019 it was the busiest he'd ever seen CYCM as dozens of locals turned up. The Battery

Farm's blistering set of 'doom punk' at CYCM in 2022 was also notable as the Moston punk rockers' set, which received a rapturous reception from the CYCM audience, followed a Q&A session with the club's new CEO Natalie Atkinson in which she had stressed the importance of business planning and commercial strategy. Where else would you find hardcore doom punk and business strategy juxtaposed so magnificently inside a football ground?

When the Honey Drops became the first soul band at CYCM in December 2022, they paused mid-set to ask the audience if they were looking forward to the match, and there were plenty of groans – not because things were that bad on the pitch (for a brief period earlier that season FC United topped the Northern Premier League) but mainly because, more often than not, CYCM is so enjoyable that it can feel like a chore to leave its warm embrace to go and stand on the terraces on a cold, grey afternoon in Moston. Being able to watch talented musicians, writers, comedians, poets and actors perform for free inside a football ground on a Saturday afternoon feels very special indeed. After all, going to the match is about much more than just watching the match, as CYCM's founder observed all those years ago.

* * *

The first midweek match of the season saw a trip to Merseyside to take on Marine in a fixture which provides one of those rare occasions when Mancs and Scousers can congregate in a football ground without the need for segregation.

Marine are a community-focused club and clearly on the up thanks to the windfall from their FA Cup run in the 2020/21 season which saw Tottenham visit the Marine

Travel Arena in the third round in January 2021, when spectators were unable to attend as we were in the midst of another wave of Covid and another lockdown, but it was broadcast live to millions of viewers on the BBC.

To help replace the lost revenue from being forced to play the tie behind closed doors, Marine came up with the innovative idea of selling virtual tickets with the opportunity to win some prizes. The initial intention was to sell out their 3,185 capacity stadium but, in the end, they sold more than 32,000 of the £10 tickets – mostly thanks to the generosity of Spurs fans – and earned more than £500,000 from the cup run which was life-changing for a club then playing in the eighth tier.

This has allowed Marine to invest in their ground and facilities over the last few years and also enabled them to increase their football budget to the extent that they were able to put all of their first-team squad on contracts for the 2023/24 season, which includes a few ex-FC United players such as Chris Doyle and Fin Sinclair-Smith.

On a glorious late summer evening, FC United's defending in the first half resembled Antony Gormley's dozens of life-sized, cast-iron male sculptures that are dotted along nearby Crosby beach and we were 4-0 down by half-time – the first time we'd ever trailed 4-0 at this stage of a game.

As I waited for a half-time pie, three women were nattering away in front of me and, as the queue inched forward, one of them spotted an advert for women's walking football sessions just to the right of the serving hatch. 'We'll have to give that a go, girls, what do you reckon?' 'Yeah, why not, it'll be a laugh that.' In an increasingly click-driven world it's nice to see that old-school advertising still has a place too.

FC were better in the second half and pulled a goal back, but still lost 5-1. Marine finished one place below us in the league last season but looked a decent bet for promotion. The match was watched by a crowd of 1,456 which included probably a couple of hundred from Manchester – it's not often that FC supporters are so outnumbered away from home.

* * *

Later that week FC United appointed Jennie Swarbrick as the new manager of the women's team and also the club's community manager. The latter is a role that we'd been looking to fill for more than a year. It's quite a coup for the club to get a manager of Jennie's calibre – her UEFA A Licence makes her the most qualified football manager at the club – and someone who up until recently was working with Liverpool FC Women and has also been involved in nurturing the talents of several members of the current England squad. She's also the club's first female football manager.

Meanwhile, on the same day, Manchester United issued a statement explaining that the club is still in the process of deciding whether Mason Greenwood – who had faced charges of rape and controlling and coercive behaviour until they were dropped in February 2023 – has a future at the club. This provoked understandable outrage from many United supporters with some threatening to walk away if Greenwood stays and there are some FC United co-owners who feel that the club should speak out on issues like this. There's certainly scope for us to be bolder in how we communicate our support for women's and girl's football and perhaps draw a contrast with events over in M16.

* * *

Our first Saturday away game of the season brought a trip to Stafford – the furthest south that we'd play all season without hopping on the travelators at Manchester airport. The home side were much hungrier in the early stages of the game and they led 2-0 after half an hour before a Luke Griffiths penalty meant we trailed by just one goal at half-time. FC played some good football in the second half and created enough chances to win but ultimately left Marston Road pointless as Stafford Rangers ran out 3-2 winners.

During the match a group of FC supporters unveiled a 'Greenwood Out' banner that provoked a 13-page thread on online forum The Soul is One and again revealed the divergence in supporter opinion regarding our relationship with Manchester United that's persisted throughout our 18-year existence. Some think it's important that we recognise the 'red thread' back to United and offer solidarity with match-going reds at Old Trafford while others think it's time to move on, stop being a 'tribute act' and focus on carving out an identity of our own. Much of this links in with the work that a small group of us are involved in regarding the club's identity and being clearer about who we are and what we stand for.

* * *

The following day Spain beat England 1-0 in the Women's World Cup Final in Australia. The match kicked off at 11am UK time and was watched by dozens of players and fans at Broadhurst Park ahead of the women's team's first match of the season in the women's National League Division One North against Doncaster Rovers Belles, one of the most famous names in women's football having won the Premier League twice in the early 90s.

The kick-off was delayed to give players and supporters the chance to watch the World Cup Final, and when the players eventually took to the field the South Yorkshire side romped to a 7-1 win – perhaps not surprising given the disrupted summer that FC's women's team has endured.

Later the board issued a statement reflecting on a turbulent time for the women's team and acknowledging: 'We had relied too heavily on the former CEO Natalie Atkinson's understanding of the women's football scene,' admitting there was a lack of 'sufficient knowledge and insight to effectively scrutinise this area of the club'. And despite increasing the budget for the women's team for next season, insufficient attention was paid to the wider consequences of moving up a league. It added that it had been 'an invaluable learning experience'.

Ultimately the fallout from James Mulvihill's resignation as women's team manager took a long time to recover from and left us having to build a women's team almost from scratch at a time when we should have been gearing up for a new season at a higher level.

* * *

Much has changed at Ilkeston since FC last played them in 2015, including the liquidation of Ilkeston FC in 2017 and the formation of a new club called Ilkeston Town, which began life in the Midland Football League Division One in the tenth tier. Since then they've been promoted three times and last season played in the Southern Football League before being reallocated to the Northern Premier League for this season. Ownership has changed hands a few times – including a spell from November 2021 to January 2023 when local businessman David Hilton was in control and oversaw extensive improvements to the club's New Manor Ground.

On a lovely late summer evening, the Broadhurst Park pitch looked a picture with an eye-catching circular mowing pattern. And some of FC United's football was similarly easy on the eye as we beat Ilkeston 1-0 in a terrific match against a side that came in with three wins from their first three matches.

As against Worksop we began on the front foot and created plenty of goalscoring opportunities in the first half, although what turned out to be the winning goal, scored by Nic Bollado, came from a defensive error rather than good football. The second half was a much more even contest and we did well to hold on to the lead and secure another three points which is something that we've not done very often in the last couple of seasons.

One of Ilkeston's directors, John Attewell, remarked the following day, '[I] went to Broadhurst Park last night for the first time with Ilkeston. What a superb stadium and welcoming officials. Good team too.' The type of wholesome content that the internet wasn't really invented for.

* * *

In the fallout from the 'Greenwood Out' banner at Stafford, it emerged that an FC United supporter had tweeted sexist abuse at Dr Rachel Broady, a lecturer at Liverpool John Moores University. Spotting that this was coming from an FC fan and well aware of the club's history and values – given she comes from Newton Heath – Dr Broady tweeted that 'it's sad to see @FCUnitedMcr following misogynists who abuse women online'.

Former board chair Adrian Seddon reached out to Dr Broady to apologise on behalf of the club and invite her to a game. It was also heartening to see supporters calling out this behaviour on The Soul is One and challenging the 'supporter' who made the remarks. Speaking on behalf of the board, Warren Heppolette said, 'There can't be any confusion or doubt about where we stand as a club in relation to sexism, women's rights and women in football.'

* * *

By now a common theme had emerged with FC's first three home matches of the season against clubs that had been plunged into financial crisis in the last decade, either forced to resign from their league or, more seriously, going bust and starting again, and Macclesfield, who fall into the latter category, were the visitors on the Saturday of the August bank holiday weekend.

Businessman Rob Smethurst and ex-footballer Robbie Savage resurrected the club after Macclesfield Town were liquidated in September 2020 with debts of over £500,000. They began life again in the North West Counties Premier Division in 2021/22 and after two consecutive promotions now find themselves in the seventh tier and like the phoenix clubs FC Halifax Town and Chester before them, the Silkmen will be keen not to hang around for very long in the Northern Premier League. Smethurst owns the club while Savage is the director of football.

Macclesfield regularly attract attendances of more than 3,000 and with a large crowd expected at Broadhurst Park they were offered an allocation of 850 tickets in a segregated away end and, although they didn't sell them all, the presence of around 600 visiting fans added to the atmosphere on what was a tremendous matchday on and off the pitch.

Ben Hughes's report in the *Non-League Paper* described the match as having a 'real arm-wrestle feel throughout' as momentum shifted from one side to the other. But Luke Griffiths's last-minute penalty gave FC a hard-earned 2-1 win and was just reward for a second half in which they carried a greater goalscoring threat – although we could have done without the five minutes of added time. So far this talented young side have been a joy to watch at Broadhurst Park with a willingness to take more risks in the final third of the pitch than we've seen in recent seasons.

* * *

'Stainton Park has rarely been a happy hunting ground for FC,' read the preview of FC United's bank holiday Monday trip to Radcliffe on the club's website. And that certainly didn't change today as we were steamrollered 5-0 by an impressive Radcliffe who were devastating going forward, with Anthony Dudley scoring a hat-trick. They've now won all their first six league matches of the season – scoring 24 goals in the process – and are six points clear at the top of the table. They'll take some beating on this showing.

While we've got a 100 per cent record so far at 'Fortress Broadhurst', away from home we've conceded 13 goals in three matches, which is worrying, and are 11th in the table with nine points from six matches and a goal difference of minus five.

The match was watched by a crowd of 2,338, the highest for a Radcliffe match at Stainton Park, although the ground record is still held by the crowd of 2,473 who watched FC United beat Castleton Gabriels 3-0 in September 2005. Stainton Park was one of several grounds around Greater Manchester that hosted home matches in FC's early years when Gigg Lane was unavailable.

Fan-owned phoenix club Bury AFC played their home games at Stainton Park for three seasons following their formation in 2020, before a merger with Bury FC and a return to Gigg Lane this season, and this has clearly not done their landlords any harm financially.

* * *

Jennie Swarbrick attended August's board meeting to provide an update on the women's team and also the club's community work only a couple of weeks into her role as community manager. Jennie updated the board that we now have 25 players registered to play for the women's team this season including assistant manager Elsie Baxter.

Earlier this month we didn't have any registered players and Jennie said she's proud of what we've achieved in assembling a squad in such a short space of time and added that we have built relationships with the likes of Burnley and Huddersfield that have enabled us to bring in some players on loan.

On the community side, Jennie highlighted the success of the kids' holiday activity camp – giving children aged seven to 11 years, and in receipt of free school meals, free access to a range of sporting activities including football, cricket and rounders along with food and refreshments – which had run at Broadhurst Park throughout the summer holiday and had been fully booked. She stressed it was all about having some fun in the sun and keeping healthy at the same time.

According to the latest data on exercise levels, only 40 per cent of children and young people across Greater Manchester do the recommended daily average of at least 60 minutes of physical activity with around one third averaging below 30 minutes. And around one in four children across the conurbation leave primary school overweight or obese. Access to green space and activities like this is important.

In addition, the sports camps are a good way of enthusing the next generation of the club's supporters and when Jennie asked the kids for ideas on how we could improve matchdays at Broadhurst Park, their suggestions included an ice cream stall and an eSports competition. While our matchday offering for follicly challenged middle-aged men is pretty much boxed off with cask ales, mushy peas and pre-match sets by post-punk guitar bands, it's clear that it could do with a bit more thought when it comes to younger fans.

A recent online survey of FC fans asked what the one thing responders would improve about the club. While things like 'style of football', 'results' and 'money' predictably came out on top, it was interesting to note the response of one fan who reckoned we should look to provide a 'matchday experience for under-25s not based around alcohol'.

Jennie had also noted, in her first two weeks at the club, that the 3G pitches adjacent to the stadium tend to be free in the late afternoon and she often sees kids trying to sneak on to the pitches at this time and reckoned that we should encourage them to come and play football for free during this downtime and let them feel part of the club as it would potentially reduce the incidences of anti-social behaviour at Broadhurst Park and nearby.

Steve Durrands was also attending his first board meeting. He's a long-standing co-owner and a qualified accountant who had agreed to take on the role of part-time financial controller – to offer some much-needed leadership of the finance function – at a rate of pay that was well below what we'd usually expect to pay for an experienced accountant.

Steve updated the board that the club made an operating loss of £14,500 in July – the first month of the 2023/24 financial year – which was £20,700 worse than the operating profit of £6,200 that we had budgeted for. Although, he noted that around half of this variance from budget was explained by a timing issue relating to sales of the new home shirt and women's kit.

3

We've sold out of pies, love

DREAMS OF Wembley and the build-up to our first FA
Cup match of the season on the first Saturday in September
were interrupted by a reminder that 'the competition must
at all times be referred to as "the Emirates FA Cup" in all
written and verbal communications'. So a preview of Course
You Can Malcolm, which had already been posted on the
club's website and included a reference to the plain old 'FA
Cup', was hastily amended lest we incur the wrath of the
FA and a possible fine.

Prior to the match, at CYCM, the north Manchester
theatre company Malandra Jacks performed a taster of their
new show *Census* which is about Moston and is set to do a
four-night run at the Contact Theatre in town. They're not
the first theatre company to play at CYCM: the wonderful
Moston Active Drama performed the first scene from *She's
Just Nipped Out For Fags* at one of the early editions of
CYCM and have been back many times since.

On the pitch FC beat Barnoldswick Town 1-0 in the
FA Cup's first qualifying round on a beautiful late summer
afternoon. It was a largely forgettable encounter that had
the feel of a pre-season friendly rather than a cup tie, but

a Nic Bollado header with quarter of an hour to go put us through to the next round just as I was beginning to consider options for getting to and from Barnoldswick by public transport on a Tuesday night. We pocketed £2,250 in prize money for the win, which was nice.

The following day the women's team got their first point of the league season with a goalless draw at home to Norton & Stockton Ancients Ladies. And an email to co-owners announced that Nigel Brookes, a long-standing co-owner, was to become FC United's operations coordinator responsible for overseeing off-field activities for the club's various football teams and would report to general manager Danny Davis. It's part of a restructuring of the senior team following the departure of former CEO Natalie Atkinson.

* * *

Later in the week the BBC reported, 'Manchester United shares have seen their biggest ever one-day fall,' after news that the Glazers were considering taking the club off the market and trying to sell it again next year as they were reportedly holding out for an offer of £10bn. The Glazer family had announced last November that it was considering selling the club and exploring 'strategic alternatives'.

While there was reference to 'fierce opposition from some fans' there was no mention of the longest-running and most visible protest against the Glazers' ownership – the only one that's continued throughout the family's 18-year tenure – FC United. In recent years we've tended to be less vocal as a club in calling out the Glazers' ownership of United – and promoting supporter ownership as an alternative model – than we once were and some FC supporters feel that it's time that we found our voice again.

It's 20 years this month since the Glazers began buying shares in United and George Baker, a former board member who now sits on the communications committee, reckoned, 'We need to remind people that not only do we still exist but we still believe in everything we stood for when we formed.'

The following day the club issued a statement headlined '20 Years of Glazer Ownership: Two Decades of Discontent at Old Trafford vs the rise of FC United' that called for 'the restoration of Manchester United to its former glory, grounded in the principles of genuine footballing heritage and traditions' and argued for 'improved fan engagement and representation', adding that 'putting the interests of supporters first is paramount in this journey towards renewed success'. It also drew a contrast between the 'corporate greed' of the Glazer era at United and supporter ownership at FC United where 'fans have a meaningful voice'.

* * *

On one of the hottest days of the year FC United beat old foes Bradford Park Avenue 2-0 to maintain our perfect record at 'Fortress Broadhurst' so far this season with both goals scored by Jay Fitzmartin, including an early one which left the Yorkshire side chasing the game on a sweltering afternoon when you'd prefer not to be chasing anything. A new song, hailing the fleet-footed winger, signed from Atherton Collieries in the summer, is born to the tune of the 60s classic 'It's My Party'.

Bradford were relegated from National League North last season and are already struggling to find their feet in the Northern Premier League this time. Their financial position is also precarious as they reported a £455,000 loss in their 2022/23 accounts and their owner, Bradford-born Gareth Roberts, told the local newspaper in February that he could not afford to keep funding the club for much longer as he has 'not got a bottomless pit of money' and acknowledged that he was 'looking around for other directors to come in, who could sponsor the club'.

Park Avenue were long-standing members of the Football League before dropping into non-league in 1970 and enduring a decline which ended with the club being liquidated (that word again) in 1974 and subsequently returning as a Sunday league side. But it wasn't until 1988 that the 'old club' was reformed and joined the West Riding County Amateur League from where it eventually rose to Conference North after defeating FC United in the play-off final in 2012, Tom Greaves (who went on to become FC's record goalscorer) scoring a dramatic winner in the last minute of extra time – one of many intriguing battles we've had with the Yorkshire side down the years.

It's international weekend which means that UEFA article 48 – preventing clubs from screening matches that kick off at 3pm on a Saturday afternoon – is suspended and, after securing Bradford's agreement, we are able to stream the match live to an audience beyond the 1,711 spectators inside Broadhurst Park. The live stream is watched by viewers in Canada, Finland, Netherlands, Norway, Poland and Thailand as well as the UK.

The following day FC's women's team lost 5-0 away to York City Ladies in a match played at Tadcaster Albion's ground, which is a lovely venue but offers a reminder that FC United are the only club in National League Division One North whose women's team plays its home matches in the same stadium as the men's team. York City are unable to host their women's team matches at their own 'multipurpose' community stadium which opened in 2021 – preferring instead to host the York Knights rugby league team – thus forcing their women's team to make a 24-mile round trip to play their 'home' matches. It seems odd to refer to a stadium being a 'community' venue when it's unable to host the football team that seeks to nurture footballing talent from half of the local population.

* * *

Later in the week an email to co-owners invited us to 'join the FC United board and shape our future together' ahead of this year's annual general meeting which will take place on 26 November. It offered a reminder that, as per the club's rules, applications to stand for the board must be received by the club by 12 October. Any adult co-owner who has been a member of the club in the two seasons preceding the AGM can stand for election to the board with the endorsement of not fewer than five other members.

* * *

'At least we can ditch that "Fortress Broadhurst" shite now,' quipped one supporter as we made for the exits, after a comprehensive 4-0 thumping by Warrington Rylands meant we exited the FA Cup at the second qualifying-round stage and could dispense with the red rosettes and tinfoil FA Cups for another year.

It was, as many remarked, a 'winnable' tie on paper and an opportunity for us to earn a few bob in prize money but after Rylands went ahead against the run of play just after the half-hour mark, we rarely looked like getting back into the tie and were thoroughly outplayed in the second half.

The post-match reaction on the unofficial forum was full of the usual 'questions need to be asked' and 'lessons need learning sharpish' and calls for a more physical approach to stop 'opposition strikers walking right through us'. Some supporters feel that Neil Reynolds has had more than enough time to show his credentials – his fifth anniversary as manager is fast approaching – but in reality, due to Covid, he's only been in charge for two full seasons so far.

The last time we lost an FA Cup tie 4-0 at home was against Brighton in a second-round replay in 2010 and the Sussex side piled on the misery for the red two thirds of Manchester this weekend by beating United 3-1 at Old Trafford to put another bald manager under the cosh from supporters.

The following day the women's team also conceded four goals at Broadhurst Park but fought back from 4-2 down to beat Chester-le-Street Town Ladies 5-4 – their first win of the season – with Chaneece Reeves scoring a hat-trick. 'I need a week off after that game!' laughs manager Jennie Swarbrick after a topsy-turvy encounter in which FC were 2-0 up after only 12 minutes but then trailed 4-2 before half-time.

* * *

'Them skills are sick, man.' The lads near me in Broadhurst Park's main stand were quite rightly heaping praise on Avro academy's diminutive winger Harry Salt who scored two of his side's goals (and could have had another with an audacious overhead kick which was just over the bar) as they beat FC United's academy team 3-1 in the first qualifying round of this season's FA Youth Cup. Harry's second goal was good enough to win any match – deftly controlling the ball on the edge of the penalty area with his right foot before firing it into the bottom corner with his left.

FC began the game strongly and were the better side in the first 20 minutes before a defensive howler gifted Avro their first goal, and a second followed shortly afterwards, leaving FC chasing the game. They stuck at it in the second half and grabbed a late consolation goal but Avro deserved their win. The centre-back and captain Dominic Doyle was my man of the match for FC.

The tie was watched by a crowd of 330, all accommodated in a busy main stand, and it was noticeably more diverse than a typical matchday at Broadhurst Park, with lots of families and youngsters in attendance cheering on players on both sides – Avro are based only a few miles away near Oldham.

And, in a feat of multitasking that I can only admire, many of the youngsters were also tuned into Manchester United's Champions League game against Bayern Munich while keeping an eye on their contemporaries on the pitch.

The evening offered a reminder that FC's fanbase is far from representative of either Moston or Manchester when it comes to age, gender or ethnicity. In terms of ethnicity, the figures are particularly stark with 96 per cent of co-owners who took part in the club's 2021 survey identifying themselves as white whereas, according to the 2021 census, 57 per cent of Manchester's population is white. In terms of gender, 88 per cent of those who took part in the survey were male, but the figures on age are more encouraging with 17 per cent of the club's membership in 2023/24 under the age of 16 compared to around 20 per cent of Manchester's population. It's crucial we continue to fulfil our manifesto pledge to 'encourage young, local participation'.

* * *

Dimitri brought his synth-based one-man band all the way from junction 33 of the M1 between Rotherham and Sheffield to wow the CYCM audience before our match against Whitby Town on 23 September with a set that included a tongue-in-cheek sneak preview of the new Champions League anthem. The 'former nightclub owner' sported an Italian football referee's jersey and the Serie A theme continued beyond kick-off as Whitby rocked up in what looked like an 80s Sampdoria kit.

On the 34th anniversary of Mark Hughes's glorious volleyed goal in the Manchester derby, Michael Donohue scored an equally stunning goal midway through the first half to give FC the lead, but the visitors equalised before half-time after a defensive mix-up. On the balance of play it felt like a fair result although Whitby could have nicked it towards the end.

The following day the women's team were beaten 3-0 by Durham Cestria at Durham University's sports ground.

* * *

I'm nearly nudged off the pavement by an SUV as I wander up Lloyd Street in the centre of Manchester past a row of cars out of which suitcases and boxes are being transferred into nearby buildings. It's that time of year when the population of Manchester rises by around 100,000 as students arrive for the start of a new academic year.

I daresay plenty of these students will be interested in football and I wonder how many will make their way to Broadhurst Park in the coming months, remembering that encouraging 'young, local participation – playing and supporting' is one of the club's core principles. West Didsbury and Chorlton FC, who play in the North West Counties League, are proving an appealing option for students – admission is cheap, it's close to Fallowfield where a lot of students live, and there's a vibrant atmosphere as they regularly attract crowds of more than 1,000.

But FC fan and former Manchester University student Jake Worrall reckons that West 'feel a bit hipster and appeal more to people that aren't really into football'. And 'being in Chorlton helps as there are loads of decent bars and cafes to go before and after matches' whereas schlepping all the way out to Moston to watch FC is probably not as attractive.

Jake started at Manchester University in 2014 and he recalls how the following year he brought a group of about 30 students to one of FC's first matches at Broadhurst Park after setting up an FC United stall at the university's freshers' week. 'We got quite a bit of interest in that first year,' says Jake, 'but when we tried it again in 2016 no one turned up.' From the initial group that came to a game in 2015 Jake reckons that about four or five became regular match-goers – including Jonathan Cardoza (aka Baz) who went on to become the compere of Course You Can Malcolm and is a member of the finance and risk committee. Jonathan had already listened to FC matches on FCUM Radio at home in Bahrain before choosing to come to Manchester to study.

When we moved into Broadhurst Park, a group of younger FC supporters known as the Giddys, which included Jake and Baz, were a visible presence towards the front of the St Mary's Road End terrace with their colourful, inventive and occasionally politically infused banners and flags. Their 'Drop Points Not Bombs' banner at Stockport in December 2015 – a peace-loving reference to airstrikes on Syria at the time – caused quite a stir among those supporters who prefer those entering a football ground to leave their politics at the turnstiles.

Jake grew up in Sussex and was nine years old when he came to his first FC United match. He was aware of the Glazer takeover from television news coverage at the time and he knew that his dad strongly objected to it. Shortly after watching a feature about FC United on television they came to their first FC game, the 3-3 thriller with Cheadle Town at Stockport the day after George Best died in late November 2005. They were both hooked and for the next few seasons they regularly made the long trip up to watch FC.

One of the most memorable was the FA Cup tie at Norton & Stockton Ancients in October 2010 when a Mike Norton hat-trick sealed a 5-2 win for FC and a youthful Jake was pictured on the front page of the *Non-League Paper* celebrating one of the goals. 'We'd stopped over in Manchester as it was impossible to get all the way back to Sussex by train that night so we got a shock when we spotted the cover of the *Non-League Paper* at Piccadilly station the following morning,' smiles Jake.

Post-university, Jake has remained in Manchester and works as a software engineer at the BBC; he's used these skills to help the club, as a member of the commercial committee, initially as an observer but now as a full member. At first he found it a bit daunting as, being one of the committee's younger members, he was unsure what he could contribute but over time he's grown into the role and feels it's useful to have 'a business background'.

He helped to move the club shop on to the Shopify platform, which has made purchasing FC merchandise online a much more pleasurable experience than in the past. 'The old shop website was built ages ago,' says Jake, 'and it lacked flexibility and was expensive to run.' There is a wealth of sales and customer data available through the

Shopify system and Jake has set up several automated reports to monitor sales. 'But we don't use this data as much as we should,' he adds.

Jake was also involved in the recent implementation of an online ticketing system and assessed the pros and cons of two ticketing systems that were trialled at two home matches during the season. 'It was a detailed exercise,' he explains, 'that assessed a range of factors like user experience, data and the key features of each system.' He is conscious too of the need to ensure that whatever we do on the commercial front doesn't stray into 'outright commercialism'. 'There are some similarities here with the BBC and the importance of its role as a public service provider,' he says.

So, having been a committee member, would he be interested in stepping up to the board in future? 'Yes,' he says. 'I almost see it as a duty to the club that if you have skills and experience in a particular area that would be useful to the board, then you should stand for election.' Although, he acknowledged that the time commitment could put people off. 'I'd love to be able to reduce my hours in my current job and devote more time to FC,' he says, then adds with a smile, 'but I don't think I'll be able to do that for a few years yet.'

If Jake was to step up to the board in future, then he would be following in the footsteps of his dad Tim, who was board chair when I first began attending board meetings in 2016. We owe much to Tim Worrall who, along with Sam Mullock, steered the club through a very difficult period in the summer of 2016 when it could easily have folded. 'I'm very proud of what my dad did when he was on the board,' says Jake.

* * *

The agenda for September's board meeting was rejigged to allow co-owner John Herring to update the board on the recent people and culture review and its recommendations without him having to sit through the rest of the meeting. John is also director of organisational development and culture at the NHS Greater Manchester Integrated Care Board and had been invited to lead the review which had taken place in June and July this year.

The review included a survey and interviews which involved board members, football staff, other paid staff, partners and volunteers. The highest-scoring area in the survey was around vision and clarity, with staff and volunteers indicating that they were inspired by the club's vision, and the key themes they picked out were fan ownership, community, affordability and the 'alternative' nature of the club.

As regards sustainability, while many people also see the ground as an anchor in the local community to be proud of, there is – not surprisingly given the club's financial issues since it moved into Broadhurst Park – a concern about the long-term financial sustainability of the club. And, interestingly, when it came to 'excellence', the responses highlighted that 'excellence has all sorts of definitions beyond being successful on the pitch'.

However, there were areas of concern in the survey with many people feeling that the culture and behaviours on display at the club 'did not enable them to be their best, lead to good team working or enable the vision'. And some felt that they weren't adequately supported and were part of a team that didn't have each other's back. John noted that the scores in this section of the survey were particularly low compared to his experience in assessing other organisations.

John also mentioned that two areas of the club were regularly cited as being problematic – the 3G pitches and the stadium itself. The report highlighted that there is an ongoing issue regarding the 3G pitches with local youngsters trying to gain access to them for free – as noted by Jennie Swarbrick at last month's board meeting – but many staff don't feel equipped to deal with this and hence it had tended to go largely unmanaged. And the cleanliness and upkeep of the stadium was also cited as an issue, particularly as it is a 'shop window' for prospective players, staff, volunteers and sponsors.

John's report made several recommendations including the development of a statement of 'just cause' – which ties in with the current work on the club's branding and identity – and also agreeing a set of values and behaviours across the club that everyone is committed to. It also suggests developing an 'owners' charter' that recognises that with football club ownership comes responsibilities, and this is something which was touched on in a structural review, undertaken by three of the club's co-owners, in 2018 but hasn't been properly addressed.

The board thanked John for a valuable piece of work and agreed that the staff team should lead on implementing all the report's recommendations. But they recognised that the owners' charter will probably be the trickiest recommendation to implement given a previous failed attempt to implement a 'code of conduct'. In many respects the club is in a unique position – in having more than 2,000 co-owners but a lean staffing structure – which means that there is an absence of 'best practice' that we can refer to and Warren Heppolette reckoned that we might have to dip into the philosopher Jean-Jacques Rousseau's *The Social Contract* for a steer on this.

There was good news on the financial front this month as the latest management accounts highlighted that the club made an operating profit of £20,300 in August – £6,900 better than budget – and reported an operating profit of £5,800 after the first two months of the 2023/24 financial year, although this was £13,800 worse than the operating profit of £19,600 we budgeted for.

* * *

'We've sold out of pies, love, but we've got pizza – pepperoni or cheese.' I end up with a half-time slice of 'cheese' pizza for three quid that's probably not big on nutritional value but feels quite exotic for the Northern Premier League, especially at a ground that only installed floodlights four years ago, such is Warrington Rylands' rapid ascent of the pyramid.

It was almost exactly 19 years to the day since an 18-year-old Wayne Rooney scored a hat-trick on his Manchester United debut as they beat Fenerbahçe 6-2 in the Champions League – still the finest debut I've ever seen.

Rooney's agent Paul Stretford pocketed £1m as part of the transfer which was, at the time, the biggest fee received by a British agent, and he later went on to become the owner of Rylands FC, a former works team who are now known as Warrington Rylands.

I'd missed the first few minutes of the match as the train that was meant to bring us into Warrington Central was stranded at Sheffield and so I ended up wandering across town from Warrington's Bank Quay station having taken another train – a scenic route that took in the town hall and law courts – but didn't miss anything of note on the pitch by the sounds of it.

Despite having the lion's share of possession, FC United rarely looked like scoring and lost 1-0. The post-match reaction on The Soul is One was largely measured. 'We were desperately unlucky tonight. Thought we ran them ragged after they scored.' 'A good performance minus the lapse for the goal.' But also a bit deflated too. 'The club is very flat at the moment and clearly needs a lift.' 'People are getting used to being beaten away and are now just shrugging their shoulders.'

* * *

'Are you all right there, sir?' There's a huge police presence around town ahead of the Tory party conference which begins on Sunday especially around St Peter's Square and the Midland Hotel, where most of the movers and shakers will be staying. So even momentarily pausing while on a lunchtime stroll round Manchester city centre to gaze at a building can arouse suspicion. The hotel, together with the adjacent Manchester Central conference venue in a former railway station, has been fenced off to allow conference-goers to move between hotel and conference hall without having to mix with the riff-raff.

Back in 2015, shortly after we'd moved into Broadhurst Park, government minister Damian Hinds took a break from the Tory conference to visit FC United to, as a club press release put it, see the 'success of the club in raising funds and building a community facility in Moston'. When Hinds later tweeted a photo of himself and club officials on the Broadhurst Park pitch, it aroused the anger of many FC fans – plenty of whom had been on a protest march in Manchester against the Tories only a few days before.

The club, at the time, viewed 'talking to government ministers and other politicians' as an 'essential part' of relaying its message regarding the benefits of community ownership but many fans would have preferred us not to be cosying up to members of a government busy implementing austerity measures that were damaging communities like Moston and leaving the football club as one of the few community assets in the area.

FC's radical history is a source of pride for many supporters who perceive the club to be left-leaning. And some people, who have little interest in football, have been attracted to the club by its inclusive ethos and values.

* * *

Just as we'd learned to spell his name right on social media, Chiekh Thiam, perhaps the most exciting player of the first few weeks of the season, left us to join Warrington Rylands. Once again we're reminded of the sage advice that Kris Stewart from AFC Wimbledon gave us at the Apollo in May 2005 to not get too attached to your players at this level of football. Players tend to come and go with much greater regularity than higher up the pyramid. Kris also said that owning our own football club would be incredibly hard work and he wasn't wrong there either.

But it's a case of 'one in, one out' as we bolstered our forward line by signing Jake Charles, who has represented Wales at youth international level on an initial month's loan from Scarborough. He's also the grandson of former Wales international John Charles who became the first British footballer to play in Italy when he signed for Juventus in 1957. Maybe Jake will also get the opportunity to play in Italy in the Fenix Trophy later this season, who knows, but for now he went straight into the team at Workington.

FC's visit to Workington on 30 September was the first time we'd played the Cumbrian side since April 2015 after clinching the Northern Premier League title with a 1-0 win against Stourbridge a few days earlier. We lost that day, in front of a bumper crowd of 2,603 at Borough Park, but it didn't matter as we'd already been promoted to the sixth tier for the first time in our history.

And we lost again at Borough Park 2-1, despite creating a hatful of chances and having a goal controversially disallowed. 'Completely pissed off … a familiar story of playing well but not putting chances away,' summarised one regular on The Soul is One, and another sounded equally hacked off, 'Wasn't expecting the season to peter out so soon.' 'I'm really enjoying watching this team, especially at home, but I've pretty much dropped my expectations to not making the play-offs already,' said another.

The controversy at Workington was nothing compared to the hysteria that followed a disallowed Liverpool goal at Spurs a few hours later. It provoked hours of debate in the following days, in tones usually reserved for serious news stories involving death or destruction, about the merits of VAR, with an official statement from Liverpool that referred to 'sporting integrity being undermined' and their manager Jürgen Klopp calling for the match, which Liverpool lost 2-1, to be replayed. I've never fully got over Brian McClair's goal being incorrectly disallowed in Manchester United's FA Cup quarter-final against Nottingham Forest in 1989 but this is on another level. Rarely a day goes by without me being a little bit more assured that I made the right decision to quit the Premier League circus in 2005.

4

Something much bigger than the individual

'A LONG-OVERDUE twatting and a solid three points,' opines one of the regulars on The Soul is One as the men's team begin October with a Tuesday night 250-mile round trip to the North Yorkshire coast and return with all three points after thumping Marske United 5-2. Astonishingly, given our away form so far this season, we were 4-0 up after 20 minutes – scoring four in a frantic five minutes which had our social media volunteers struggling to keep up – before eventually snaffling our first away points of the season.

'We're a good side when things click,' reckoned another poster on the unofficial forum. The post-match thread stretches to a measly four pages compared to nine pages after last week's defeat at Warrington Rylands. Such is life on the internet.

Marske were bottom of the table coming into this one, and the game was a far cry from FC's first visit to Marske by the Sea two years earlier when we were knocked out of the FA Trophy by the village side who were playing in the division below us at the time.

The women's team also commenced October with a long-distance win as they beat Leafield Athletic 1-0 in the FA Women's National League Plate with Chaneece Reeves scoring the winner midway through the second half.

* * *

An email to co-owners announced that 'our men's team players, management and backroom staff have recently joined the supporter ownership cause' by becoming co-owners of FC United, and it was accompanied by a picture of the team brandishing their membership cards. Forward Charlie Ennis says, 'Co-ownership makes this club unique and special – it makes us all feel a part of something!' I wonder how many other footballers around the country also co-own the club that they play for? Could player-ownership become a thing?

Meanwhile, we have lost a board member as Gemma Avery announced 'with a heavy heart' that she would be resigning from the board as due to personal circumstances she felt 'unable to dedicate the time I feel the position needs'. It's a shame as even in her relatively short period at the club we've benefited from Gemma's expertise in communications and marketing – particularly in the work that we've been doing on the club's brand and identity of which she's been an integral part.

It leaves us with four board members – Dave Ashurst, Warren Heppolette, Paul Butcher and Bhavna Mistry – but with Warren, Paul and Bhavna having to stand down at next month's AGM, Paul already having indicated that he's not going to stand for election again and some uncertainty around how Bhavna can be brought back on to the board, it's difficult to predict what the make-up will look like post-AGM.

* * *

The travel budget continued to get a hammering as we made our third long-distance trip of the week, on the first Saturday of October – this time to Morpeth – and beat the hosts 4-1 in the third qualifying round of the FA Trophy. For the second time in four days we were 4-1 up away from home at half-time. It's a competition in which we've usually struggled – aside from the 2014/15 season when we made it through to the quarter-finals before losing 1-0 to Torquay – so here's hoping for a decent draw in the first round proper on Monday. We pocketed £2,450 for the win which is not to be sniffed at.

The following day the women's team lost 2-0 at home to Stockport County Ladies in front of 249 spectators – our biggest crowd of the season so far.

* * *

The Tameside Stadium in Ashton-under-Lyne holds plenty of fond memories for FC fans down the years – one of seven grounds across Greater Manchester where we played 'home' matches in the years prior to moving into Broadhurst Park – and was, most famously, where we clinched the Northern Premier League title in 2015 and won promotion, for the first and only time in our history, to National League North. According to Karl Ladley's wonderful book *FC United of Manchester: The Complete Record 2005–2022*, we were unbeaten in 13 'home' matches at the Tameside Stadium, which included 11 wins.

But we didn't win there on Tuesday, 10 October as we exited the Manchester Premier Cup at the first hurdle, losing on penalties to Curzon Ashton after a 1-1 draw at the end of 90 minutes, although it was a creditable performance against a side currently sitting in fifth place in National

League North. Max Cane scored FC's goal – an equaliser in the 75th-minute, after Curzon had taken the lead a few minutes earlier.

* * *

Thursday, 12 October is the closing date for motions and candidacies for the board to be submitted ahead of November's AGM and the early indications are that we will have five co-owners standing for election to the board: Warren Heppolette will be standing again with Nick Boom (from the strategy and governance committee), Matthew Haley (from the communications committee), Simon Preston (the chair of the commercial committee) and Paul Hurst (from the co-ownership committee) also standing. This is an excellent advert for the committee structure, which is seen as a potential source of future board members.

* * *

The home match against Morpeth Town on 14 October was the 900th time that an FC United team had taken to the field in a competitive fixture and, as if keen to recognise this landmark, FC made a brisk start with Jan Palinkas scoring from a corner in the first minute. Having beaten Morpeth 4-1 only seven days ago, even the most curmudgeonly among us scented a win but by half-time we trailed 3-1 despite having had 71 per cent of possession according to the matchday stats.

Luke Griffiths pulled a goal back early in the second half but, shortly after, as a squally shower swept in, FC's keeper Pat Boyes spilled a high ball and Morpeth bagged a scruffy fourth goal. They notched a fifth near the end too and it was the cue for some home fans to head for the exits. FC's X account had given up sharing the usual match stats by the end – the only one that mattered was that we lost 5-2.

Before the match, James Young, a United fan and writer for *United We Stand*, had kicked things off at CYCM with some poetry. James is no stranger to FC having been in Milan to watch us in the Fenix Trophy in June – a trip he wrote about in the *UWS* summer special. He was followed on stage by Prawn Prison – a one-man punky 'electronic spoken word project based in Manchester' – with some wry observations on modern life which were accompanied by a synth-based soundtrack.

There was a lovely interview in the programme with Emmanuele Quarta from the Italian fan-owned club ASD Ideale Bari, who were formed in 2012 – partly inspired by FC United – and currently play in Italy's seventh tier. When asked what is most rewarding about being part of a fan-owned club, Emmanuele replied, 'We are all part of something that is much bigger than the individual,' and added that 'when matchdays come around there's a sense of pride when our players enter the pitch' as it is 'the crowning of a full week of people working together to make that happen'.

* * *

FC's finance manager Hannah Gorman left this week after nine years working at the club having joined as an apprentice, prior to us moving into our own ground, when our office was at Hope Mill in the centre of Manchester. In addition to number-crunching, Hannah has been a familiar face behind the bar or on the turnstiles on matchdays.

A year ago the club's CEO, club secretary, commercial manager, finance manager and events and hospitality manager posts were all held by women but they have all now left the club (or, in the case of the club secretary post, been made redundant). Retention of key members of staff has been a perennial problem for the club – the advice of AFC Wimbledon fan Kris Stewart back in 2005 about not getting too attached to players could equally apply to staff members it seems.

And women's team captain Corie Mather has left FC 'to take up an opportunity elsewhere'; a couple of days later, she became Wythenshawe FC Women's latest signing and went straight into the squad for their FA Cup tie at home to Barnsley on the Sunday. Chaneece Reeves took over as FC's captain.

* * *

What is it about storms and trips to Basford? Our 1-1 draw on our first visit to the Nottingham club in February 2020 occurred the day before Storm Ciara battered the country and this season's trip came the day after Storm Babet did its worst. In 2020 the two sides were challenging for promotion with Basford second in the table and FC in fourth but this time around the table has a very different look with Basford second from bottom and FC hardly pulling up any trees (unlike Babet) in 13th place after last week's drubbing by Morpeth.

The geographical uncertainties of non-league football mean that it's the first time we've played Basford since the 2021/22 season. Clubs in the Midlands are susceptible to being shuffled north or south at the end of a season depending on who gets promoted and relegated. Last season Basford and Ilkeston competed in the Southern League Premier Central, at the same level, but were moved into the Northern Premier League for this campaign. So instead of away trips to the likes of Needham Market and St Ives, they face long treks to Morpeth and Workington instead.

'No worries about the weather,' posted FC's official X account after Basford's 3G pitch passed a morning inspection, but for those of us reliant on public transport to get to Nottingham the news was less cheery as, with large parts of Derbyshire flooded and a major incident declared across the county, there were no trains running between Manchester and Nottingham. So no surprise that the match was watched by a crowd of only 507 (nearly 400 down on the crowd in 2020) and despite, again, having the lion's share of possession it finished 1-1 – an early goal for the home side equalised a few minutes later by a penalty converted by Luke Griffiths.

'There's only one Bobby Charlton,' sang the FC fans in the second half following the sad news that Sir Bobby Charlton had died aged 86. I'm too young to have seen him play but was raised on tales of Law, Best and Charlton from my dad. Bobby was a United legend – that he scored 29 league goals the season after surviving the Munich air crash still astounds me – and many reckon that he's England's greatest ever player. 'Football is more than a game. It has the power to bring happiness to ordinary people,' he once said.

* * *

FC's women's team beat Cheadle Town Stingers 5-4 on penalties, after the match finished 2-2, in the Women's FA Cup third qualifying round at Broadhurst Park, to make it through to the first round proper. FC twice came from behind in normal time to take it to penalties. 'The resilience of the team is fantastic,' said manager Jennie Swarbrick in her post-match interview.

The win will see us collect £4,000 in prize money. Last season the women's team also made it through to the first round proper and won more than £8,000 in prize money, which was significantly more than the men's team garnered in their equivalent competition.

* * *

Assistant manager Brian Richardson updated the board that there had been a small overspend on the football budget up to mid-October which is mainly due to injuries to contracted players. However, Brian is confident that we will be able to recover the overspend over the remainder of the season as injured players return to full fitness and/ or we are compensated through our players' insurance policy.

Brian works closely with financial controller Steve Durrands to monitor our performance against the football budget and provides regular updates for the board. He added that the start to the season for the men's team has been disappointing but noted the league is 'very tight' and when we factor in the number of injuries we've had so far he felt that 'we have done well in most games' and remained 'confident results will improve in the coming months'.

But confidence was in short supply a few days later after a dispiriting 2-0 loss at home to bottom club Atherton Collieries. 'He's got to go,' 'the football's shit' and 'he couldn't even come over to the fans at the end' were some of the more printable comments I overheard on my way out of the ground. The 'he' being manager Neil Reynolds. We've now garnered a mere five points from our last seven games, which is relegation form. Once again FC had most of the possession but a lack of penetration in the final third of the pitch and some excellent last-ditch defending by Colls left us deflated again.

* * *

Friday, 27 October marks the fifth anniversary of Neil Reynolds's first match in charge of FC United but apart from a post on the club's X account which refers to 'sharp suits, European trophies and an unrelenting commitment to the club', it passes without official comment. Which is a shame as it's a landmark that ought to be celebrated and there's much more than the 'sharp suits' that we could have referenced.

It's easy to forget the mess the club was in when Neil took over in October 2018 as he inherited a team that was bottom of National League North, top-heavy with contracted players and overspending on its playing budget. Chief executive Damian Chadwick had also resigned – less than two years into the job – shortly after Tom Greaves's departure as manager, and the club was being managed by an interim group of volunteers. After a miserable start to the season and with little financial wriggle room to change things, we appeared pretty much nailed on for relegation.

Tom Greaves had taken over as caretaker manager when Karl Marginson had departed in October 2017 and, like Ole Gunnar Solskjaer at United, he was a victim of his own success as he managed to turn things around – including a memorable win against Salford City on Boxing Day – and was subsequently offered the job on a permanent basis. But after five defeats in the first six matches of the following season he resigned.

Reno's arrival marked the first time that FC had appointed a manager with actual managerial experience and a UEFA B coaching badge. He joined from Bamber Bridge, who he had led to promotion to the Northern Premier League the previous season on a shoestring budget and straightaway he made an impact, putting a strong emphasis on fitness and using the latest technology to track progress.

Within a couple of weeks, supporters had raised over £4,000 to purchase a set of hi-tech tracker vests for the squad.

The new manager spoke about looking up the table rather than down and after creditable draws at home to Brackley and Alfreton, FC enjoyed something of a purple patch in the first half of November with impressive away wins at Blyth Spartans and Hereford, scoring six goals in the process and playing arguably our best football during our four seasons in the sixth tier with the newly recruited captain Mike Potts impressing in midfield.

But that form didn't last and those of us too young to remember Manchester United's relegation to the Second Division in 1974 experienced our football club being relegated for the first time. Remarkably, despite the shambles he inherited, Neil managed to bring the playing budget back into line by the end of the season, which was a significant achievement that contributed to the club generating an operating profit that year.

Neil oversaw the recruitment of an almost entirely new squad ahead of the 2019/20 season and, after a slow start, it blossomed into the most enjoyable campaign in years – a young FC United side playing attacking football and, like all the best United sides, seemingly never knowing when it's beaten. Tunde Owolabi's 34 goals were one of the highlights and included a club record as he scored in seven consecutive matches. When Covid curtailed the season in March 2020, FC were in second place in the Northern Premier League (and the league's top scorers) and appeared destined for the play-offs. But, alas, it was expunged from the record books, the season that never was.

The 2020/21 season barely got going before another lockdown brought it to a halt in November after only seven league matches. But Neil memorably led FC to the first round proper of the FA Cup, for only the third time in our history, where we played Doncaster Rovers at Broadhurst Park in a match broadcast live on the BBC.

Even if we were ultimately soundly beaten by an excellent Doncaster side and, sadly, no spectators were allowed in the ground, it still felt like a joyous occasion – a celebration of everything that we stand for as a football club. And the prize money from the cup run, not to mention the £32,500 we got for the live screening of the match, was crucial to the club's survival as we headed into the longest football-less period of the pandemic.

The 2021/22 season was Neil's first full campaign in charge and – despite finishing a disappointing ninth in the league and ten points adrift of the play-off places – it ended memorably as we won the inaugural Fenix Trophy in the Italian seaside resort of Rimini and were therefore the only British club side to win a European trophy in 2021/22.

Last season FC finished only five points outside the play-off places (and that was after incurring a three-point deduction) and there were some outstanding performances including beating the eventual champions South Shields home and away.

With a third of the 2023/24 season gone, we're in the bottom half of the table but, as one of the more measured posters on The Soul is One put it, 'We have a ground (albeit with years of repayments to make) to be proud of and a young team in red at three o'clock most Saturdays who, by and large, give their all week in, week out – they and the manager need our support.'

The official club post on X attracted plenty of likes but not surprisingly there were a few unhappy replies including one from @renoout, '5 years of excuses and it's still crap … ta ra Reno', which was accompanied by a picture of

the infamous 'three years of excuses and it's still crap …
ta ra Fergie' banner from December 1989. Although the
anonymous poster possibly hadn't thought this through
properly as Alex Ferguson, far from heading for the exit,
subsequently went on to be manager of United for another
24 years.

* * *

'I'm going to do a song for you called "Colonel Gaddafi's
space shuttle".' The multi-talented Gideon Conn is a firm
CYCM favourite having played twice for us many years ago
at Gigg Lane – indeed he was the first musician or band
to be invited back – and he played a lovely acoustic set,
sprinkled with wry humour, on his return to Malcolmses
on 28 October.

In his programme notes Neil Reynolds described
Tuesday night's 2-0 loss at home to Atherton as 'the most
dejected I've felt in a while'. So an FA Trophy tie against the
runaway league leaders Radcliffe, who had thumped us 5-0
in the league in August, was hardly the perfect pick-me-up,
and when we went 2-0 down after barely half an hour I was
fearing the worst.

But FC were tenacious in the second half and Michael
Donohue's well-deserved late equaliser took the game
to penalties. It's a shame it didn't go to extra time as
the momentum was with us but we missed one of our
penalties, Radcliffe didn't miss any and that was the FA
Trophy done and dusted for another year. But there was
enough in that second-half performance to build on in
the coming weeks.

The following day FC's women's team were thrashed
6-0 at home by Hull City Ladies in the FA Women's
National League Plate to complete a thoroughly miserable

weekend for red-shirted football teams from Manchester with 'United' in their name.

* * *

The focus of October's board meeting was the club's academy, which is provided in partnership with SCL Education and currently offers a full-time education and training programme for boys aged from 16 to 18, with 90 per cent of students drawn from within a three-mile radius of Broadhurst Park. The classroom space under the St Mary's Road End terrace, which was redeveloped in the summer of 2022, can accommodate up to 120 students.

A year ago the club suffered a heavy financial blow when it only managed to recruit 52 students for the 2022/23 academic year – less than half of the target of 108 we'd set for the first year of our three-year business plan – which left us with a fall in revenue for the academy of £119,000. In hindsight, this target was too ambitious, with a plethora of post-pandemic challenges affecting the education sector particularly in areas of high deprivation such as north Manchester.

Neil Reynolds, who had managed an academy prior to joining FC United and as well as being the men's first-team manager was also the club's academy principal, subsequently resigned from the latter role at the end of December 2022 and, during the remainder of the year, we were also able to find savings in travel, food and kit costs as a result of the lower student numbers.

The club's community committee and the board subsequently led a review to establish the reasons for the shortfall in student numbers and identify things that it could learn from in terms of its future academy recruitment, and it resulted in a revamped operating model for the academy which resulted in SCL employing the head of academy, Tom Conroy, and coach Chris Taylor, and a stronger focus on educational attainment and good outcomes for students. While the club maintains overall strategic control of the academy, its day-to-day operation is overseen by SCL under a facilities and marketing agreement which offers the club greater certainty regarding its income and mitigates the risk of a drop-off in student numbers.

In light of the recruitment difficulties in 2022, some supporters had wondered if we should be providing an academy at all as it can often appear something of a luxury for a seventh-tier club to have one. However, the club is legally obliged to provide educational and sporting opportunities for young people in north Manchester.

There are terms in both our funding agreement with Sport England – which helped pay for the construction of the ground – and the partnership agreement between FC United, Moston Juniors and Manchester City Council that commit the club to providing education. This includes providing space for education in a dedicated room and developing links with education providers to increase access to football and provide educational opportunities for young people.

Stuart Allen, SCL's director of operations, had been invited to October's board meeting primarily to explore how to make FC's academy more appealing to young footballers and learners – including developing a plan for recruiting students for the 2024/25 academic year – and also discuss other potential educational opportunities such as adult education.

* * *

The Rochdale Pioneers Museum – regarded as 'the home of the worldwide cooperative movement' – contacts the club as they're running a new feature on their social media around the different types of co-operative around today and would like to feature FC United in this.

Aside from being the birthplace of the co-operative movement in 1844, Rochdale holds a special place in FC United's history as it was the setting of perhaps the club's finest moment to date when we beat the Dale 3-2 in our first appearance in the FA Cup first round on Bonfire Night in 2010. Some 4,000 FC supporters crammed into Spotland's Willbutts Lane stand on a raucous night of non-stop singing – with Jon Champion commentating on the match on ESPN memorably describing how it felt like the whole stand was shaking – and Michael Norton's injury-time winner was the cue for a delirious pitch invasion.

And later on that night there was a beautiful moment as hundreds of us piled off the train at Victoria station and the words of our punk anthem 'I am an FC fan' (to the tune of the Sex Pistols' 'Anarchy in the UK') echoed round Manchester's finest railway station, much to the bemusement of punters heading in the other direction after a night out in town.

5

Making friends
not millionaires

THERE WAS a bit of history on the first Saturday of
November when 18-year-old Max Woodcock, who came
on as a substitute in the second half, became the first player
born after our first match – against Leigh RMI in July 2005
– to play for FC United. But despite a valiant effort in the
second half we lost 2-0 to Hyde United in a game watched
by a crowd of 1,711, which included a noisy group of away
fans who were congregated mostly in the Lightbowne Road
End of the main stand as segregation was in place for this
fixture.

Course You Can Malcolm was short of volunteers this
weekend, as quite a few supporters had already headed out
to Poland for the first Fenix Trophy match of the season
in Kraków on Monday night, so this was a rare Saturday
afternoon without any pre-match entertainment under the
St Mary's Road End.

The mood on The Soul is One was predictably
downbeat. 'I think for the rest of the season now we might
benefit from prioritising not getting beat,' wrote one of the
manager's regular critics. And while one poster bemoaned
the fact that we've now got a trip to Kraków when we ought

to be focusing on preparing for a tough match at Lancaster, another reckoned, 'What better way to prepare for a game by trying out new tactics in a meaningless game? Better to try them there than in a competitive fixture.'

Today was also Big Coat Day (the title comes from the reply by an FC United fan to a reporter at Wimbledon in the summer of 2005 referred to in the opening paragraph of this book), the club's annual collection of coats and warm winter clothing to help homeless and vulnerable people across Greater Manchester.

It's been a regular feature of the club's community programme since 2005 and down the years we've worked with several charities to help those most in need. This year we're partnering with Winning Hearts and Minds – an organisation that works to improve heart and mental health in north Manchester – and the British Heart Foundation. There was a big storage container outside the ground before kick-off for people to drop off items, which looked pretty full about half an hour before kick-off.

Each winter it's reckoned that around 5,000 excess deaths occur in the north-west of England simply because of a lack of heating or warm clothing. These are deaths that are entirely preventable and Big Coat Day is the club's way of trying to help out locally.

The following day FC's women's team were thrashed 6-0 for the second time, away at Middlesbrough FC Women.

* * *

As the clocks go back, the nights draw in and the golden colours of autumn adorn country lanes, so splashes of red begin to appear on jackets, jumpers and coats, and football clubs typically do everything they can to be seen to be paying their respects to the 'fallen'. It's poppy season again so it's no surprise to find someone on the members' forum questioning why 'we didn't observe Remembrance Day' at yesterday's match as it is our last home match prior to Remembrance Day.

It's a reasonable question as we've often used the last home match before Remembrance Day to hold a minute's silence in the past – the televised FA Cup first-round tie against Doncaster in 2020, for instance, was played four days before Remembrance Day and was preceded by 'The Last Post' and the laying of a wreath on the pitch. This time around, however, the board had decided not to mark the occasion on the pitch but still to have donation boxes for the Royal British Legion in reception and the main bar for those who wish to wear a red poppy.

It's been a thorny issue for the club down the years and another poster bemoaned the 'poppyisation of football' and a remembrance period that now seems to last for 'the thick end of a month'. In 2014 I wrote an opinion piece for the matchday programme that criticised the relatively recent trend for football clubs to emblazon shirts, websites and merchandise with the red poppy. Many supporters saw it as an attack on the wearing of poppies and some even felt sufficiently offended to write to the club to complain.

* * *

FC United began this season's Fenix Trophy campaign with a trip to Poland to take on Kraków Dragoons – the second time we've travelled to Poland in the competition having made our Fenix debut in Warsaw against AKS Zły in October 2021.

This season's tournament is the biggest so far with 12 non-professional clubs from ten European countries taking part. Five clubs from last year's event, including FC, are competing again this year – BK Skjold, Prague Raptors, KSK Beveren and Kraków Dragoons are the others – meaning that there are seven new teams involved this year and five new countries with Norway, Finland, France, Romania and Wales represented for the first time.

There are also two other English teams taking part with fellow fan-owned clubs Enfield Town and Lewes FC competing in Europe for the first time. But like the Champions League, we've been kept apart from teams from the same country in the draw for the group stage. Perhaps just as well as we've lost to both sides in friendly matches in recent years.

The format of this year's tournament is similar to last year with an initial group phase featuring four groups of three teams that play each other home and away before the four group winners head to the 'Final 4' phase in the spring or early summer of 2024. FC have been drawn in Group C with French side Vinsky FC and Kraków Dragoons. It's possibly the easiest draw we could have got as Vinsky are the lowest-ranked side in the tournament – they currently play in the 11th tier of French football – and the Dragoons lost all four matches in last season's competition.

The Polish side are a multinational club, founded in 2016 to provide a means for immigrants to more easily integrate into the local community. Krakow Dragoons' innovative approach, resulting in a team that is more diverse than many professional clubs in Poland, has attracted plenty of media attention at home and abroad.

There were 230 supporters in KS Prądniczanka's stadium in Kraków and a further 340 watching a live stream of the match, free of charge, on Fenix Trophy TV. Prior to kick-off, the FC line-up had been announced on social media to the accompaniment of 'Turn On the Lights Again..' by Fred Again and Swedish House Mafia, and this turned out to be somewhat prescient as the match was plunged into darkness by a power cut in the 20th minute with FC 1-0 up.

'We're FC United, we'll play in the dark,' chorused the travelling FC fans but, after a lengthy stoppage, it was agreed that everyone – at least those not flying back to Manchester in the morning – would return the following day, at noon, to resume the match. And, in bright sunshine the following day, FC eventually ran out 4-1 winners.

The use of 'pyro' by FC fans – which set off the ground's fire alarm prior to the lights going out – hacked off several supporters who ended up with damaged clothes and singed scalps, as one of FC's volunteer safety stewards highlighted on the members' forum. The club's former safety officer reckoned that the perpetrators 'have no regard for the safety of others around them' and he urged fellow supporters to 'call them out'. The arrangements for the match in Kraków, posted on FC's website a few days beforehand, had included a warning that 'anyone bringing flares which may damage the pitch or stands risks being ejected from the ground'.

'No pyro, no party' has become a matchday mantra for many younger supporters and there's no doubt that flares have added to the atmosphere at plenty of FC matches down the years – Rochdale, Bradford Park Avenue in the play-off semi-final in 2011 and the night we won promotion in 2015 spring to mind – and, like a lot of clubs, we've often used those colourful images to sell our matchday atmosphere and the passion of our supporters. But it's not for everyone and, as the club's owners as well as its passionate supporters, we must bear that in mind and police ourselves accordingly.

* * *

Perhaps uniquely in modern football, FC United's founding manifesto includes the commitment that it 'will strive wherever possible to avoid outright commercialism', so it's unsurprising that it has perennially struggled on the commercial front. And the club's relationship with commercialism is perhaps one of its most misunderstood aspects – even by its own supporters.

Without a big-time investor to splash the cash, sponsorship and advertising income is essential to FC remaining competitive on the pitch and being able to challenge for promotion. When you consider that FC United is the largest supporter-owned club in the country, boasts crowds and a social media following that wouldn't look out of place in League Two and has a profile that extends way beyond Manchester and England (with supporters from all over Europe regularly visiting Broadhurst Park), it's something of a puzzle that we struggle so much to find sponsors.

We were limited in terms of advertising opportunities as tenants at Gigg Lane but struggled to capitalise on new opportunities when we moved into Broadhurst Park. 'We should have gone commercial as soon as we moved into the new ground,' reckons Paul Haworth, who became the club's interim part-time business development manager from January 2024 and later its full-time commercial manager. But it wasn't until after the pandemic that we finally got round to employing a dedicated commercial manager when Frances Fielding joined the club.

Frances made an impression but she was here less than a year before moving to Manchester United, and then Danny Davis came in but his role changed soon after Natalie Atkinson departed as CEO, so we've not surprisingly struggled to gather momentum on the commercial front.

Paul reckons that 'we are effectively a League Two club operating on a Northern Premier League budget and staff team' when it comes to commercial activity. Due to financial constraints, 'We expect one person to be responsible for all the club's revenue lines, be a salesperson, account manager and marketing team.' Which isn't easy.

And because of our history we face challenges to growing our commercial income that don't exist at other clubs. 'Yes, we'd all like a £50,000-a-year sponsor for the men's first team but without shirt sponsorship being available we have to find other assets for businesses to sponsor,' said Paul.

Paul feels that from a commercial perspective there is little to be gained from comparing us to the likes of Atherton Collieries or Ashton United. 'Our ground and facilities and support are much better. We built this ground with the intention of it one day becoming a league ground,' he says. 'Look at Barrow, as a League Two club, they are more than happy to train here.' And most non-league clubs with facilities like ours tend to be ex-league clubs like Macclesfield.

Our revenue model, however, is very different to the likes of Barrow, who generate a significant amount of income by selling players at a profit and also receive television money by being in the EFL. Barring a run in the FA Cup we don't receive any broadcasting income and the amount we earn through the sale of players tends to be limited – the four-figure sum received for Regan Linney, for instance, is tiny compared to the transfer fees in the EFL. But our running costs are relatively high – for example, we spend about £60,000 a year on electricity. So it's important we maximise the profit we make from sponsorship and advertising, selling merchandise and hosting functions and events.

It wasn't until 2022 that FC set out its overall approach towards sponsors and corporate partners when it adopted an ethical sponsorship and corporate partnership policy. The policy states, 'The club will not have relationships with organisations or industries whose principles, policies or conduct are in obvious conflict with the club's values or where, in the club's view, public perception of such organisations and industries might undermine the club's reputation or credibility and/or damage our relationship with our stakeholders.'

And it sets out a list of activities that the club would seek to avoid working with: business activities that cause damage or harm to local communities either nationally or internationally, but with specific regard to Manchester in particular; criminal activity; weapons or weapons systems manufacture, sale or distribution; tobacco manufacture; human rights violation, including modern slavery; business activities in perennial breach of UN Global Compact; overt tax avoidance (e.g. use of low/no tax jurisdictions in corporate structures); and generating revenue from the sale of pornography. Conspicuous by its absence from this list is gambling as there was a feeling that objecting to a gambling firm sponsoring the club would smack of double standards given that it has operated a fundraising half-time draw – a form of gambling – almost since day one.

The policy is also clear that it excludes any sponsorship arrangements that the club 'is required to fulfil by virtue of being a football club operating in the English football pyramid and its related competitions' which includes, for instance, the need to refer, as we've already seen, to the FA Cup as the Emirates FA Cup in all our official communications – despite the fact that Emirates is a flag-carrying airline of a country with a human rights record that would breach FC's ethical sponsorship policy. There was a recognition, also, that in some cases the application of this policy may require subjective judgement and in situations where it's not possible to achieve consensus it would be escalated to the board to decide.

The ethical sponsorship policy had been written after a members' survey in 2021, completed by over 700 co-owners, had given the board a steer on a host of issues. Eighty-eight per cent of co-owners surveyed felt that the club continued to fulfil its manifesto commitment to 'avoid outright commercialism' and 57 per cent remained opposed to shirt sponsorship under any circumstances. At its first general meeting in 2006 an overwhelming majority of co-owners had backed a resolution 'that no FC United of Manchester playing strip will carry shirt sponsorship'. But interestingly, 16 years on, 28 per cent said they might back shirt sponsorship 'under certain circumstances' and 15 per cent were in favour of it 'as long as it was a good deal for the club'.

Which signifies some softening of views on shirt sponsorship and it was notable that among those supporters who had been following the club for less than ten years the objection to shirt sponsorship under any circumstances fell to 41 per cent. It will be interesting to see where supporter opinion on this sits in five to ten years' time.

The issue of shirt sponsorship is an old chestnut that's been debated on a regular basis throughout the club's history – particularly at times when finances have been tight. In 2023 a poster on the members' forum wondered if we'd investigated how much a potential shirt sponsorship deal could be worth. But for many supporters a shirt sponsor remains a red line not to be crossed no matter how much cash it might bring in. 'If we have to sponsor the shirt, the club has failed,' replied one member, while another questioned, 'If you have to sacrifice everything you've believed in to survive ... have you survived at all?'

But others recognised that many newer co-owners clearly don't view shirt sponsorship in such stark terms and one member wondered if, initially, inviting a charity or non-governmental organisation to sponsor our shirt might be an agreeable halfway house. Another, with wry humour, reckoned, 'Given the state of our finances the RNLI may be a good choice.'

Interestingly, Paul Haworth thinks the whole issue around shirt sponsorship has become something of a red herring, 'It's not the silver bullet that people think it is. We've got other commercial assets that are much more valuable than the front of a football shirt.'

Paul feels that our vote to have no shirt sponsorship in 2005 signified a fightback against the increasing commercialism of football. 'Let's be honest, most of us didn't have a problem with sponsors' names appearing on shirts,' he says. 'Many of us were happy to wear a [Manchester United] shirt bearing the name of Sharp.' The issue we had was with commercialism increasingly taking priority over the interests of fans.

'We rarely get any coverage on television or in the national press so it's really mainly the people in the ground that see a sponsor's logo on the shirt,' says Paul, 'so we're better off offering potential sponsors the opportunity, say, to have their logo splashed across one of our stands – it's much more eye-catching than a logo on a shirt.'

And with our extensive social media reach, businesses can get their name in front of many more pairs of eyes by advertising on our channels. 'We've already started doing this by running adverts for some of our sponsors on social media during half-time of games this season and haven't had any complaints from fans so far,' adds Paul.

Paul feels that the current sponsorship packages that we've put together for the men's and women's teams offer much better value for businesses than shirt sponsorship. 'Once we sell these packages things will look a lot different on our social media, matchday programme, website and around the ground,' he adds. 'We've valued the men's team sponsorship package at £50,000, and if we were to find a sponsor, supporters would likely see the benefit of that in terms of an increased playing budget which would hopefully make a difference on the pitch.'

For me, what started off as a red line in 2005 has been overtaken by a growing realisation that we formed FC United to demonstrate that supporters can own and run football clubs and it's entirely up to us to decide on the details of whether we want a shirt sponsor or not. The red line for me is the dilution of supporter ownership.

Stadium naming rights also appears to be off-limits with supporters as 68 per cent of respondents to the survey said that they wouldn't consider it under any circumstances. However, 72 per cent said that they would be prepared to consider sponsorship of one of the stands at Broadhurst Park. There's always been some affection, among fans of a certain vintage, for the 'Wonderfuel Gas' sign above the old Stretford End prior to the redevelopment of Old Trafford in the early 90s so perhaps this wasn't a surprise.

On the same evening as FC's trip to Kraków, it was clear that the club's ethical sponsorship policy would be tested as a *Panorama* documentary entitled 'Boohoo's Broken Promises' was broadcast on the BBC which revealed that, despite the fast-fashion retailer Boohoo's promises to reform its supply chain, it was pressuring suppliers to cut costs and meet shorter deadlines on orders. Why was this of interest to FC United? Well, Boohoo is the parent company of PrettyLittleThing who became FC's 'official women and girls' football partner' in a five-figure sponsorship deal announced in January 2023.

At pretty much every lower-league club in the country the announcement of a five-figure sponsorship deal with a local company would be a cause for celebration. But news of FC's deal with the fast fashion retailer PrettyLittleThing, the single largest sponsorship deal in the club's history, involved oodles of work behind the scenes to ensure that the announcement went smoothly.

PrettyLittleThing had initially approached FC United in the autumn of 2022 and said they were interested in supporting women's and girls' football in Manchester following the popularity of the UEFA Women's European Championship in 2022 and the success of the victorious England team. They were attracted to FC United's ethos as a supporter-owned club, how rooted we are in our local community, and also the progressive nature of the club with its then predominantly female senior leadership team. They had already sponsored an FC United match but were clear that they wished to offer more substantial support to the club this time round.

The deal would see PLT's logo feature on all marketing materials produced by the club to promote women's and girls' football, a full-page colour advert in every matchday programme and half a dozen pitchside advertising boards. A brand that specialises in 'killer looks' and the 'latest trend-led pieces' for modern 20-something women had hooked up with a non-league football club with an increasingly middle-aged male support.

However, the Boohoo Group, of which PrettyLittleThing is part, had been accused of modern slavery in July 2020 after an undercover investigation by the *Sunday Times* discovered that the company were paying their garment workers £3.50 an hour at a factory in Leicester – less than half the minimum wage at the time for those over 25. The workers' rights group Labour Behind the Label also found that staff were 'forced to come into work while sick' during the pandemic, which was later linked to an increase in Covid cases in Leicester.

Given this controversial recent history, co-owners would be bound to have lots of questions about the deal so it was crucial that we explained the rationale behind it and were prepared for as many questions as possible prior to the announcement. FC's ethical sponsorship and corporate partnership policy specifically mentions that the club will avoid working with organisations involved in human rights violation (including modern slavery) and overt tax avoidance.

This approach by PLT was referred to the club's commercial committee (and the board was also made aware) and due diligence was undertaken on PLT and Boohoo Group to ensure that it complied with the club's ethical sponsorship and corporate partnership policy before giving Natalie Atkinson and Frances Fielding the green light to commence discussions.

As the board and CEO's communications business partner, I was asked to draft the press release for this announcement and spent a couple of weeks digesting the mumbo jumbo of countless corporate reports, trying to understand the carefully crafted legalese of reviews by Alison Levitt and Sir Brian Leveson (the latter best known for leading the inquiry into press ethics after the phone-hacking scandal), and browsing through a stack of news articles about PLT and Boohoo, none of which were complimentary. And then to complicate matters further, in late November 2022, on Black Friday, Labour Behind the Label organised a protest outside PLT's HQ on Dale Street in the centre of Manchester which was covered on the local BBC news.

It was the toughest piece of work I've been involved in since volunteering for the comms team in 2016 as it wasn't difficult to imagine the fallout and 20-page forum threads if we had ballsed up the announcement.

In May 2021 the revelation that the Far East Consortium (FEC) had made a donation to FC United's food hub, which had supported its local community through the pandemic, and an FEC representative had secured a place on a working group responsible for setting out a strategy for the club's extensive work in its local community provoked a furious reaction from many FC supporters who were sickened that the club that prides itself on 'making friends not millionaires' had entered into any relationship whatsoever with a Hong Kong-based property development company that was registered in the Cayman Islands.

The FEC had partnered with Manchester City Council in a joint venture, known as the Victoria North project, said to be 'worth £4bn', to regenerate the Irk Valley area as the city centre pushes north from Victoria station like an invading army.

One co-owner pointed out that the homeless charity Lifeshare, which had been turfed out of its home for over 30 years by the redevelopment, had been working for several years with FC United on its annual Christmas Comforts and Big Coat Day events (both set up to support local homeless people) and, for this reason only, the club should have given any involvement with the FEC a swerve. It led to a long-running debate about the operation of the club's food hub and the resignation of one of the board members who was accused of lying to co-owners.

It could be argued that the FEC's involvement in FC's food hub was an act of 'sportswashing', albeit on a much smaller scale than the Abu Dhabi takeover of another local club, that had many supporters understandably highlighting that if companies like this were happy to pay their fair share of tax in the UK, then there would be no need for food hubs to exist in the first place.

On a personal level, I didn't approve of the club doing this deal with PrettyLittleThing – no matter how much money it would bring in, it didn't sit right with me that we should enter into a commercial relationship with a company with such a controversial past. But, at the same time, I could see how delighted Natalie and Frances were to secure this deal, which also had the backing of the board, so it was important to shelve personal opinions and do what's right for the club.

In the end, a detailed Q&A document to support the press release announcing the deal stretched to 3,000 words. It acknowledged that while PLT 'have had serious issues in the past with its supply chain', the process of due diligence that we'd been through had assured us that it had 'reformed its supply chain since 2020 to such an extent that PLT now represents a suitable partner for the club and, importantly, one which complies with our ethical policy'.

There was also the crucial question of whether this deal represents 'outright commercialism'. Nearly two decades after we had outlined our opposition to it in the club's founding manifesto, we still hadn't defined exactly what we meant by 'outright commercialism'. All we'd got to go on was a five-point test developed by a former board member several years ago that hadn't been approved by the board or even discussed at a board meeting.

However, in light of the size of this sponsorship deal, the board felt that it was important to demonstrate that it avoided being seen as 'outright commercialism' and, in the absence of any other guidelines, the board and commercial committee had considered each of the questions posed in the five-point test and concluded, particularly in light of the club's current financial situation, that the deal avoided that classification. The five questions were answered as follows:

- Is the deal explicitly barred by any existing rule or resolution of the club? *No.*
- Has any prior vote by the membership implicitly agreed to the deal through its direct consequences (e.g. FA Cup entry/televised games)? *No.*
- Does the deal detract from, contradict or sit at odds with the other principles (values) outlined in the club's manifesto? *No.*
- Is the deal necessary in light of the club's financial situation, be that in the short, medium or long term? *Yes.*
- Is there any alternative and realistic option for raising the revenue that this deal proposes, within the same time frame? *No.*

In the end, the announcement of the deal, despite my worst fears, was largely well received by supporters and there was an appreciation for the detailed rationale that we'd offered. There was also recognition that there are always likely to be questions with commercial deals of this magnitude as few companies are 'whiter than white' when it comes to ethical concerns. As one of the club's original steering committee members (and former board member), Luc Zentar, pointed out on the members' forum, it's almost impossible in the modern day to be completely ethical so the question increasingly becomes one of how much we're prepared to compromise. 'The fact that we're even having this discussion and are able to make changes if we collectively decide to do so is what is so special about FC,' he concluded.

This was also the first time either Little Mix or a member of the Kardashian family had been mentioned in an FC United press release. Beat that, Wrexham.

Importantly, the deal included a termination clause for 'any material breach of terms that might impact on the club's revenue or reputational damage' and a few weeks after the *Panorama* documentary aired, the board confirmed that the deal wouldn't be extended beyond its initial one year which, while it left a big hole in the club's commercial revenue, felt like the right decision in the circumstances.

Current board chair Nick Boom reckons that 'the deal was always on the margins' of what we were comfortable with as a club and adds that former CEO Natalie Atkinson 'really pushed for it as she was passionate about the development of women's and girls' football and was convinced that it was going to be a long-term deal'. But following Natalie's departure and a change of senior personnel at PLT, the club's relationship with them cooled and then the shocking revelations in the documentary clearly risked reputational damage for the club.

On the other hand there are sponsors who've been with us for years and Nick highlights a recent conversation with Ray Vaughan, the co-founder of Chauntry Ltd, who provide booking systems for car park operators across the world and have supported the club since 2005. Ray estimates that his company has contributed around £250,000 to FC down the years as sponsors of the youth team; this sponsorship has played a crucial role in the development of the club's academy. What initially began as support for youth football coaching sessions has developed into an on-site academy that provides full-time education and football coaching for 16-to-18-year-olds across north Manchester.

Paul Haworth believes that a partnership approach to the club's commercial deals is the way forward. 'We need to look after our sponsors,' he says. 'Too often in the past we took the money and then didn't do anything, it was purely transactional.' He explains that he's recently done a deal with a local paint manufacturer, in which they've agreed to sponsor us and also supply us with some free paint and, in return, we've offered our function room as a venue for their Christmas party. 'There's an ongoing conversation with them about how we can help each other and that's important,' Paul adds.

There are perhaps more advertising boards around the ground now than there have ever been in our time at Broadhurst Park, with adverts for a local brewery, a paint manufacturer, a scrap metal dealer, a city centre pub, a clothing company, and a firm that provides consultancy to the local health service. It's a useful measure of the extent to which the club engages with its local business community. 'I want boards right the way round the ground that advertise businesses and products that our supporters are interested in and want to buy so that there's something in it for everyone,' explains Paul.

* * *

Manchester United's 4-3 defeat to FC Copenhagen in their 'must-win' Champions League match on 8 November included a bit of FC history as the Portuguese player Diogo Gonçalves became part of a select group of players – which includes Jamie Vardy, Anthony Pilkington and Ché Adams – who have scored against both FC United and Manchester United. Gonçalves was Broadhurst Park's first goalscorer in May 2015 when FC played a young Benfica side to mark the ground's opening.

* * *

There's a chill in the air, a bright-blue sky and the crunch of leaves underfoot. Saturday, 11 November felt like the first proper big coat day of the season – perfect for whiling away a few hours in Lancaster.

As well as boasting perhaps the finest name of any football ground in England, Lancaster City's Giant Axe home is also handy for the town's railway station – barely a five-minute stroll away – and is overlooked along one side by trains pulling into and out of the station. It's a ground where we've rarely done well and today was no different. The home side hit the woodwork twice and while FC huffed and puffed in search of a breakthrough we seldom looked like scoring and a goalless draw was probably a fair result in the end.

The match was watched by a crowd of exactly 1,000 spectators – many of whom were still queuing to get in several minutes after kick-off – which was the Dolly Blues' largest attendance of the season so far and more than 500 in excess of their average so far for the campaign.

After the match I wandered into the town centre where around 100 people, many with candles, placards, banners and Palestinian flags, had assembled in the Market Square to listen to speakers calling for a ceasefire in Gaza where Israel had killed more than 10,000 Palestinians since Hamas's massacre of more than 1,000 Israelis on 7 October. It was one of many such gatherings around the country on Armistice Day – the perfect day to call for such a ceasefire.

I joined the throng and stood near a woman with a placard displaying the words 'oppose genocide'. It was difficult to make out what some of the softly spoken speakers were saying and, later on, there was an awkward moment when the gathering was disrupted by a small group of young FC United supporters who came marching down the road, singing FC songs, behind a large union flag which bore the club's badge.

I'm not sure they were aware that this gathering was taking place in the square and they quickly moved on but there was an awkward moment where, not surprisingly, some of the peace marchers thought they were about to come under attack from a group of flag-wielding football hooligans and the majority began chanting 'free, free Palestine' to drown out the songs of the FC fans.

I don't think any malice was intended by the young lads but it could easily have become a flashpoint on a day when a huge demonstration in London calling for a ceasefire in Gaza came under attack by right-wing thugs. Up to 800,000 people joined the march in London – including some FC United supporters who'd made the trip to the capital rather than Lancaster – and it was the largest such event in the UK since 15 February 2003 when more than one million people – including me – had marched through London to Hyde Park to protest against the planned invasion of Iraq.

Later, as the peace marchers left the square and began marching through the centre of Lancaster behind a banner which read 'Palestine can't breathe', they sang, 'From the river to the sea, Palestine will be free.' Interestingly, if this had been sung at the nearby football ground earlier in the afternoon it would possibly have landed one or both clubs in trouble, not only with the football authorities but the police as well.

Earlier in the month, clubs across the country had been sent guidance by the FA 'relating to the continuing conflict in the Middle East', which urged 'everyone in football to exercise restraint when expressing views that could be seen as causing offence to any community' and, in particular, to refrain from using the phrase 'from the river to the sea' which had been highlighted as causing 'deep offence' to Israelis. It warned that any use of this specific phrase by clubs would result in the FA 'seeking guidance from relevant authorities, including the police'.

* * *

The following day, the biggest cup tie that any FC United side has played so far this season – with £6,000 in prize money up for grabs – saw a magnificent victory for the women's team as they beat York City Ladies 2-0, in front of a crowd of 230 at the University of York's athletics stadium, to progress to the second round of the Women's FA Cup for the first time in the club's history. It was a well-deserved victory with both goals scored by Ella Ritchie.

Quite a turnaround from the 5-0 defeat to York a few weeks ago and manager Jennie Swarbrick hailed it as the team's finest performance of the season so far. There was even a rare thread on The Soul is One about a women's match with the comment 'Brilliant result! Swarbrick is working wonders' summing up the mood.

Earlier in the week the club had launched its Wildcats programme for girls aged five to 11 to try out football for the first time, in a non-competitive environment, and also keep active and make new friends. The sessions are run by FA qualified coaches and are part of a national programme sponsored by Weetabix. FC's events will take place each Thursday evening at Broadhurst Park and will hopefully offer young girls a pathway into football that could lead to them playing for the FC women's team.

Sunday, 12 November was also the deadline to ask questions on the members' forum of the five candidates standing for election to the board at the forthcoming AGM. It allows those who will be unable to attend the meeting a chance to put their questions and it's become an important part of our democratic process. A total of eight questions have been asked ahead of this year's AGM, with candidates invited to give us their thoughts on topics including how we boost attendances, the success of the club's committee structure, our participation in the Fenix Trophy and the perennial problem of how to improve the retention of staff.

* * *

'We're delighted to announce that we've signed a striker who brings a top pedigree and a proven track record in the NPL,' posts the club on X as it announces the signing of experienced striker Bobby Grant and shares an interview with him in FC's training gear after he'd trained with the rest of the squad the night before. The 33-year-old spoke of how he had 'jumped at the chance' to join FC after speaking to Neil Reynolds about his plans for the club.

It's not quite that November day in 1992 when Manchester United signed Eric Cantona but it's quite a coup to sign a player of this calibre – Grant has plenty of Football League experience having played for the likes of Blackpool, Accrington Stanley and Rochdale and also, more recently, had a spell as player-manager of Radcliffe – and a potentially season-defining moment.

But later the same evening, incredibly, the deal was off as within minutes of the announcement Grant had messaged Reno to inform him that he'd decided to sign for another club after receiving a more attractive offer.

When the club later posts on X that the deal is off, it becomes one of FC's most popular social media posts ever as it garners more than one million views and the story attracts national media interest. 'Player signs for non-league FC United – then quits hours after interview in club tracksuit' announces the *Daily Star* on its website the following day.

The saga created something of a siege mentality going into the home match against Guiseley the following day, which FC went into without a centre-forward following Grant's late snub. We won 3-2 thanks to a last-minute penalty by Declan McLoughlin, which brought a welcome three points and our first win at home since September.

* * *

FC United shared six goals with Bamber Bridge at the Sir Tom Finney Stadium on 21 November after goals from Max Woodcock and Charlie Munro had put them 2-0 up after 20 minutes. Brig levelled the scores shortly after half-time before Dontai Gabidon restored our lead but we couldn't hang on and it finished 3-3 in the end despite the home side going down to ten men after ex-FC United skipper Michael Potts was sent off early in the second half. You can't help feeling it was a case of two points lost rather than one gained. Although, unbeknown to us, even this solitary point would be lost later in the season.

* * *

FC's annual general meeting on Sunday, 26 November is one of two set-piece members' meetings during the year and a cornerstone of the club's democracy. The club's rules stipulate that it must hold at least two general meetings a year and for it to be able to do business there must be a quorum of either '20 members or ten per cent of the members entitled to vote at the meeting whichever is the lower'.

The AGM provides an opportunity for co-owners to vote on motions on a range of issues and also stand for election to the board and is also the meeting at which the board reports to co-owners on the club's financial performance in the previous financial year – in this case the 2022/23 year. The financial statements are made available for co-owners to review prior to the AGM.

Prior to the pandemic all general meetings were held in person but the lockdown of spring 2020 forced us, like workplaces all over the country, to look at other options for holding meetings and, for a while, all board and general meetings were held online. But since the last of the Covid restrictions ended in 2021 we have switched to a hybrid model which allows co-owners to attend either in person or online.

This meeting was also the first time that FC United's co-owners had been able to vote online at an AGM. The club had been looking at online voting options for a while and the co-ownership committee had been asked to find a cost-effective solution. Conversations with other supporter-owned clubs and supporters' trusts ensued and the Election Runner platform, which had already been used for several years by the Exeter City Supporters' Trust, was eventually selected as the preferred option.

Instead of faffing around with ballot papers, forms and envelopes, voting online is a relatively simple process that involves members being sent an email following the general meeting or AGM containing a link to an online ballot paper that they are able to access via unique log-in details which are also supplied in the email.

Co-owners voted in favour of two resolutions at the AGM – firstly that the club should implement a 'fund the foundations' scheme to raise funds to help repay the debts incurred in the building and development of Broadhurst Park, and secondly a resolution that the club should have the ability to change its home, away and third kits on an annual basis. To be passed, resolutions require a simple majority (i.e. more than 50 per cent) of those co-owners who voted.

There were also several members' votes which, although not binding, are designed to offer direction to the board. Perhaps the most significant of these saw 82 per cent of co-owners vote in favour of raising the qualifying age for concession price admission from 60 to 65 while 95 per cent backed the motion that 18-to-21-year-olds should be treated as a separate admission pricing category with an admission price of £5 from next season. As with resolutions, members' votes also require a simple majority of those members who vote in order to be passed.

There was also overwhelming support to continue with the 'pay what you can afford' season ticket scheme for 2024/25 with the same minimum price of £175 for adults, £135 for concessions and £21 for under-18s. This pioneering scheme was first introduced in 2009 when the club 'did a Radiohead' by replicating the 'pay what you like' business model the band had used for its *In Rainbows* album – although we didn't actually go quite as far as

Radiohead as we recommended minimum prices for season tickets.

In doing so FC United became the first football club to offer fans the chance to set their own season ticket price in the hope that those who can afford to pay a bit more will do so and, in the process, subsidise those who pay less. If fans were struggling to pay the minimum price, then they were encouraged to contact the club to arrange to pay in instalments.

And down the years some supporters have donated season tickets to those in financial hardship. It was all about putting supporters at the heart of the club rather than being banished to the fringes.

The club's founding manifesto commits it to doing everything it can to keep admission prices as affordable as possible. While the £13 admission price for adults is cheap in comparison to top-flight football, there was a recognition that it may not be so affordable for young adults who've chosen not to go into higher education and may be in low-paid jobs and are faced with a substantial increase in admission price from £3 to £13 when they turn 18. In contrast, those who stay in education at the same age are charged the reduced concession price of £9.

At the other end of the age scale someone aged 60, who may still be in a relatively well-paid job towards the end of their career, is also able to get in for only £9. It's an interesting debate that mirrors concerns that young people are increasingly getting a raw deal in wider society as governments are perceived to prioritise the finances and wellbeing of older generations.

A few days after the AGM the vote count took place at Broadhurst Park and the turnout of 33.3 per cent (615 votes from 1,845 eligible members) was more than five times the number of co-owners (108) who had voted at the previous year's AGM.

All five candidates who stood for election – Matthew Haley, Nick Boom, Simon Preston, Paul Hurst and Warren Heppolette – secured sufficient votes to be elected to the board for a two-year term and each received at least 447 votes (72.7 per cent). The option to reopen nominations – aka RON – received only 42 votes.

A post-AGM review by the co-ownership committee noted, 'The number of people viewing the AGM online exceeded the number attending in person so we may need to consider for the future the fact that online is the primary audience and what that means for presenters.'

Following the AGM, a crowd of 390, the biggest of the season, watched FC's women's team take on Hull City Ladies in the second round of the Women's FA Cup – the kick-off having been pushed back to 2pm to allow sufficient time for the meeting. It was a belting match against a side that had thrashed us 6-0 at Broadhurst Park only a couple of weeks before and currently sit in third place in National League Division One North. Eve O'Carroll gave FC the lead in the 23rd minute but Hull equalised before half-time and eventually ran out 3-2 winners.

It was FC's first appearance in the second round of the Women's FA Cup and this season's run has earned the club £12,000 in prize money. Only a couple of years ago we would have needed to reach the quarter-finals to earn that much prize money, which illustrates again the extent to which commercial interest in the women's game has grown on the back of the Lionesses' success in the European Championship in 2022.

* * *

As November drew to a close, FC announced the signing of striker Jordan Buckley from Warrington Town for an undisclosed fee. This will be Jordan's second spell at FC having left the club in the autumn of 2019 in search of regular first-team football after the free-scoring Tunde Owolabi had quickly made the number nine shirt his own at Broadhurst Park.

6

It's just the big clubs
being greedy again

'HOW GOOD is 85-rated footballer Jack Grealish in real life?' asks a video that YouTuber Abisola Emmanuel 'Eman' Balogun – better known as SV2 – shared with his 3.8 million followers in early December in which he took on ex-Aston Villa star Jack Grealish in a football challenge for an app which allows young players to showcase their skills to a wider audience – showing again how social media platforms have become the go-to route to getting noticed.

What's this got to do with FC United? Well, the 'challenge' was filmed on the pitch at Broadhurst Park. Over the last few years several advertising and media agencies have been keen to use our ground for film shoots and special events and it's become an important source of income for the club – in 2023/24 it generated £35,000 from hire of the main pitch. The ground – particularly the St Mary's Road End and the main stand – offers an impressive backdrop and is a relatively inexpensive option for film shoots. Grealish was the latest in a string of star footballers – including Sergio Agüero, Phil Foden and Jadon Sancho – who've taken to the Broadhurst Park turf for filming and photoshoots.

The SV2 video provided some excellent footage of Broadhurst Park, but there was some nervousness among the club's communications volunteers about how sharing a video featuring a Manchester City player might go down with FC supporters. However, the board confirmed it was comfortable with sharing it as 'film shoots are a key pillar of our business model', as Nick Boom put it, and there was a feeling that co-owners would understand the importance of us promoting our facilities.

Many young people access football content through YouTube nowadays and some clubs like Hashtag United – with 648,000 subscribers to their channel and nearly 130 million views – generate a significant chunk of revenue from sharing match highlights, interviews and features on the platform. In contrast, FC United's YouTube channel, which was set up in 2012, currently has 5,650 subscribers and has been viewed 312,000 times.

* * *

With the country gripped by freezing temperatures and the majority of matches in the Northern Premier League postponed, it was nice to pick up three points on the road as we beat Gainsborough Trinity 3-1 on the first Saturday of December. It was the Lincolnshire side's first defeat of the season at their Northolme ground, which claims to be the oldest stadium in the world to be continuously used by one team as it's been the Holy Blues' home since 1884.

Following the match, a message on the NPL Group Facebook page from Tom Parkinson said, 'The FC United fans are a credit to their club. They brought at least 200 today and never stopped singing.' Tom added, 'Unfortunately for us they went back with all three points but they made the atmosphere today. Well done, guys and all the best for the season.'

* * *

Thomas Street in Manchester's Northern Quarter has been closed to the public while it's transformed into a canopied catwalk ready to welcome more than 600 guests – including David Beckham, Kate Moss and Kristen Stewart – for Chanel's much-anticipated Métiers d'Art show, which the French fashion house has brought to Manchester to give its glitzy global brand some northern grit.

On 7 December, as people gathered near Thomas Street to glimpse the celebrities, a few protesters had also gathered, unimpressed with the council cosying up to a luxury fashion brand while many Mancunians are struggling to put food on the table or heat their homes. If they have a home at all. This time last year, a 33-year-old man had died while sleeping rough in freezing weather only yards from this spot – highlighting again the city's homeless problem. One placard read 'Food or heat not luxury consumer goods' and urged the council to 'get your priorities sorted' while another referred to 'over 250,000 children living in poverty in Manchester'.

There had been no difficulty accessing the boardwalk at Broadhurst Park earlier in the week for the first meeting of the newly elected board following the AGM. The board had agreed that Nick Boom would be the new chair with Warren Heppolette as vice-chair and had also agreed to invite Bhavna Mistry back. Bhavna had originally joined the board as a non-executive director in June but, as per the club's rules, had to stand down at the AGM.

Each board member had also agreed to oversee the work of one of the club's six committees although it acknowledged that it lacked expertise regarding the club's community work and had therefore agreed to co-opt someone – ideally a community leader with knowledge of the local area – to assist in developing our community programme and provide oversight of the community committee.

Meanwhile, Bhavna had undertaken a review of the club's merchandising operation encompassing both the actual and online shops and other outlets such as the National Football Museum and she presented her findings and recommendations to the board.

The report identified that merchandise sales in the first nine months of 2023 were around a third up on the same period last year but there is much that we can improve. The review found that while products are generally neatly displayed in the club shop, displays often 'feel tired' and the shop window is limited in space. There's also a lack of signage around the ground to direct supporters to the shop – it's easy for newcomers to miss it – and the report suggests that we should consider opening the shop on non-matchdays to maximise sales, especially in the run-up to Christmas.

Of course, a significant proportion of sales happen online these days and the review found that while our online shop compares well to other clubs at our level, we could improve the quality of the images we use of items on sale. As the report mentioned, 'We select what we want with our eyes.'

The National Football Museum in Manchester city centre has recently begun stocking a selection of FC items in their shop but Bhavna's report noted that we had not replenished stock on a regular basis, which had affected sales.

The report made several recommendations that were accepted by the board and the commercial committee was invited to prepare an action plan to implement them, including the preparation of a business case for the recruitment of a paid shop manager.

An important change to the board meeting business means that from now on there will be a standing item on the agenda for the board to receive and discuss reports from the club's committees. Nick Boom stressed that the committees are an extension of the board, operating under delegated powers, and it's important that the board has oversight of their work through its committee leads.

* * *

Heavy overnight rain put our home match against Marine on Saturday, 9 December in doubt but a pitch inspection around 1.30pm deemed the surface playable and the forecast, at the time, was for no more significant rain until much later in the afternoon. But within half an hour another spell of rain swept in, puddles began to form on the pitch and five minutes before the match was due to kick off the referee called it off.

The Coalition of Kindness community group, led by FC's former community liaison officer Vinny Thompson, had organised a collection of food items and Christmas presents prior to the match for people struggling during the ongoing cost of living crisis. And despite the lack of any football, the collection was well supported by fans of both clubs including Marine supporters who travelled in numbers and dropped off items.

A typically 'classy gesture' – as FC board member Matthew Haley remarked – from supporters of a club that regularly collects for local food banks at its own home games. Vinny described the collection as 'a magnificent effort' and added, 'We can't thank everyone enough. Great respect to both sets of fans for their contributions. The donations will put smiles on the faces of people who need them most this Christmas.'

The *Liverpool Echo* cottoned on to the story later in the week and remarked, 'The support from both sides shows the solidarity between Liverpool and Manchester, despite their long-standing rivalry on and off the pitch, in the fight to end austerity.' But a week later Manchester United fans could be heard chanting 'feed the scousers' at Anfield.

Another strand of the club's community work had seen staff and volunteers at FC United visiting local schools to talk to pupils about their role at the club as part of an initiative run by the North Manchester Business Network called What's My Job, designed, in a fun way, to challenge how children aged nine and ten think about the world of work and their future in it. As the programme's website explains, it's important to do this as early as possible as even at the age of seven almost half of children base their job aspirations on people they know.

A few weeks earlier the club's operations coordinator Nigel Brookes took part in the programme and kids at a local school tried to guess what he did at FC United. 'It was lovely to hear some of them say they recognised me as they come to Broadhurst Park with their families, showing we are becoming further embedded locally,' said Nigel.

* * *

Marske United issued a statement on 10 December explaining that their licence to play in the Northern Premier League had been suspended and the NPL had requested further information 'regarding the recent change in structure following the departure of the previous chairman'.

Their forthcoming fixtures against Worksop and Lancaster have therefore been postponed.

Marske had hoped to bring in new investment by opening a share scheme 'to guarantee survival to the end of the season and beyond' but the plans were postponed when the club learned that it would take six to eight weeks to establish and they would be unable to play during that time and would therefore have no money coming in.

* * *

In FC's early years we took pride in our '90/90 atmosphere' at Gigg Lane with 90 per cent of supporters singing for 90 per cent of the match. It was the sonic-negative of what we'd grown accustomed to in the Premier League. Instead of newcomers turning up at Old Trafford in awe of multi-millionaire superstars, we sang about how 'we don't care about Rio', and the 'Govan socialist' who'd famously labelled us as 'attention seekers' quite rightly copped for some stick too.

The atmosphere at Broadhurst Park these days isn't quite what it once was but away from home our support, more often than not, is relentless. Such was the case at Worksop Town on the third Saturday of December – one of those afternoons when as each opposition goal goes in the noise generated by the FC fans is cranked up a notch.

At half-time, with FC trailing 2-0 and the ground enveloped in a beautiful wintry sunset, an elderly bloke approached me and said, 'You lot have been great.' I paused momentarily as I wasn't sure what he was referring to until he added, 'The non-stop singing, it's great, I've really enjoyed it.'

He went on to reminisce about his days following nearby Rotherham United and how he used to travel everywhere with the Millers. But he's in his mid-70s now so when he can't get to an away match he'll often come to watch Worksop. And he waxed lyrical about having seen Bobby Charlton play for United back in the day along with Duncan Edwards who he reckoned was 'the greatest ever'. It was a lovely chat and his warm words about FC United provided one of those timely reminders that despite our current travails there's still much to be proud of. It often takes an outsider to offer some much-needed perspective.

The second half continued in the same vein with the home side scoring twice more in the last ten minutes to win 4-0. The fourth time that we've been thumped by four goals or more this season. A tongue-in-cheek rendition of 'Don't blame it on the sunshine … blame it on the budget' filled the Bassetlaw air. At the halfway point of the season we're in 16th place with our eyes increasingly drawn more to the bottom of the league than the top. Beating Worksop 3-0 on the opening day of the season feels like a distant memory.

There was little seasonal cheer on The Soul is One with one regular contributor posting, 'I back Neil and I sincerely hope he can turn this around but if not the board are going to face some unpleasant decisions at the end of the season.' There was also much talk, as there invariably is when we lose, about FC's playing budget and one poster reckoned that 'if the numbers being quoted' by some of the Worksop fans were correct, then their playing budget is 'around eight or nine times higher than ours with one of their star players on nearly as much as our full weekly budget'.

Post-match, a group of us hunkered down in the micropub on Worksop station were fearing that this might not be the weekend's only drubbing for a team in red with big United due to play at Anfield the following day. Liverpool were top of the table and United were coming into the match on the back of a 3-0 thumping by Bournemouth the previous weekend. 'Is anyone watching it tomorrow?' someone asked and there were head shakes and mumbled replies with important tasks such as 'a pile of ironing' and 'Christmas shopping' appearing to take Sunday afternoon priority. I didn't realise there were so many domestic superstars in our ranks.

The following day the women's team were thrashed 6-0 at Broadhurst Park by table-topping Barnsley in their final league match of 2023 and ended the year rooted to the bottom of the National League Division One North table with only four points from 11 matches and a goal difference of minus 37. Manager Jennie Swarbrick said that the target for the remainder of the season was simply to avoid relegation – the team currently sitting three points below safety but it's effectively four points if we factor in a vastly inferior goal difference.

* * *

Like an unflushable Boxing Day turd, the European Super League is back in the news after the European Court of Justice ruled that FIFA and UEFA had 'abused a dominant position' by threatening to expel clubs who took part in the ESL from major competitions when plans for a breakaway league were announced in April 2021 but then subsequently shelved after widespread supporter opposition. Shortly after the ECJ's statement, a set of revamped proposals were announced for how an expanded ESL would look, including men's and women's leagues with promotion and relegation and matches broadcast free on a digital streaming platform.

Almost exactly 31 years earlier, *90 Minutes* magazine had interviewed me and a mate – for their weekly 'ask the fans' feature – outside the away end at Stamford Bridge about talk prior to that weekend's Premier League fixtures of the big clubs planning to form a European Super League. I said something about it being all about greed and profit ('it's just the big clubs being greedy again') and how it definitely wasn't for the fans – the type of insight that regularly nets me a handful of likes on social media three decades later – and *90 Minutes* deemed our comments to be sufficiently interesting to include in the following week's magazine along with a picture of us both looking young and vaguely handsome – if you'd had half a dozen pre-match pints in an Earl's Court boozer perhaps.

The 2021 plans for a European Super League ignited a welcome debate about the ownership of football clubs and the BBC ran a brief piece on fan ownership at FC United for *Football Focus* which featured staff, volunteers and board chair Adrian Seddon talking about the benefits of supporter ownership. Then, after protests by United fans memorably forced the postponement of the biggest match in the English football calendar – United v Liverpool – *Channel 4 News* visited Broadhurst Park to film a piece on Manchester's fan-owned football club.

But fan ownership alone isn't the answer. As the chair of supporter-owned Lewes FC, Stuart Fuller, told *The Guardian* in 2021, while most of his club's 1,600 co-owners 'like the idea of being an owner, they don't want to join the board. They're happy for somebody else to do it. That's the major issue you have with fan ownership.' As we've seen at FC, supporter ownership demands commitment, scrutiny, hard work, attention to detail and, above all, participation to make it work. It's exhausting at times. And it's a collective effort – you can't just sit back and let others get on with it. There's a world of difference between fans passively consuming an on-screen product versus match-going supporters actively participating in the running of their clubs.

FC United published a statement the following day declaring that the club 'is disappointed to hear about the renewed proposal for a European Super League' and adding, 'We're once again calling for better supporter representation across the game we all love ... we strongly advocate clubs being fully owned by their supporters.' The statement continued, 'While a potential ESL may not affect FC United directly we will continue to speak out on issues that are important to football fans while offering affordable football for everyone at our fan-funded Broadhurst Park ground.'

The statement attracted a smattering of interest on X and one FC supporter quote tweeted it with the comment, 'But it's OK to post about a European competition that is pointless and makes the club come further and further away from "affordable football".' A reference to the Fenix Trophy and a reminder that the tournament isn't everyone's cup of tea.

* * *

Ahead of the visit of Stafford Rangers on the Saturday before Christmas there was a cheeky seasonal message from FC on X, 'Happy Christmas from everyone at the club to all our supporters around the world, especially Alan Gowling!' Back in 2005, shortly after FC's formation, the former Manchester United player famously remarked on BBC Radio Manchester that 'it'll all be over by Christmas' – something which we always remind him about at this time of year.

FC bossed the first half and were two goals up at half-time as a double rainbow hooped over Moston and was photographed by several supporters. The first goal was a long-distance screamer by Declan McLoughlin that went on to win FC's goal of the season award. But when Curtis Jones chested the ball into his own net early in the second half it made for a nervous last half an hour in which both sides could have added to their tally but it eventually finished 2-1 to FC. The visitors remained rooted to the bottom of the table while FC stayed in 16th place with 28 points from 22 matches – which is surprisingly only three points fewer than we had after the same number of games last season.

Prior to the match there was a festive extravaganza under the St Mary's Road End as the usual pre-match Course You Can Malcolm event was accompanied by FC United's first Christmas market, with mulled wine, mince pies and some exclusive merchandise on sale. And the result brought some festive cheer on The Soul is One with one supporter posting, 'Really enjoyed the game. Hopefully get some momentum going now and have a good second half of the season,' and another remarking on 'some real positives' with two big local derbies coming up against Ashton United and Radcliffe.

*　*　*

Late afternoon on Christmas Eve brings news that Jim Ratcliffe, the founder and CEO of the petrochemicals giant INEOS, has agreed a deal to buy 25 per cent of Manchester United for £1.25bn. 'It's the Christmas present many Manchester United fans will have been hoping for,' reports the BBC.

A statement by FC United later in the day cautioned that while 'Ratcliffe's involvement' at United 'could see some positive changes, we do not believe it will be enough to change the deep-rooted issues at Manchester United or in modern football where supporters are regularly treated with disdain'. And it went on to describe the Glazers' ownership of United as 'an unmitigated disaster' for the club 'with almost £2bn taken from the club and its supporters' and noted that despite Ratcliffe's purchase, 'the Glazer family will still hold a controlling stake in the club' and therefore 'be free to continue extracting large dividends while ignoring supporters' views'.

While Failsworth Jim paid more than £1bn for a minority stake in United, you can become a co-owner of FC for little more than £2 per month. So far this season more than 2,300 people have signed up – we've always had more than 2,000 members throughout our 18 and a half years – and we remain the largest football club in England, by number of members, that is wholly owned by its supporters.

The use of the term 'co-owner' is deliberate and signifies active participation in the running of the club rather than the more passive notion of being a 'member'. Over in M16, Manchester United has around 400,000 members who pay at least £35 per season simply for the right to be able to apply for match tickets. But, in contrast, FC United co-owners are invited to participate in the running of a football club that strives for on-pitch success and also empowers its local community. We all have skills, knowledge and experience to offer, whether it's in laying bricks, crunching numbers, designing websites, writing content, fixing electrics or as a senior executive in a multinational corporation.

And around £2 per month represents remarkable value for money when you consider the level of transparency about the running of FC United that's available to co-owners. Only last month the regular board meeting 'summary' report that documents discussions at each board meeting and is typically emailed to co-owners within a few days of the meeting stretched to nearly 8,000 words – a level of openness that would scare the living daylights out of the likes of the Glazers, Ratcliffe and Sheikh Mansour. Arguably, no group of football supporters anywhere in the UK are as well informed about the running of their club.

Being a co-owner of FC United offers an opportunity to break the mould and demonstrate that you don't have to be the mega-rich CEO of a multinational petrochemicals company or a member of the Abu Dhabi royal family to co-own a Manchester football club. And we don't have to fit the lazy, patronising stereotypes drawn up for us by the rich and powerful.

* * *

Prior to the fixture computer doing its business, each club sensibly gets the chance to nominate their preferred opponents on the various bank holidays through the season to avoid long journeys over a holiday period. So when we've been in the same division we've often ended up playing Ashton United over Christmas and Easter.

And Boxing Day sees us make the short trip to Ashton-under-Lyne for a local derby at Hurst Cross which, like Gainsborough's Northolme which FC visited a few weeks ago, is also one of the oldest grounds in the country. Last year we thumped Ashton 4-0 at Broadhurst Park on Boxing Day but this was a much tighter and feisty encounter that saw Jordan Buckley sent off in the second half – our first dismissal of the league season and the furthest we'd ever been into a campaign without having a player sent off. In the final few minutes manager Neil Reynolds was also shown a red card for his reaction to the referee's decision not to intervene after a strong challenge on Aaron Bennett.

Bennett was the match winner as he scored a stunning solo goal four minutes from time to seal an impressive 2-1 victory for the Reds. This was FC's third success in four matches and we now sit seven points from the play-off places. Reno's delight at the result was clear as he sprinted across the pitch to celebrate with the supporters at the final whistle.

* * *

It's no surprise given the amount of rain that's fallen on Manchester in the last few days that a 10.30am pitch inspection on Saturday, 30 December deemed the surface to be unplayable and so for the second time this month a high-profile home match is postponed. A crowd of more than 2,000 had been expected for this meeting with table-topping Radcliffe but the fixture will now be rescheduled for a Tuesday night. It's another blow to the club's cash flow particularly as the men's team's next match at Broadhurst Park is not until 20 January against Marske United and there is a strong possibility, given Marske's current plight, that this one might not go ahead either.

7

Elvis impersonator: Bradford Park Avenue

THE FIRST week of the new year saw Marske United resign from the Northern Premier League with immediate effect. A club statement said that this tough decision had been taken 'after exhausting every available option to raise the £120,000 in funds required to get the first team to the end of the season'. Instead the money raised will provide the club with 'a solid foundation to rejoin the football pyramid at a lower level next season'. The good news is that Marske will survive but for the next few months its first team will not be in action.

The club acknowledged that while it had 'punched above its weight for many years', resulting in a rapid rise through the leagues, it had 'unfortunately stretched itself too far and lived beyond its means'. And it highlighted how the challenges of increasing wage, travel and maintenance costs had brought an 'existential threat' to the club.

A statement from FC's board expressed the club's 'solidarity and sympathy with the supporters, volunteers and players at Marske United' but recognised that our match against Marske at Broadhurst Park on 20 January will now not go ahead, leaving us without a home league fixture throughout the month of January in addition to having already had two Saturday home games postponed in December. It's 'far from ideal' for our cash flow and this financial impact will also be felt by those clubs who were due to host Marske over the remainder of the season.

* * *

Our first match of 2024 sees us make the trip to Derbyshire to take on Ilkeston – our first visit to the New Manor Ground, with its quirky clock tower, since October 2014 when a solo goal by Ché Adams, who went on to play in the Premier League and represent Scotland at international level, contributed to a comfortable 3-1 for the hosts. And the Robins won comfortably again this time round with two second-half goals giving them all three points in front of a crowd of 1,017 – Ilkeston's highest of the season so far. With Jordan Buckley suspended after his sending off at Ashton we carried little threat going forward and it was another of those games where we could have stayed on the pitch until midnight and still not scored.

A few days later Marine announced that they'd signed 'experienced forward' Bobby Grant. But what about the training gear he took from FC? There's no need to worry as operations coordinator Nigel Brookes explained that he hadn't de-registered Grant as an FC United player as he had a feeling that he would end up at another Northern Premier League club. So when Marine got in touch to ask us to de-register him, Nigel took the opportunity to ask for our kit back and Nadim Hammad, FC's marketing officer and a mainstay of the office team, subsequently collected it from Marine's CEO in Manchester city centre. 'We can confirm the kit has been repatriated,' we posted on X.

Recalling those 'here's what you could've won' moments on *Bullseye*, Grant would go on to be an excellent signing for the Mariners, scoring 12 goals in 22 appearances in a run of form in the second half of the season that saw them win promotion to National League North via the play-offs.

* * *

Mid-January in Bradford and it's prime big coat weather – bright sunshine and a few degrees above freezing. The bus station is closed ('they're fixing the ceiling mate' a security guard informs me) so I nip into the Wetherspoon pub across nearby Centenary Square to use the toilets without attracting attention amid the hubbub of shoppers and theatre-goers enjoying lunchtime refreshment.

Across the square, in front of the city's gothic City Hall with its fabulous Florentine bell tower, a man stands alone holding a Palestinian flag with the words 'Free Gaza' written on the back of his fluorescent green jacket. On the same afternoon more than half a million people will march in London to demand an immediate ceasefire in Gaza.

Nearly 25,000 people – 70 per cent of them women and children – have been killed in Gaza since 7 October. 'Gaza is devastated,' states the charity Medical Aid for Palestinians, adding, 'Israel's indiscriminate bombardment and siege have reduced entire neighbourhoods to rubble … History is watching. Humanity demands an immediate ceasefire.'

There are days when football feels both utterly irrelevant and completely necessary as something that is almost a universal language wherever you are on the globe and I'm reminded of the '24 Hour Peterloo Peace People' banner that appeared at Old Trafford on the same day as the huge march against the Iraq war in February 2003.

As I cross a busy road, a crowd is gathering at the entrance to the Alhambra Theatre for a matinee performance of *Cinderella* – starring Billy Pearce – and the aroma of a nearby curry house teases my nostrils but there's no time for hanging around as I press on up Little Horton Lane intent on making it to the Horsfall Community Stadium, a couple of miles south of the city centre, in time for kick-off.

On arrival, the signs above the three turnstiles at the Cemetery End invite supporters to pay by 'cash', 'card' or 'crypto' but the turnstile below the latter sign was closed so I settle for paying by card instead. Today's match against Park Avenue isn't quite a relegation six-pointer but the reshuffling of the league table after Marske's resignation – their results expunged from the record – allied to last week's insipid performance at Ilkeston has had us eyeing the teams below us.

The home side take an early lead with pretty much their only shot at goal in the first half but FC come back strongly in the last 15 minutes of the half and goals from Declan McLoughlin and Jordan Buckley put us 2-1 up at half-time. I move into the stand that runs parallel to the home straight of the athletics track that circles the pitch for the second half and the singing is non-stop throughout the half with FC eventually triumphing 4-2 with two excellent goals from Aaron Bennett and Trevon Bryan – the last an 18-year-old making an impressive debut on loan from Bolton Wanderers.

As darkness descends over West Yorkshire, the atmosphere is so good that it even feels a little bit like the memorable play-off semi-final in 2011 when FC, backed by more than 2,000 raucous travelling fans, had beaten Bradford 2-0 and made such a racket that their chairman claimed that his side had been 'intimidated' on their own turf.

A steward with dark, slick-backed hair and a bit of a quiff was serenaded as Elvis Presley by the FC fans for much of the second half. He looked nothing like Elvis but it was good fun nonetheless with the steward revelling in the attention.

That's our fourth win in our last six matches – a decent run of form since the beginning of December that includes three away victories. But as happened after the fine away wins at Gainsborough and Ashton in December, any momentum is quickly lost as our next league match has already been called off with Marske's resignation from the league.

* * *

The following day the women's team moved off the bottom of the table after a goalless draw with York City Ladies at Broadhurst Park in their first match of 2024. It was a fair result but FC had chances to win it, particularly in the first half. The best came when captain Chaneece Reeves burst forward from midfield like Bryan Robson and was one-on-one with the York keeper but her shot lacked power and was comfortably saved – it would have been a goal of the season contender had she scored. Nevertheless, it could be a crucial point come the end of the season and manager Jennie Swarbrick has labelled the mission for the rest of the season as 'the Great Escape'.

The attendance of 321 was the highest for a home league match so far this season, bettered only by the 390 who watched the FA Cup second-round tie against Hull City in November, and there was plenty of vocal backing for the team as they pressed for a winner in the last few minutes. Following misogynistic comments directed at former England player Eni Aluko by Joey Barton on social media earlier in the month, FC had staged a 'women in football' campaign on social media in the run-up to this fixture.

At the turnstiles I bumped into FC's chair Nick Boom who'd brought along his young daughter Alex for her first match at Broadhurst Park – although she'd seen FC's women's team play before away from home – and he was keen to show Alex around the ground and make it as equally a special occasion for her as our first visit to Old Trafford had been for us all those years ago.

* * *

The club announced on 17 January that it had agreed to extend Neil Reynolds's contract as men's first-team manager for a further two years to April 2026. A Q&A document, providing additional detail for co-owners, explained, 'We firmly believe he is the right manager to lead the club towards achieving our long-term ambitions on the pitch. Neil has a proven track record of success, unwavering dedication, and a deep passion for FC United … we see Neil as an integral part of our vision.

'In Neil (and Jennie), we have two exceptional and forward-thinking managers who prioritise continuous improvement and share our passion for the club. They understand that hard work and dedication are essential as we can't simply rely on throwing money at problems.'

The decision attracted much criticism from supporters, with the club currently 16th in the league. The previous board had agreed the extension in principle last October and it was due to be revealed around the time of Neil's fifth anniversary at the club but a sequence of poor results, including defeat at home to Atherton Collieries, meant the announcement was postponed. Chair Nick Boom felt that the new board needed to be fair to Neil – without a clear set of objectives for the club's football teams it's difficult to assess Neil's performance objectively so it's important that we put a football strategy in place before making a decision on his future.

In many respects this situation is similar to the backing supporter-owned Exeter City gave their manager Gary Caldwell in November last year when they were only a point above the relegation places in League One having not won a league match since mid-September. The club's board and its supporters' trust backed Caldwell, stating that they appointed him on the basis that 'this would be a long-term appointment with the aim of helping us grow and develop all aspects of the football club' and this 'had not changed' a year on. 'We don't cane our managers,' the club's chair Nick Hawker told *The Guardian*.

* * *

Given the temperature barely got above freezing in the third week of January in Manchester, it wasn't a great surprise that the friendly against Stalybridge Celtic on 20 January was called off on the morning of the game. It had been arranged as a fundraiser after Marske's resignation from the league had left FC with a blank Saturday. Despite the best efforts of ground staff and volunteers – and the frost covers which had been in place throughout the week – the pitch hadn't been able to thaw properly and was deemed unplayable.

At this level of football, with no television revenue and much smaller commercial income streams, postponed and cancelled matches have a substantial impact on clubs' finances and losing this friendly, along with the home games against Marine and Radcliffe in December, at which we would have expected bigger-than-average crowds, seriously affects our ability to generate the level of matchday revenue that we had anticipated in our business plan. It's not quite as bad as the six-week period we went without a match, home or away, in the winter of 2009/10 but to lose three Saturday home fixtures in December and January is a hefty blow.

Last season we didn't lose any home games to the weather – although the biggest home encounter of the season, against eventual champions South Shields, was postponed in the aftermath of the Queen's death in September 2022 – but in losing three games so far this season it feels like we've either been really unlucky or the pitch requires some serious attention this summer. This comes less than four years since supporters raised more than £30,000 in a magnificent response to the 'No Drain No Game' crowdfunder to fund urgent pitch renovation work in the summer of 2020.

The Broadhurst Park pitch had received minimal investment since the ground had opened in 2015 and half of the total raised in 2020 was spent on fixing drainage problems. Although £15,000 to install new drains might seem a lot for a club of FC's size, the postponement of a Saturday afternoon match to a midweek night was estimated, at the time, to cost the club around £8,000 in lost income so it represented an astute investment.

FC supporters were back in similar fundraising mode as, following news of the postponement of the Stalybridge game, they donated what they would have spent on admission, food and drink at Saturday's match (and considerably more in some cases) both online and in person. By 4pm 421 virtual match tickets had been purchased online, bringing in nearly £4,000 in revenue, and 869 virtual half-time draw tickets at £1 each had also been snapped up. By the end of the day total donations had risen to around £8,500.

A similar fundraising friendly against Chadderton on a blank Saturday in December 2018 – when, a few days ahead of Christmas, the club had needed cash to be able to pay staff and players – was watched by a crowd of 289, so to sell more than 400 'tickets' for a match that wasn't even played was a tremendous effort. In fact, the virtual 'crowd' of 421 is higher than the average attendance so far this season of four other clubs in the Northern Premier League Premier Division. Board member Dave Ashurst tweeted late on Saturday afternoon that this 'special set of fans continue to amaze'.

* * *

The following week, board members Paul Hurst and Nick Boom attended a hearing with the Northern Premier League's disciplinary panel regarding a charge that FC fielded an ineligible player in the 3-3 draw at Bamber Bridge in November. We had offered Dontai Gabidon a contract a few days prior to the match but due to an administrative error in registering this change in the player's status we were found to be in breach of the league's rules and were deducted the point we gained from this fixture and fined £200 (with £100 suspended for 12 months).

The club had requested a personal hearing and argued that a points deduction was inappropriate in this instance – Dontai would have played in the match regardless of whether he was contracted or not so the team hadn't secured an unfair advantage – but it was to no avail.

Paul had been involved in preparing a club statement to the league regarding the charge and he took a day off work to attend the hearing with Nick at a hotel by the M1 near Ossett. 'It was very Alan Partridge-esque,' he smiles. The panel included league officials and two directors of NPL clubs not in the same division as FC and after making the club's case Nick and Paul were asked to leave the room while the panel made its decision. 'It only took them about four or five minutes,' says Paul. He and Nick were then invited back in to learn that the club would be deducted a point. 'We spent so much time preparing for that hearing,' Paul adds.

The board subsequently issued a statement saying that it took 'full responsibility for the error' and accepted the charge and penalty and apologised 'to our supporters, players, first team manager and coaching staff' and added, 'We are in the process of conducting an internal review to ensure we drive improvement within our football administration.'

Volunteer club secretary Nigel Brookes and board member Dave Ashurst had offered to resign over the matter but the board had declined to accept their proposals. The statement added that 'the task of club secretary is often a thankless one and with the Football Association and league handbooks both running to hundreds of pages, errors are sometimes made'.

The board's football lead Simon Preston described the whole episode as a 'baptism of fire' for those board members who'd only recently been elected. 'I had quite a few sleepless nights around this time,' he says, 'particularly when it came to communicating the point deduction to supporters.' He also added that we've now put in place 'a four eyes checking procedure' before any documents are shared with the league in future and will also work with the NPL to improve administration issues across the competition.

There was obvious disappointment among supporters and co-owners, particularly as this was the second consecutive season that the club had incurred a points deduction, but there was acknowledgement that 'mistakes happen' and that 'nobody needs to be hung out to dry'.

Matchday secretary Adrian Seddon felt that the punishment was 'harsh but fair' given that we'd made several administrative mistakes in recent years including being deducted three points the previous season for fielding an ineligible player. He pointed out that we had said at the time that we would put in place measures to reduce the likelihood of such errors occurring in future but hadn't really followed through on this – so we've only ourselves to blame.

Last season's infringement related to the use of loan players and was a clear breach of a rule that was set out in the league's rule book. However, as Paul pointed out, the requirements relating to the start date of contracts aren't documented in the rule book but instead the league had directed us to a circular that it had sent to clubs last summer which specified this requirement – it was this correspondence that we had missed in this instance.

Adrian reckoned that the role of football secretary is 'one of the most thankless jobs in football' and described how Nigel, as a volunteer, is expected to be on hand at training every Tuesday and Thursday night and has to register every player we sign, with some loan players having to be registered each month. Adrian explained that this can be a time-consuming process and described how for one recent signing Nigel had to complete four separate pieces of paperwork: a registration form for the league; a contract form; a transfer agreement; and a transfer form.

He added that 'all these forms have to be correctly filled out, signed and witnessed' and the details on all the forms must match 'or else the whole thing is rejected and you start all over again'. Similarly, when it comes to inputting the information on to the FA computer system, if there are any discrepancies between the information provided and the manual forms, then it all gets rejected. 'I wouldn't fancy that job and I hope anyone who bumps into Nigel tomorrow at Matlock puts an arm round him and says they've got his back,' Adrian added.

* * *

Matlock Town away is always one of the first matches that I look out for when the fixtures come out. The view from the terrace behind the goal towards the hilltop folly of Riber Castle – made famous in Shane Meadows's film *Dead Man's Shoes* – is surely one of the most picturesque from any football ground.

Despite that, the only time I've seen us win away at Matlock came on an unseasonably sultry April day in 2012 – when striker Ben Deegan played in goal for the entire match and fan-favourite Jerome Wright scored a second-half winner that kept us on course for a play-off place. I'd stopped overnight in Derby then and had a chance to book the same hotel, for another stopover in Derby this weekend, but the majority of the recent online reviews – 'bath had pubes in it on arrival, view of car park, only good thing is the location' – suggested that, 12 years on, the hotel was struggling a bit so we opted to stay elsewhere this time.

There were reduced admission prices on offer for supporters arriving at the ground before 1pm – prior to the match Matlock were creating a promotional video and so wanted as many early arrivals as possible – but we eschewed that for a gentle stroll along the river from Matlock Bath (where we had disembarked the rattler from Derby) and then a walk up the hill to visit a pair of micropubs near the Derbyshire County Council offices. Besides, I suspect the last time I was in a football ground that early was back in the late 80s at Old Trafford when we used to queue at the Stretford End turnstiles from before 1pm.

The crowd of 1,349 was Matlock's biggest so far this season and the atmosphere was tremendous throughout with non-stop singing from the FC fans on the covered terrace behind the goal and a nearby group of home supporters making a decent racket too with the accompaniment of a drum. But it was a wretched performance by FC who barely mustered a shot on goal and were comprehensively beaten 3-0 by a side only one place above us in the league who had only recently lost their leading goalscorer.

The women's team lost their 'must-win' game at Chester-le-Street Town Ladies the following day – they were the only team below us in the league prior to the match – 2-0.

* * *

The first board meeting of 2024, on 29 January, saw the board set out its key missions for the next few years:

- To create a positive culture across the club that provides a supportive environment and promotes a strong sense of community among staff, volunteers, co-owners and supporters.
- To increase matchday attendances by 500 over the next three seasons across the men's and women's teams.
- To develop a football strategy that aligns with the club's values and goals and provides direction and purpose for all the teams that represent FC United.

- To establish a sustainable community programme that addresses the needs of our local community.
- To drive commercial success by exploring avenues for revenue generation and commercial partnerships that ensure the club's long-term financial stability.

Each mission was allocated a board sponsor, and chair Nick Boom emphasised the importance of a collective effort from the board, staff, volunteers and co-owners to achieve these missions and added that we need to explore ways to actively involve co-owners in this process.

Will Jacques from the finance and risk committee was also in attendance to take the board through the risk register which he had been working on for the last 18 months. He described this process as 'tortuous' particularly as, during that time, we had a change of CEO or general manager and nearly all the relevant staff have changed too.

Essentially the risk register is a spreadsheet that currently identifies 109 risks, each of which is recorded including a description of the risk, the risk owner (usually a board member, senior manager or committee), any work that's currently being done to mitigate the risk and an action plan for further mitigation, and each risk is scored according to severity and likelihood.

Of particular importance for the board is the heat map which identifies the biggest risks that the club currently faces – currently a list of 12 – and these include: the inability to attract or retain board members; uncontracted players; poor cash flow management; and an inability to attract or retain holders of key staff roles or the sudden loss of a role holder.

Will recommended that the risk register should be formally reviewed by the board every six or 12 months with individual risks being reviewed by their risk owner on a quarterly basis with a particular focus on the highest scoring ones in the heat map.

Board members had also been asked to review the performance of their committees ahead of this month's board meeting with particular emphasis on the following: whether the terms of reference for each committee are fit for purpose; whether the work of each committee is aligned with the club's business plan; and if there are any gaps in skills or expertise on the committees that need to be addressed.

Since their formation two years ago, the committees have made a huge contribution to the running of the club and Nick felt that without their support the board would be unable to function effectively. But there was agreement that there needs to be more liaison between the board and committee chairs regarding the priorities for each committee and the fact that the receipt of reports from the committees is now a standing item on the board meeting agenda should help with this.

Finance controller Steve Durrands apologised to the board for the lateness of the management accounts, which are currently running one month behind schedule following an extended period without a finance manager while the club sought a replacement for Hannah Gorman. Problems with a corrupted data file had further complicated matters with the production of November's accounts, leading to a laborious manual exercise to rectify the situation.

Usually we'd be reviewing the December management accounts at January's board meeting but instead the accounts for November highlighted that we made an operating loss of £3,100 in-month, £11,500 worse than budget, but still reported an operating profit of £20,900 after the first five months of the 2023/24 financial year.

Steve said the latest cash flow forecast highlighted that the financial impact of losing three Saturday home matches in December and January has, as expected, had a significant impact on our cash flow. Nick stressed that we don't have access to a bank overdraft or extended borrowing facilities so we must manage this situation ourselves and the board had requested to see weekly updates on the club's cash flow.

Observing this meeting were co-owners Chris Boulderstone and Graham Voaden with Graham tuning in online from Cornwall. And tonight also marked the debut of a piece of technology known as a 'meeting owl', which allows co-owners to observe meetings online with a 360-degree view that focuses on whoever is speaking. The non-feathered 'owl' was kindly purchased and donated by the club's London and southern supporters' branch of which Graham is a member.

* * *

Tuesday, 30 January saw us host our first home match since before Christmas against promotion-chasing Marine who were much the better side and after taking the lead early in the second half there was little doubt that the Lilywhites would bag all three points. Their second goal, scored by ex-FC United player Fin Sinclair-Smith, was a cracker and reminiscent of his late winner for FC against Guiseley in the FA Cup in 2020, which had put us through to the first round proper of the competition for only the third time in our history and had sparked scenes of joy at a socially distanced Broadhurst Park.

Sinclair-Smith added a third soon after and it all felt a bit too easy for a side that was brimming with confidence and, even at this stage of the season, appeared nailed on for a place in the play-offs. There were a few boos at the final whistle, which was harsh as Marine were probably the best side we played all season at Broadhurst Park. But after two comprehensive 3-0 defeats in a matter of days we desperately need to get back to winning ways next Saturday.

8

The most forward-looking team in Britain

SECOND-HALF GOALS from Jordan Buckley and Jan Palinkas gave FC a comfortable 2-0 victory over Gainsborough Trinity on the first Saturday of February and our first home win of 2024. And one of the rare occasions this season when, as supporters, we've been able to relax a little in the closing minutes.

The day before the game we'd announced the signing of goalkeeper George Murray-Jones on loan until the end of the season from Manchester City, who had also agreed to carry on paying George's wages during this loan period. 'Thank you to all parties for making this possible and welcome to FC George,' said a post on X.

Meanwhile, over on Bluemoon – the self-styled 'leading Manchester City forum' – despite all the success the Abu Dhabi-owned club has enjoyed over the last decade, there's a discussion thread devoted entirely to FC United which stretches to more than 400 pages. And a poster on there was far from happy with the signing of Murray-Jones.

'WTF!!! Why the fuck are we helping these fucking parasites out?! They couldn't actually come out and say thank you to MCFC, they had to say "all parties" … I just hope he's shite.'

Spoiler alert: he certainly wasn't. And the reason for the reference to 'all parties' was simple – FC's central defender Charlie Oliver is a coach at City's academy and had helped to make the loan deal possible.

Our first home match on a Saturday afternoon for six weeks also provided a much-needed boost for the club's coffers. Before the game, general manager Danny Davis showed me the app on his phone that tracks how much cash the various bars around the ground have taken. 'If we get to £7,000 this afternoon, I'll be pleased,' he tells me. This excludes revenue from the sale of food which is provided by an external catering company who pay us a share of their takings.

Danny Lafferty was named man of the match and in a post-game interview Neil Reynolds described the central defender as 'an outstanding man'. Which raised eyebrows among those FC fans who had spotted a few days earlier that Lafferty had liked a post on X by the right-wing extremist known as Tommy Robinson which alleged that 'the vile specimen' suspected of attacking a woman and two children with an alkaline substance in south London is an 'asylum seeker' from Afghanistan already convicted of sex offences 'in our country'. A couple of weeks earlier Lafferty had also liked an anti-Islamic post on an X account called 'Extremist Patriot Channel'.

It reminded me of the time, seven years ago, when we signed a player but then announced, before he'd even played a game, that 'due to unforeseen circumstances Andy Watson has cancelled his registration with the club'. It turned out that Watson had been retweeting extremist right-wing content which several FC fans had strongly objected to and he left the club without even setting foot on the pitch and promptly locked his Twitter account.

It's impossible to police the internet but surely when players join FC United they must be aware that they are joining a football club which states in its founding manifesto on the back of its membership cards that we will 'strive to be accessible to all, discriminating against none'?

In 2021 we became one of the first non-league clubs to sign up to the anti-discrimination charity Kick It Out's Equality Charter which committed us to 'work towards the eradication of discrimination in football and the promotion of equality, inclusion and diversity'. At the time Neil Reynolds said that his team and coaching staff were 'proud to support this initiative' and added, 'There is absolutely no place for racism, not only in the game but also in wider society and I am looking forward to working with everyone to show how our club will not tolerate any form of discrimination.' The charter also mentions that, as a club, we will 'encourage all our club members to take a pro-active stance in the fight against discrimination'.

Back in October we'd been proud to announce that 'our men's team's players, management and backroom staff' had become co-owners of the club that they play for. Lafferty hadn't joined the club then, and it's unclear if he subsequently became a member after joining but, either way, liking extremist right-wing content on X is miles away from taking 'a proactive stance against discrimination'.

A group of FC fans known as 'The Committee' (@CommitteeFCUM) – described in its X bio as the 'uncentral committee of the FC United Gobshite Brigade' – replied to Lafferty on X the day after the Gainsborough match to congratulate him on his excellent performance but advised him to 'perhaps stop liking tweets by T*mmy

R*binson' and added that 'racists who seek to divide the working class on racial/religious lines aren't welcome in society and certainly not at FC United'.

* * *

Home matches are like Wilmslow Road buses and having waited ages for one we've now had three in the space of a week as we take on runaway league leaders Radcliffe on 6 February in a rearranged match after the original fixture at the end of December was postponed due to a waterlogged pitch. It was another wet day in Manchester but fortunately the rain had stopped by late afternoon and the pitch, although heavy, was deemed fit to play.

After all that, it was an excellent match – possibly the best so far this season at Broadhurst Park – and FC, captained by Danny Lafferty, were the better team in the first half and should have been in front by half-time, playing with an intensity rarely seen this season. Aaron Bennett once again ran his socks off and was subbed off in the second half as the heavy conditions began to tell and FC ran out of steam in the final quarter. Radcliffe created several excellent chances and it was no surprise when Jordan Hulme grabbed the winner seven minutes from time much to the delight of the visiting fans at the Lightbowne Road End.

There was a late shout for a penalty after a Radcliffe defender appeared to handle the ball in the penalty area but the referee wasn't interested – which resulted in Neil Reynolds ending up on his arse as he charged down the touchline to register his displeasure – and that was that. One of FC's best performances of the season against a side that is now 11 points clear at the top of the table, with two games in hand, and seemingly destined for National

League North next season. Another midweek home defeat but this one was chalk and cheese compared to the week before against Marine and the team were applauded off the pitch like victors.

The attendance was 1,635 – one of our best midweek crowds for a while – and was boosted by a couple of hundred away fans. But it would almost certainly have been in excess of 2,000 had the match been played on 30 December. The minute's silence prior to kick-off on the 66th anniversary of the Munich air disaster was impeccably observed by everyone.

* * *

More heavy rain later in the week meant there was pretty much no chance of our away match at Whitby on Saturday, 10 February going ahead but the home side had to get a referee to come to the ground at half past eight on Saturday morning to officially call the game off. The FC players' coach had been due to set off from Broadhurst Park at 9.45am.

Frustratingly it was too late for any money to be reimbursed for the official supporters' coach which had been booked by Pete Wharton and cost £1,700. While the club itself hasn't directly lost any money on this – the coach is paid for by supporters – it means, as Pete pointed out, that those fans have less money to spend the next time they're at Broadhurst Park.

Pete made the point at February's board meeting, where he was an observer, that more consideration should be given to supporters when it comes to announcing the postponement of matches. In this case, with virtually no prospect of the game going ahead and the away team and its supporters faced with a trans-Pennine round trip of 250 miles, it ought to have been postponed the day before, which would probably have allowed those fans who had booked on the official supporters' coach to at least get some of their money back. The board's football lead, Simon Preston, promised to raise this with the NPL and, depending on the outcome, the club may make representations to the league.

* * *

The first leg of United's 1991 League Cup semi-final against Leeds, played on a cabbage patch of a pitch at Old Trafford, cropped up on my X timeline the other day. And with the classic kits (I love it when a United side plays in red shirts and black shorts), the pitch cutting up badly after yet more wet weather, and a second-half kerfuffle that threatened to remove the 'F' from the tournament's name, the Fenix Trophy Group C clash between FC and French side Vinsky on 13 February had the feel of that 1991 rumble in the Rumbelows about it at times.

It was a decent match, perhaps better than most of us expected given that Vinsky are the lowest-ranked team in the tournament, and the eventual 4-1 win for FC flattered the hosts as the game had been level at 1-1 five minutes from time. The French side, sitting deep and counterattacking in numbers, became the first away team to open the scoring in a Fenix Trophy match at Broadhurst Park and led 1-0 at half-time.

Off the pitch we were trialling the use of electronic tickets for this fixture and it was the first time I've got into a football match armed only with a QR code on my phone. Welcome to the 21st century. But the crowd of only 406 was disappointing and reflected a lacklustre campaign to promote the game. We'd averaged more than 700 for the three midweek Fenix ties in previous seasons and a crowd of

870 had watched our first Fenix encounter under the lights at Broadhurst Park against Brera in May 2021.

It didn't help that Vinsky didn't bring any fans. The club, based in the town of Magnanville not far from Paris, was formed in 2017 by YouTuber and French football personality Vincent Maduro (aka Vinsky360) from whom the club takes its name. Maduro's aim was to bring the day-to-day life of an amateur football club to a wider audience and while Vinsky have attracted a huge online following, very few fans actually turn up to watch them in person. Maybe a glimpse into the future of football? On the pitch they've gone from strength to strength with three promotions in three years and they currently compete in the regionalised 11th tier of French football.

As ever with the Fenix matches, there was significant media interest with the *Manchester Evening News* making a rare visit to Broadhurst Park along with a journalist from *France Football* magazine and several YouTubers. 'It's a unique competition and we're a unique club so people should be interested,' said board member Warren Heppolette.

And that was illustrated again the following day as a group of 14 visitors from the Philippines were given a tour of the ground by FC volunteer Des Gallagher – the first of a recently established official tour that will be run under the badge of the club's Sporting Memories Group which meets every Friday afternoon at Broadhurst Park and has been a staple of our community programme for many years. There are already a couple of other tour bookings in the pipeline and the board has also approved the creation of a club museum – subject to cost – that would also form part of the tour in future.

* * *

Former Manchester United player and assistant manager Mike Phelan was the guest at this week's meeting of the Sporting Memories Group. He spoke and answered questions for two and a half hours and received a standing ovation at the end of a thoroughly enjoyable session. These days Mike runs his own company coaching kids at grassroots level and Des Gallagher, who organises the Sporting Memories sessions, described him as 'a very humble man who knows that football has been good to him and is prepared to put that good back into the game at grassroots level'.

Sporting Memories is a national charity that seeks to bring older people together to share their memories of either playing or watching sport in a supportive environment that helps to maintain and improve mental health in an age group that often suffers from loneliness and social isolation. It was formed in 2011 and now has more than 100 groups across the UK, including FC United's, which has been meeting at Broadhurst Park since 2016 and is the only one in the country to meet weekly.

Des understands the importance of FC's Sporting Memories Group better than most. He's a founder member of FC United and a long-standing volunteer who has given his time to the club in many ways down the years from pouring pints on matchdays to working in the office during the week. Des began attending the Sporting Memories sessions at Broadhurst Park several years ago when he had time alone that he needed to fill.

For many of the people attending the sessions, including Des, simply knowing that there is a place where they can meet like-minded people on a weekly basis can make the world of difference to their outlook on life. Des saw the significance of these sessions and he began to organise speakers for the group and publicise it around the club and local area.

Manchester's older population (defined as people over the age of 65) was estimated to be nearly 50,000 in 2021 and around nine per cent of its total population but in Moston that proportion is 13 per cent and among the highest in the city.

The group has gone from strength to strength with a regular attendance of around 25 to 30 people – three times the number who attended when Des joined the group – and it has welcomed several high-profile speakers down the years. The club recently applied for a grant which could allow the group to take part in activities further afield in future, providing a change of scenery and an opportunity for attendees to stretch their legs.

* * *

Kate Ireland became possibly the first Course You Can Malcolm turn to cycle to the gig, ahead of the match against Warrington Rylands on 17 February, and she wowed us with an intriguing tale of Glaswegian sibling rivalry and love. She was followed on stage by musician Matt Hill, who was making his third appearance at CYCM and served up a lovely folk-tinged set that closed with a cover that he introduced as: 'One of the great summations of Marxist theory – it's written by Dolly Parton and it's called "9 to 5".'

Unfortunately the weather did its worst again and the heavy rain which arrived during the first half eventually forced the match, which was goalless, to be abandoned midway through the second half despite both teams being keen to play on. We know it rains quite a bit in Manchester but patience is wearing thin by now – that's three Saturday home matches postponed and one abandoned in the last ten weeks.

Abandoned matches have been very rare in FC's history and because of this the club hasn't had a policy on handling postponements and abandonments up until now but the board felt, in light of this unprecedented streak, that it represents good practice for the club to have clear guidance in this area and had therefore asked general manager Danny Davis to draft a policy which was subsequently reviewed at February's board meeting.

There was also recognition that as we increasingly begin to feel the impacts of climate change it might also be worth factoring lost revenue (as a result of games being postponed and rearranged for midweek nights) into our budget setting and potentially also allowing for higher pitch maintenance costs. Although chair Nick Boom acknowledged that the best way to deal with this would be to build sufficient cash reserves to enable us to comfortably negotiate the financial impact of any postponed fixtures.

* * *

FC's academy team beat Newcastle Benfield 3-0 in the quarter-finals of the National League U19 Alliance League Cup on 21 February with goals from Alex Canning, Jayden Wilson and Raphael Ikediashi – the latter scoring only a couple of minutes after coming on as a second-half substitute to seal the win. The match was played in stormy conditions on the 3G pitch and the young Reds were convincing winners so are now only one match away from the final, which will be held at St George's Park, the FA's national football centre in Burton, in May.

Volunteer photographer Lewis Mckenna's stunning photograph of Raphael's rain-soaked goal celebration captured perfectly what it means to this talented group of young players to make it this far in a national competition.

The academy team are also top of Division H of the National League U19 Alliance – nine points clear of nearest rivals Buxton with a game in hand – and are unbeaten in the league and have only lost one match so far in any competition this season.

* * *

FC lost 3-0 at Morpeth Town on 24 February and remained 17th in the league table. The crowd of just 484 at Craik Park was the lowest to watch a Saturday afternoon league match involving FC so far this season.

The referee booked five FC players and also sent off goalkeeper George Murray-Jones for dissent. After the match the referee talked FC's matchday secretary Adrian Seddon through each incident and Adrian reckoned that while you could make a case that each one merited a booking there wasn't really a bad foul in the entire game.

Adrian's role is focused entirely on the administrative tasks that enable matchdays to run smoothly, which includes liaising with the opposition and officials in the days leading up to a match regarding kit colours, ticket prices, car parking and arranging boardroom and media representation. On the day of the game Adrian meets the opposition secretary and also liaises with the referee and other officials and he's in the room when manager Neil Reynolds finalises his team and then exchanges team sheets with the opposition secretary.

At half-time and full time he sends the score to a media address and also consults the referee at the end of each match to agree on the cautions that have been dished out. 'I won't tell you how many naked referees I've seen,' he laughs.

The following day the women's team beat Cheadle Stingers 1-0 in the Manchester FA Women's Challenge Cup in another match played on the 3G pitch. 'It wasn't easy and it certainly wasn't pretty but we dug in and got the job done,' said a relieved manager, Jennie Swarbrick.

* * *

FC United often receives emails from Manchester United fans seemingly unaware there are two football clubs bearing the name 'United' in the city. Especially when Manchester United lose, which happened rather a lot through the 2023/24 season, and within minutes of them being beaten at home to Fulham on 24 February, an email entitled 'Sack ten Hag' and sprinkled with angry-face emojis informed the board of FC United that 'You. Are. Stupid.'

Meanwhile, around the same time, an 'anonymous billionaire' detailed precisely how 'to make Manchester United the greatest in the world' in an 8,400-word email entitled 'My Big Plans For Manchester United' and addressed to 'Sir Jim Ratcliffe and Manchester United Board Executives'. It advised them to 'read carefully to the end' but unfortunately it had been sent to the board of FC United of Manchester rather than Manchester United FC so they didn't get a chance to.

When Erik ten Hag was eventually sacked in October 2024 the same inbox was busy with people interested in applying for the vacant managerial position at Old Trafford with one applicant outlining how he'd 'guided Derby County from the Championship to becoming one of the world's elite clubs' on Football Manager and looked forward to 'bringing further success to Old Trafford'.

And another from a 'certified practitioner in ten psychometrics', initially sent to jim.radcliffe@ineos.

com and subsequently forwarded to an FC United email address, told us of how his 'discovery of a 4th Law of Iceberg Communication Theory' could improve 'Man U's competitive edge' and added, 'I look forwarding to receiving your thoughts when convenient and would mention that my wife and I are off to Majorca tomorrow until the 16th.'

And, as if that's not enough football club confusion, it's still a source of much amusement that football-related conversations with strangers often involve enquiries about 'Gary Neville's lot' whenever I mention FC United. Given Salford City's meteoric rise to the Football League – turbo-charged by a Singaporean billionaire – it's easy to forget that FC United were playing them, in English football's ninth tier, not that long ago. But there the similarities between the two clubs tend to peter out. In a Venn diagram of mine and David Beckham's lives, the only circles that intersect are captioned 'co-owns a football club in Greater Manchester' and 'had a curtains hairstyle in the 90s'.

* * *

February's board meeting began with an update on progress so far regarding each of the five key missions identified at last month's meeting and there was recognition of the need for a coordinated strategy to growing our attendances, which could include: bringing friends to games; speaking positively about the club; supporting the women's team as well as the men's; promoting the club on social media; sharing information in the workplace or pub; and distributing leaflets and displaying posters.

Chris Boulderstone, who runs the club's junior membership scheme, had submitted a proposal, which got the unanimous support of the board, for the formation of a junior members' committee that, while it won't have any formal powers, would allow younger supporters to feel more involved in the running of the club and provide a means for them to ask questions and submit ideas to the board. The board also agreed to ensure that board members are available to attend junior committee meetings.

Anyone under the age of 16 can join the club as a junior member for an annual fee of £3 – we had 400 junior members in 2023/24 – and this provides access to regular events through the year, the chance to be a mascot for the day and lead the players out on to the pitch, and also join the matchday 'ball crew'. It's been one of the club's biggest success stories down the years with several former junior members going on to play important roles in the day-to-day running of the club and also become committee members. The club's offering to junior supporters exceeds what most other clubs do.

The management accounts for December highlighted that the club made an operating loss of £10,600 in-month, £14,300 worse than budget, and reported an operating profit of £12,600 after the first six months of the 2023/24 financial year, which was £25,100 worse than the operating profit of £37,700 we budgeted for.

Despite the postponement of two Saturday afternoon home fixtures in December, gate receipts and food and beverage income generally performed well in December compared to budget as the Marine match was postponed only a few minutes before kick-off. However, sponsorship and advertising income was £4,000 below budget in December and merchandising income was down by £4,400 compared to budget as sales didn't go as well as expected in the run-up to Christmas. The lack of home matches at which to sell merchandise didn't help.

The board and management team are continuing to monitor our cash position – which remains tight – on a weekly basis with a focus on reducing costs wherever possible. Nick stressed again that we don't have any cash reserves or access to borrowing facilities so we must manage our cash flow extremely carefully and remain focused on getting through this tough period.

Michael Wehner, who is a member of the club's co-ownership committee and was observing this meeting online from Detroit in the USA, said it had given him a 'deep appreciation' for how the club is run.

* * *

The biggest share of the money raised to fund the building of Broadhurst Park home came through community shares which provide an alternative means for co-operatives like FC United to raise finance. The shares are ultimately withdrawable, subject to financial performance, but cannot be sold or transferred between investors, unlike shares in a typical company, and represent an innovative way for people to invest in businesses or organisations that they believe in such as shops, pubs, libraries, renewable energy schemes and sports clubs. According to Co-operatives UK, more than £200m has been raised by more than 126,000 people in community shares in the UK since 2012.

FC United's share offer was launched in 2010 and invited existing co-owners and others who shared the club's vision to 'be part of a better way for football' and help the club to raise £1.5m towards the £3.5m total cost of building a new ground in Newton Heath, the original home of Manchester United. That amount increased later on when the Newton Heath plans fell through and Broadhurst Park in Moston became the site of the club's new ground.

Without community shares it's highly unlikely the club would have secured the all-important grant funding from Manchester City Council or Sport England or the Football Foundation that also contributed to the £6.5m total cost of its new ground.

When the community share offer closed in February 2015, it had raised just over £2m from 1,522 of the club's co-owners. Some supporters poured sizeable proportions of their savings into their football club with little expectation that they would receive any of it back – the purpose of any community share scheme is to support a business which puts something back into its community rather than to make a financial gain.

FC United were the first football club to raise money in this way and Dave Boyle from Supporters Direct wrote at the time that 'far from being the backward looking nostalgics they're sometimes painted as, FC United are actually the most forward-looking team in Britain' as it had managed to raise capital without going cap in hand to a wealthy businessman or bank.

It was a pioneering scheme that inspired supporters of other clubs like Portsmouth, Wrexham and Lewes to use community shares to raise much-needed funds for their clubs. Indeed, the Portsmouth Supporters' Trust saved their club from extinction by acquiring majority ownership of it in 2013 by raising more than £2m in community shares. Although this spell of supporter ownership was relatively short-lived as, later on, supporters voted in favour of Walt Disney head honcho Michael Eisner taking over the club.

FC's offer stipulated that 'shares are withdrawable with effect from the third anniversary of the date on which FC United takes occupancy of the completed stadium' and 'all withdrawals must be funded from trading surpluses and are at the discretion of the board having regard to the long-term interests of FC United, the need to maintain prudent reserves and the society's primary commitment to community benefit'. It also said, 'The board will not permit more than ten per cent of the total value of the shares issued to be redeemed in any financial year.'

So with the value of community shares identified as £1,853,125 in the club's balance sheet at the end of the 2022/23 financial year, the board could have chosen to repay up to £185,000 of community shares this year. But having reported an operating loss of £228,000 in 2022/23 there was no trading surplus from which to fund withdrawals of community shares and it was therefore agreed at February's board meeting that the club would write to community shareholders to inform them of this.

In the five financial years since the third anniversary in 2018 of the ground being completed, the club twice reported an operating surplus – in 2019/20 and again the following year – but the board decided in both instances that it wasn't in the club's long-term interests to fund the withdrawal of community shares given that we were in the midst of a lengthy football-less period, due to the pandemic, with considerable uncertainty around the club's future finances.

Arguably, securing £2m of investment in community shares was the straightforward bit – what lies ahead now are the hard yards of carefully managing the club's finances so that, year after year, it generates a financial surplus that is sufficient for the club to make repayments on its debt and potentially reimburse those community shareholders who would like to access some or all of their investment.

9

Is there anywhere in this ground that doesn't have poetry?

SALFORD-BASED MARKETING specialists the Behaviours Agency had kindly agreed to assist the club for free in developing a clear brand identity for the club, both verbal and visual, that sets out our values, what we stand for and how we'd like people to see us – which will shape the club's visual and verbal communication and, in particular, make it easier for us to communicate on social media without having to refer to the board for guidance. This work is being overseen by a working group led by Helen Johnston, an experienced communications professional, who is a former board member and a long-standing volunteer for the club's communications team.

'Brand' is a word that will sit uneasily with some FC United supporters but, as Helen points out, every organisation, whether it knows it or not, has a 'brand' and at FC it's important that we are clear what the club stands for – a football club owned by the fans, for the fans, that is also rooted in its community.

The agency had come up with a couple of options for new visuals – which received strong support from the working group – that drew on Manchester's 'Cottonopolis' past with a 'threads' theme that weaves together our red, white and black colours to create a bold letter 'M', which would look great on our communications and also felt 'punk' enough to work on merchandise and T-shirts.

Although it wasn't part of the agency's brief they'd also had a go at refreshing the club badge which has remained unchanged since 2005. As everyone refers to the club as 'FC United' rather than 'Football Club United', they suggested removing the words 'football club' from the badge and using 'FC United' instead. But given the furious reaction of many fans to Manchester United's controversial decision to drop the same words from its badge in 1998, it's highly unlikely that FC's co-owners would be willing to contemplate such a move, particularly as the reinstatement of the words 'football club' at the very front of our club's name took on great symbolism and is something that we still sing about to this day in 'This Badge Is Your Badge' to the tune of Woody Guthrie's radical folk anthem 'This Land Is Your Land'.

> *This badge is your badge*
> *This badge is my badge*
> *Three stripes and three sails*
> *Oh, what a fine badge*
> *They tried to take it*
> *But we replaced it*
> *On the shirt of United FC*

When considering the club's visual identity, it's also important that we think about how we present the club physically, as well as digitally, to the outside world. In the immediate vicinity of the ground, signage is poor. Standing at the bus stop across St Mary's Road only a few yards from the ground, for instance, there are no visual clues as to what you're looking at and it's possible to walk up St Mary's Road straight past Broadhurst Park and not even realise that you've just walked past a football ground.

And across the other side of the ground along Lightbowne Road, which provides vehicular access to the ground, while there is a noticeboard that advertises the club's next match, it's so poorly designed that it's almost impossible to read if you're passing by in a car – you really need to stop and take a look. It's almost like we're trying hard not to advertise ourselves to our local community.

Perhaps we could also use billboards around town to promote the club? The new 'M' design would look great on a billboard with a strapline about us being '100 per cent fan-owned' or 'Manchester's community football club' on it. Or how about a mural in the Northern Quarter? There's a surfeit of bland advertising around the Northern Quarter these days, including one with a selection of City players advertising a Japanese lager.

In May 2020, in conjunction with the North Manchester Business Network, we were offered a couple of spaces for free on billboards in the city centre after a local advertising agency had recognised how much the volunteer-run food hub established at Broadhurst Park since the beginning of the Covid lockdown was contributing to our local community in north Manchester.

Fan-owned Runcorn Linnets have had an eye-catching mural in the town's shopping centre since 2022 which bears the legend 'By The Fans, For The Fans' and pays tribute to 'the club's success and ongoing contribution to the community'. Interestingly, it was designed by the father of one of the club's junior team players and created by a volunteer who runs a local business that also produces signage for the club – fan power in action again.

And we could also look at distributing flyers and posters to promote the club in the local area and also in the city centre. Let's get shops and businesses around Moston promoting the club and what it stands for. At times it feels like we lack visibility in our own locality. Board member Simon Preston recalls visiting a nearby shop to grab something to eat when he was at Broadhurst Park during the week and the shopkeeper and other customers being unaware of their local football club.

A digital-first communications strategy makes sense when you consider the club's extensive digital reach with around six million visits to our website per year and nearly one million followers across a range of social media platforms including a bigger following on X (more than 88,000) than several League One clubs. And we've got a profile that stretches way beyond these shores with co-owners in 45 countries including as far afield as China, Japan, USA, Australia and New Zealand.

But it's important that we aren't overly reliant on communicating via digital technologies. A report on digital access produced by the Good Things Foundation highlighted that many of the worst-performing areas in Manchester when it comes to digital inclusion – defined as 'having access to the internet and having the skills and confidence to use the internet effectively' – lie to the north of the city centre in Miles Platting, Newton Heath, Harpurhey, Moston, Charlestown and Blackley. In other words, most of the areas closest to Broadhurst Park. Simply posting and reposting stuff on our socials, and encouraging others to do the same, isn't going to reach everyone.

* * *

Despite taking an early lead at home to mid-table Workington on Saturday, 2 March – Dontai Gabidon scoring on his return to the side after injury – we were comfortably beaten 3-1 and remain in 17th place in the league but only nine points above the relegation places. The upcoming matches against Atherton Collieries and Basford United – two of the five teams below us in the table – now take on an added importance, particularly as the rest of our fixtures in March are against teams with an eye on the other end of the table. It feels like we're getting drawn into a relegation fight.

It was Workington's first visit to Broadhurst Park and before the game some of their fans disrupted Lisa O'Hare's poetry set at Course You Can Malcolm, with one of them remarking, 'Is there anywhere in this ground that doesn't have poetry?' as they left in search of a poetry-free corner. CYCM volunteer Lynette Cawthra described it as one of the highlights of the season.

When our Broadhurst Park ground was still being built some of the money from the sale of the fanzine *A Fine Lung* was donated to the club and used to buy the goalposts on the main pitch and there had also been plans to inscribe some lines from Shelley's epic poem 'The Masque of Anarchy' on the goalposts. It was written following the Peterloo massacre in 1819 and referenced Manchester's radical tradition, which also led to the formation of FC United nearly two centuries later and it contains the line 'Spirit, patience, gentleness, all that can adorn and bless ...', the first three words of which were adopted as a tagline by the fanzine. It's perhaps just as well that these plans didn't come to fruition as it might've blown the minds of those Workington fans if anyone had pointed out that there was also poetry written on the goalposts.

Lisa had written a poem about coming to the match and its concluding line, 'No matter what the score, the pre-match buzz will always bring you back for more', felt particularly apt for CYCM. It's been lovely to have a regular poetry slot at CYCM this year and Lynette thanked volunteers Steve Pilling and Steve Turner, who've assisted with the booking of bands and acts this season, for this and described how they've brought a much-needed youthful energy to CYCM and 'rejuvenated its spoken word offering after a long period when we had struggled to get poets to come'.

Our ground and its main bar overlooking the pitch is something that we take great pride in and a recent edition of the club's weekly email newsletter *The Pink* described the main bar as 'the perfect choice' for a range of events offering 'dramatic views over the pitch' and 'an unforgettable setting for your special occasion'. It regularly hosts conferences, meetings, weddings and parties and in 2022/23 earned the club more than £180,000 in revenue. But after the match against Workington it offered 'dramatic views' of a different sort as a fight broke out between fans of the two clubs.

As ever these days, footage of the commotion found its way on to the internet and by the following morning it had been viewed more than a million times on X as accounts like @footballfights shared it with their hundreds of thousands of followers. Italian author Nicolo Rondinelli, who I'd met ahead of the postponed Marine match at Broadhurst Park in December, messaged me from northern Italy to tell me that he'd seen the footage.

Usually we'd kill for a fraction of that publicity for our function room and bar, which is the centrepiece of the club's events and hospitality, but such is the way that the

Nic Bollado scores the third goal in FC United's 3-0 win over Worksop Town and seals the club's first ever home win on the opening day of a season [Credit to Lewis Mckenna]

Dec McLoughlin's thunderbolt against Stafford Rangers was the men's team's goal of the season [Credit to Lewis Mckenna]

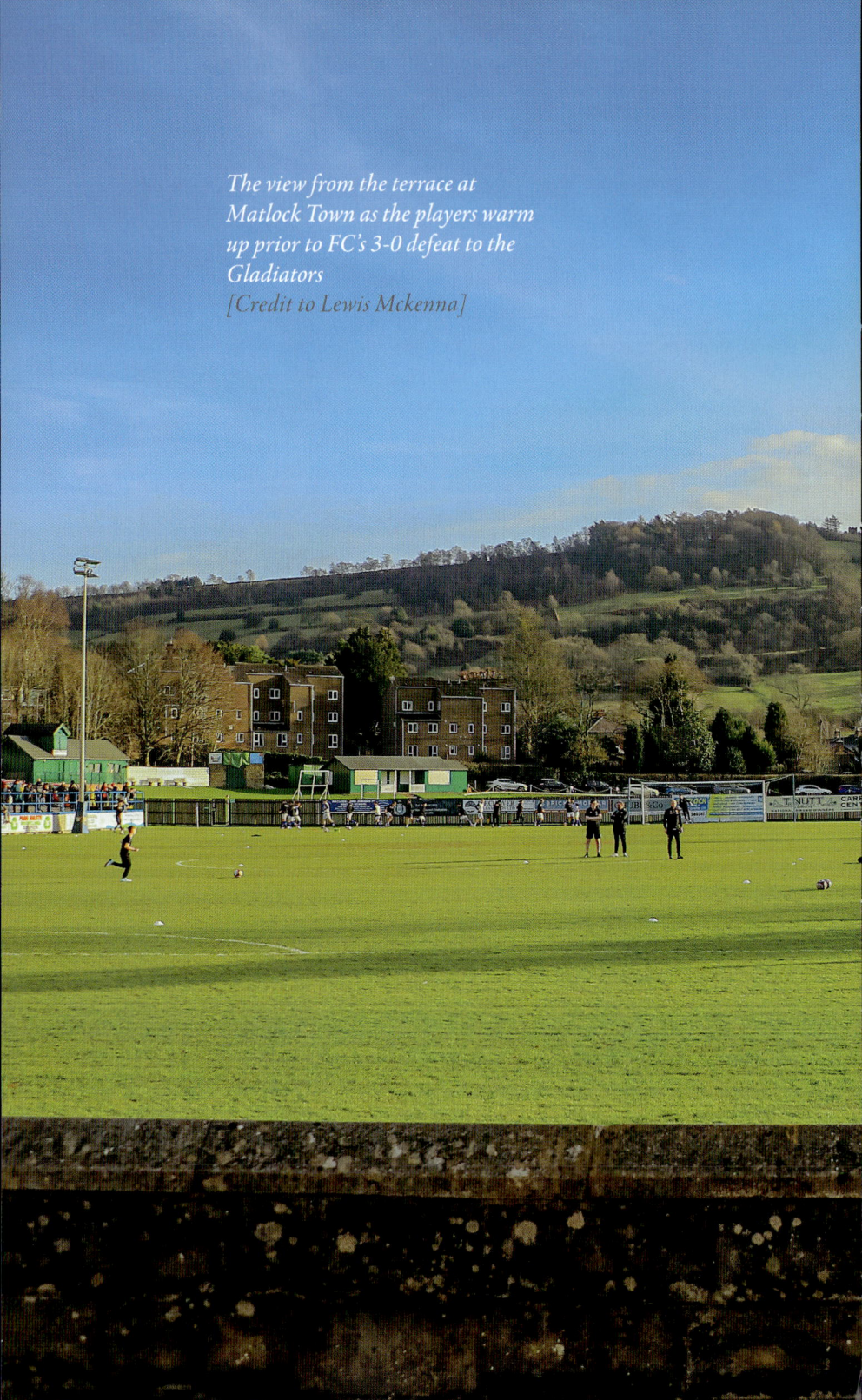

The view from the terrace at Matlock Town as the players warm up prior to FC's 3-0 defeat to the Gladiators
[Credit to Lewis Mckenna]

Joe Ferguson in action for FC at home to Warrington Rylands in a match that was abandoned in the second half due to a waterlogged pitch
[Credit to Lewis Mckenna]

'To the regiment, I wish I was there!' The function room was packed to see the cast of much-loved television comedy series Early Doors *reunited.*
[Credit to Lewis Mckenna]

Raphael Ikediashi celebrates scoring the third goal in the academy team's 3-0 win against Newcastle Benfield in the quarter-finals of the National League Under 19 Alliance League Cup
[Credit to Lewis Mckenna]

The women's team's 5-4 win against Leeds was one of the highlights of the season
[Credit to Lewis Mckenna]

The academy team celebrate winning the league after beating Halifax
[Credit to Lewis Mckenna]

Nineteen years on, FC United fans continue to display their abhorrence of the Glazer family's presence at Manchester United [Credit to Lewis Mckenna]

The women's team lift the Manchester FA Women's Challenge Cup after beating Mancunian Unity in a penalty shoot-out in a tense final at Rochdale's Crown Oil Arena [Credit to Lewis Mckenna]

FC United fans celebrate beating Lewes 1-0 in the semi-final of the Fenix Trophy in Desenzano del Garda [Credit to Lewis Mckenna]

FC United players, coaching staff and fans celebrate winning the Fenix Trophy after FC beat Prague Raptors 4-0 in the 2024 final [Credit to Lewis Mckenna]

internet works that months of hard graft can be undone in minutes. Although the announcement that 'if anyone wants to stay behind after the fight we're going to do *Play Your Cards Right*' towards the end of the 71-second clip certainly caused a chuckle or two.

* * *

'What was the score, mate? Did they win?'

'Yeah, 14-nil.'

'Four-nil? Sounds like a good win that.'

I'm strolling down St Mary's Road towards the tram stop after FC's Fenix Trophy match against Kraków Dragoons on 10 March when a bloke unloading shopping bags from his car asks me about the match. FC had thumped the Polish side 14-0, a scarcely believable scoreline, so it was no surprise to find someone thinking I'd actually said four rather than 14. I didn't hang around to correct him.

A few club records tumbled during this thumping as, for the third time in the tournament, FC racked up their biggest victory – beating the 12-0 win against Spanish side Cuenca-Mestallistes in last season's competition. And Aaron Bennett's five goals equalled the record for the most goals scored by an FC player in a single match.

There were, however, mitigating circumstances for the margin of victory. Visa complications and expenses meant that only four of the Dragoons' multinational starting 11 for the match in Kraków in October were able to begin this return fixture. And the Polish side hadn't played for nearly three months as they came towards the end of the extensive winter break in Poland's non-league season. So they were undoubtedly short of match fitness.

Despite an extensive marketing campaign on social media, the attendance, for a 3pm kick-off on a Sunday, was only 567 – less than half of the number that had attended the only other time that we had played a Fenix Trophy match on a weekend afternoon, against AKS Zły almost exactly two years ago.

The match was preceded by a Course You Can Malcolm event which marked the launch of FC's former players' association with a Q&A session with several former players including the club's leading scorer and former player-manager Tom Greaves. It was an entertaining session which showed the affection all the players still have for the club. Interestingly, when they were asked to pick a player in North West Counties football who FC ought to be interested in, Tom had no hesitation in pointing out that we'd already signed the best – Lewis Gilboy, who joined us from Bury recently.

Following the ex-players on stage were the 99 Degree who, on their return to CYCM, delivered a blistering set of their self-styled 'trashy surfabilly, spaghetti western murder balladry'. It certainly beat stopping at home and watching *Songs of Praise*. Although rumours that their rousing set had been piped into the home dressing room before the match, thus going some way to explaining the record-breaking scoreline, turned out not to be true.

The win means that FC have almost certainly qualified for the Fenix Final 4 which, it had been announced a few days earlier, will take place in Desenzano del Garda in northern Italy in May and is looking increasingly likely to feature three English clubs along with Prague Raptors, the runners-up in the first two editions of the competition.

International Women's Day had taken place earlier in the week and the men's team had chosen this match to wear the celebratory Suffragette-inspired kit that the women's team have been wearing away from home this season. The kit had been launched on International Women's Day in 2023 and its purple, green and white colours were chosen to recognise Manchester's historical connection with the Suffragette movement with a striking sash design based on the sashes worn at parades and rallies by supporters of women's suffrage. The year 2023 marked 120 years since the Women's Social and Political Union (WSPU) was formed in Manchester and began its campaign to get women the vote. It was the bright idea of one of the club's supporters and a lot of thought had gone into it.

The kit launch attracted a smattering of interest on the internet with Matt Slater, football reporter at *The Athletic*, describing it as 'an instant classic' and the BBC even took a break from dealing with the fallout from a tweet by Gary Lineker to share it on Instagram. The timing of the launch on International Women's Day in 2023 helped bring it to the notice of football supporters well beyond Manchester and although it was hoped that it might have gone viral in a similar fashion to Clapton CFC's Spanish civil war-inspired shirt a few years earlier, in the end we only sold 190 shirts. 'We didn't market it as much as we should,' says board member Simon Preston.

But it wasn't all about clicks and pound signs, as the club announced that it would be donating a portion of any profits from the sale of the shirt to Manchester Women's Aid, a charity that helps local women and children affected by domestic and sexual abuse.

This being FC United, where it can often feel like we're for ever on the verge of another online ruckus, there were some co-owners who were unhappy that the board had decided that this shirt design would not be voted on by the club's co-owners. The club's rules stipulate that at each AGM the board 'will propose to co-owners (in accordance with the established home and away kit rotation) whether or not they wish to have a new kit produced for the following season(s)' with a vote in favour enabling co-owners to subsequently vote to choose the design from a shortlist of four kit designs. However, the board felt that this new shirt 'sits outside of the process for regular home and away kit rotation' as it's for one season only.

***

On yet another damp Saturday morning the pitch at Atherton Collieries passed an early inspection so we got the pleasure of riding the guided busway to a town that was once part of the Manchester coalfield (hence the name of one of its two semi-professional football clubs). The Skuna Stadium, with its gently sloping pitch, is a classic North West Counties hotchpotch of a small main stand accompanied by various huts and cabins that house the changing rooms, bar, toilets and the boardroom. Safe to say that it's not one of the first away days you look for when the fixtures come out.

Not far from the ground there's a large mural on the end of a row of terraced houses which celebrates local athlete Keely Hodgkinson's gold medal in the 800m in the European Athletics Championships in Munich in 2022 – she's the 'pride of Atherton' and will be going for gold again in this summer's Olympics.

FC United rarely do well at Atherton and with ten minutes left it looked like it was going to be the same old story as we trailed 1-0 but an equaliser from Dontai Gabidon and then a 95th-minute winner from Aaron Bennett sent the away support into raptures – it feels like a long while since we've celebrated a pair of goals like that. An important three points against one of only four teams below us in the league that probably just about ensures that we'll remain in this division for next season.

On the bus back into Manchester, a smartly dressed bloke, heading into town for a night out, got on somewhere along the East Lancs Road and we got chatting. 'I'm not looking forward to tomorrow,' he said. 'I can't see United beating that lot.' It was the day before Manchester United's FA Cup quarter-final against Liverpool and, although similarly pessimistic, I muttered some cliched nonsense along the lines of 'you never know in the cup, anything can happen'. And lo and behold the following day saw another red-shirted Manchester football team score a late winner to send its fans into raptures. Some football weekends can be nigh-on perfect.

* * *

Season tickets for the 2024/25 season go on sale on 20 March with supporters invited to buy theirs as early as they can ahead of the club's 20th season and 'be a part of the best matchday in non-league'.

* * *

A post on The Soul is One on Friday, 22 March calls for FC supporters to boycott the forthcoming game at Macclesfield, describing their £17 admission price for adults as 'quite frankly diabolical no matter which way you look at it'. It recalled the time when we'd boycotted an away match at Curzon Ashton in 2007 after the Northern Premier League had moved the kick-off time so it could be televised, and also the FA Cup first-round tie against Chesterfield in 2015 when many of us had missed the first half to protest outside the ground at the tie being moved to a Monday night for television purposes.

The game at Curzon in December 2007 saw an almost total boycott by FC United fans after the Northern Premier League had switched the kick-off time to 12.45pm to enable the match to be shown live on the league's own television broadcaster, NPLTV. Both clubs had opposed the change in kick-off time but the league insisted that the £100,000 paid for television rights by Invision outweighed their concerns.

So a match that would probably have attracted a crowd of more than 2,000 – Curzon were top of the table at the time and FC were fifth – ended up being watched by 297 spectators with barely any FC fans in attendance. After the match FC's board issued a statement in which it congratulated fans for boycotting the tie, won 2-0, and added, 'FC United came into existence in direct response to the disregard shown for football supporters by those who put profit before the fans who support the game week in week out … as a democratically elected board we endeavour to represent the interests and will of FC United fans and we hope that the strength of feeling shown by supporters prompts greater consideration for their concerns in future.'

Which felt like wishful thinking when in November 2015 hundreds of supporters, including me, missed the first half against Chesterfield and stood outside Broadhurst Park in protest. Although it's worth noting that the £67,500 broadcasting fee received by the club for this televised fixture went a long way to keeping the club in the black in our first year in Moston.

The forum post regarding the trip to Macclesfield went on, 'As fans of FCUM we have proudly taken these stances over the years in order to send a message that greed and exploitation of fans at this and any level of football is unacceptable. It is imperative that we do the same again.' It also encouraged fans to donate their £17 to our club and urged those who will be attending to 'not buy anything in the ground' and added, 'Let's keep up the fight against the greedy capitalists who infest our game.'

Whether you'd describe Macclesfield's owner Rob Smethurst as a 'greedy capitalist' is up for debate. Talking to journalist Emma Jones on the *On Another Planet* podcast (which Jones co-hosts with Macclesfield's director of football Robbie Savage), Smethurst estimated that he has so far invested around £4m of his own money in the club he bought in September 2020 – much of this on redeveloping the ground, including a new pitch, new stand, new bars, seats, a 'fan zone' and a gym, in the hope that it will become sustainable in the future.

He explained that the cost of hosting matches at what is essentially an EFL ground is substantially higher than most clubs at this level which meant that, as he put it, 'We had to charge £17 per ticket.' Macclesfield's average crowd this season has been far and away the biggest in the Northern Premier League – nearly twice as high as FC United who are the second-best supported club – and this makes hosting a matchday considerably more expensive when you factor in the costs of stewards, doctors, safety officer, police and ambulance.

It's something that FC are familiar with from our very first season when we charged the highest adult admission price (£7) in the North West Counties League, primarily due to the cost of hosting matches at Gigg Lane, which was then a Football League ground, and also the desire to assemble a squad that could challenge for promotion. This admission price was 75 per cent higher than some clubs in the same division.

The debate that followed on the forum was largely measured as, while £17 for this level of football is undoubtedly expensive, there was a recognition that in this instance there isn't really a right or wrong answer when it comes to deciding whether or not to boycott the match – it comes down to a personal choice. Macclesfield's prices had been the same all season – it wasn't like they were deliberately exploiting the fans of FC United as they knew we would bring a larger travelling support. 'I like the maturity there has been around this,' wrote one poster, adding, 'A decade ago we'd have torn ourselves apart over this with different factions all claiming the moral superiority.' Maybe we have grown up a bit in the last couple of decades.

Adrian Seddon pointed out that Macclesfield fans 'seem to be OK with higher admission prices in return for a higher football budget' as they bid to win promotion. Their club, their rules, I guess. And he also highlighted the relatively poor experience that their supporters received when they visited Broadhurst Park earlier in the season. The match was segregated and made all-ticket for visiting fans and, although the away end is covered, the lack of any terracing means many supporters get a poor view of the match, toilet facilities are limited and, for Macclesfield's visit, there was only a single pop-up bar. All this for the adult admission price of £13 which as Adrian pointed out 'is nowhere near the cheapest in the league'.

The issue was also discussed at March's board meeting the following Monday and there was agreement that it wasn't for the board 'to determine how supporters should respond to other clubs' admission prices'. There was a feeling, however, that the club should nevertheless continue to advocate for change on key issues and chair Nick Boom highlighted how clubs like Macclesfield raising admission prices to boost their playing budget could lead to other clubs following suit in order to compete, which would result in the further inflation of admission prices.

Nick added that from the discussions he'd had with other club directors at matches, since becoming chair, it's clear that there are several other clubs who share our concerns about wage inflation and we ought to be able to collectively lobby for change and he felt that FC should play 'a pivotal role at the forefront of the supporter ownership movement, campaigning for change'.

* * *

'I like it, it's good honest fare and it's affordable – I could get into this,' one newcomer told me as we queued for a half-time brew under the main stand. A crowd of 2,304 had assembled at Broadhurst Park to watch 17th-placed FC United take on 18th-placed Basford United on Non-League Day on Saturday, 23 March, boosted by the offer of free tickets for local residents (anyone living in the M40 and M9 postcodes closest to Broadhurst Park) as part of a community day initiative. It was our second-highest crowd of the season and a tremendous attendance for a match in the seventh tier on an afternoon when there was little at stake for the home side.

Non-League Day was founded in 2010 and has become an annual celebration of English football outside its top four tiers, scheduled to coincide with an international break, thus giving fans the chance to support their local non-league team on an otherwise blank weekend. It always feels a little gimmicky to me – after all, we're trying to build something sustainable at FC that's all about people attending matches on a regular basis rather than slumming it when there isn't any big football. But there's little doubt that it's been a success in raising the profile of the non-league game and encouraging supporters of Premier League and Championship sides to give lower-league teams a go.

Dontai Gabidon put FC in front in the 12th minute and substitute Charlie Ennis scored the second ten minutes from time to seal a comfortable 2-0 win. The queues for the bars and food kiosks were noticeably longer and it was nice to see plenty of youngsters in attendance. Historically, whenever we've offered free admission like this the match has been awful, but this was a decent performance by FC and hopefully a sufficiently enjoyable afternoon to encourage a few to come back and watch us more.

The following day the main bar at Broadhurst Park was transformed into the much-loved Grapes pub as the cast of the cult television comedy *Early Doors* was reunited and swapped stories and answered questions from an audience which included many first-time visitors to the ground. Nick Boom, who was in attendance, said the cast seemed to enjoy the occasion as much as the audience, which created an 'electric atmosphere' in the room.

The idea for the fundraising event was initially brought to the board by James Quinn, who starred as Phil, the dodgy copper, in the comedy series and has also appeared in *Emmerdale* and *Coronation Street* and is an FC United co-owner and a commentator on FCUM Radio. James was instrumental in getting everyone together, and the cast had generously agreed to attend free of charge so all monies received from hosting this event went to the club. To the regiment, I wish I was there!

* * *

At March's board meeting the board asked Danny Davis to prepare a business case for a full-time commercial manager post from the start of the 2024/25 financial year for it to consider. We are now beginning to see the benefits of appointing Paul Haworth as part-time business development manager but given this appointment was for an initial six-month period only, the club must decide whether or not to make it a full-time post.

On the commercial front, it's clear that we haven't performed as well as we would have liked this year and this reflects the withdrawal of a dedicated commercial resource following the departure of Natalie Atkinson as chief executive officer and Frances Fielding as commercial manager last year. The board felt that we needed to cut costs at a time when we were enduring the worst of the cost of living crisis.

The management accounts for January highlighted that the club made an operating loss of £26,500 in-month and reported an operating loss of £14,000 after the first seven months of the 2023/24 financial year, which was no surprise as the men's first team had played only one home match in January and matchday income was therefore well down on budget.

This was Steve Durrands's last board meeting as he is stepping down as financial controller at the end of the month and the board thanked him for standing in as the club's finance lead over the last few months.

* * *

It's a long-standing joke among FC fans when the fixtures are due to come out that Whitby away will be on a Tuesday night in January. This season's trip to the North Yorkshire seaside town ended up being on a Tuesday night in late March – after the original fixture in February had been postponed – and FC returned with all three points after a hard-fought 2-1 win over the Seasiders with Aaron Bennett scoring another late winner.

* * *

By the time I'd got to the front of the lengthy pre-match queue for tickets – or more precisely a sheet of paper with a QR code on it – at Macclesfield on the last Saturday in March, one of the ticket office staff wasn't happy. 'I've been here since 11 this morning, it's not my fault you've all turned up late,' she said. I'd been in the queue since 2.40pm which I didn't think was particularly 'late' but I wasn't going to argue. Especially as we could have purchased tickets online prior to the match and thus saved ourselves the faff of double queuing.

On Friday evening it had been reported that more than 300 FC fans had already bought their tickets online but the home club had noticed that a disproportionate number had bought concession tickets priced at £13 rather than the usual adult price of £17 so they had announced that they would be doing 'checks' as fans arrived to ensure they'd purchased the correct ticket – as they are perfectly entitled to do.

An online survey prior to the Macclesfield away trip, completed by nearly 250 FC fans, revealed that less than ten per cent were happy to pay the £17 admission price and would be attending the match while 41 per cent described themselves as 'not happy about paying £17 and will not attend the match'. In reality I think most supporters, like myself, were somewhere in between – unhappy with the admission price but still keen to attend what was always going to be one of the biggest matches of our season but without spending anything else inside the ground – no food or drink or programmes, the all-important 'second spend' which is crucial for most non-league clubs.

Food and drink provides a crucial source of matchday income for many lower-league clubs and FC is certainly no stranger to this as food offerings such as 'the Bombay sandwich' attract dozens of likes on social media accounts like 'Footy Scran', while a rotating range of (mostly local) beers is always much anticipated. No wonder a typical matchday for many FC fans involves a calorific intake sufficient to fuel a podium finish in a mountain stage in the Tour de France.

In the end around 500 FC fans – our biggest away following of the season – made it inside the Leasing.com Stadium, part of a crowd of 4,298, the biggest crowd in the Northern Premier League so far this season and more than a third up on the Silkmen's average. And, in a nice touch possibly with one eye on a boycott by some FC fans, Macclesfield put £250 behind the bar at the away end so that any visiting supporters arriving early (unlike me) could enjoy a free pint or two in the spring sunshine. The bar at the away end was barely without a queue throughout the match – so much for 'no second spend'.

There is a wonderful tradition of banners at Manchester United and FC United games which goes back decades. 'Bailey whips Arsenal's Irish cream' at the 1979 FA Cup Final paying tribute to United's goalkeeper Gary Bailey remains one of my favourites – and this tradition has very much been kept alive at FC where a host of fading flags and banners permanently adorn all four sides of our Broadhurst Park home, and others are brought out on matchdays, often witty, profound, thought-provoking and sometimes all three. Sadly, a banner bearing the words 'Glazer' and '$avage' in green and gold that an FC fan brought to Macclesfield wasn't any of the above. At least the Radcliffe fans who'd displayed a banner that read 'Robbin Savage' on their visit to Macclesfield earlier in the season had shown some humour.

Meanwhile, in the boardroom, 'Robbie Savage was great with us', said Paul Hurst and had no issue with some FC fans objecting to Macclesfield's admission prices. Paul also recalls the trip to Macclesfield as being memorable for Adrian Seddon consuming six creme eggs in the boardroom.

On the pitch, the hosts, looking to cement a place in the play-offs, were by far the better side and apart from a brief spell when FC managed to string a few passes together, the first half was pretty much all one-way traffic towards the FC goal. But after barely mustering a shot all half, Jan Palinkas scored an equaliser from a corner just before half-time. Arguably, FC played much better in the second half but we didn't add to our tally, while Macclesfield scored twice more and were very comfortable 3-1 winners. As we applauded the players at the end, it was lovely to see Tunde Owolabi, now a Macclesfield player, come over and mix with the FC fans for whom he remains a bona fide superstar.

'You're nothing special, we'll see you next year,' sang our supporters at the end. 'Three-one in your cup final,' chorused the Macclesfield fans in reply.

10

Where does all the money go?

'WHERE DOES all the money go?' ranted an unhappy FC fan as we queued for the bus back into town after a defeat at home to Workington in early March. Why, when we are the second-best supported club in the Northern Premier League with an average crowd more than twice the average of most clubs in the same division, have we struggled to make much of an impression in the league in the last few seasons? Where is all the money that we generate from bigger crowds going?

As an accountant in my day job I took this rant to heart, and over the next few weeks put together what initially began as a brief 'beginner's guide to FC United's finances' but snowballed into something more substantial – a 17-page guide including tables, graphs and pie charts that attempted to help those of us who aren't financial whizzkids understand the club's finances a little better. We posted it on the members' forum and emailed it directly to co-owners later in the month and it was well received.

Spreadsheets and double-entry bookkeeping don't get the pulse racing like last-minute winners and even though, as co-owners of FC United, we have access to considerably more financial information than most football fans, many of us tend to leave the interpretation of balance sheets and profit and loss accounts to the bean counters among us. Indeed, it was a growing sense that money was ruining the game at the highest level – culminating in the grotesque phenomenon of a bunch of freeloading Floridians using Manchester United as a cash machine – that resulted in many of us leaving Old Trafford in 2005 to form our own football club. So it's perhaps understandable that some of us, even nearly two decades on, prefer to concentrate on the football rather than immerse ourselves in the money-related aspects of the club's affairs.

It feels like we've been wrestling with the club's finances ever since we moved into Broadhurst Park in 2015. The shift from renting to owning our own ground took some getting used to and despite record crowds and membership in our first season in Moston in 2015/16, only the substantial revenue generated from being involved in a televised FA Cup first-round match prevented us from posting an operating loss, as noted earlier. A substantial loss followed a year later but we were gradually able to get a grip on our finances in the following two years and in 2018/19, remarkably, despite being relegated from National League North, we were close to breaking even.

Then came the existential threat of the pandemic and a lengthy period without any football which, not surprisingly, seriously disrupted the club's financial planning, and an operating profit in excess of £300,000 in 2020/21 – as revenue was boosted by grants and other support through the pandemic and prize money and television and advertising revenue from another FA Cup run – was followed by a loss of similar magnitude in 2021/22 as Covid continued to have an impact on the club's operation but this time without any external support. And then as we emerged from the pandemic and embarked on the first year of the club's five-year vision in 2022/23, the cost of living crisis presented a substantial double challenge as it increased prices and also squeezed the disposable income of our supporters.

As a community benefit society FC United is required to submit its annual accounts to the Financial Conduct Authority (FCA) within seven months of the year end. The 2022/23 accounts, which cover the period from 1 July 2022 to 30 June 2023, were submitted to the FCA in January 2024 – having been presented to co-owners at last November's AGM – and consisted of 47 pages including a balance sheet, profit and loss account, cash flow statement, report from the board (also referred to as a directors' report) and several pages of notes which include detailed breakdowns of income and expenditure. The accounts are available for anyone to view on the FCA's Mutuals Public Register under our registered society name as FC United Limited.

FC's balance sheet, which shows the relationship between the club's assets, liabilities and equity, looks very different to most clubs at our level and at the end of 2022/23 it included fixed assets with a net book value of £5.9m (almost entirely the value of the ground), debts of nearly £1m, deferred grants of £2.4m (the grant income we received to fund the building of the ground and refurbishment since) and share capital of nearly £1.9m, which is the latest value of the community shares that part funded the building of the ground. We were the first supporter-owned club to build our own ground and it was funded, as already mentioned, through the purchase of £2m of community shares by supporters together with grants from the Football Foundation, Sport England and Manchester City Council and a loan from the council.

Meanwhile, the profit and loss account, which summarises the financial transactions of the club during the financial year, identified an operating loss before interest and taxation of £228,000 in 2022/23, which was a significant improvement on the operating loss of £345,000 reported the year before but nevertheless still a loss.

Turnover (or revenue) in 2022/23 was nearly £1.2m and was 2.5 per cent up on 2021/22 despite the impact of the wider economic climate. Matchday income in the form of gate receipts, season tickets, and food and beverage sales was the club's main source of income (£474,000) and accounted for around 40 per cent of the club's total revenue in 2022/23.

Commercial income from sponsorship and advertising of £100,000 was more than three times higher than the £30,000 generated in 2021/22 but merchandise income was slightly down in 2022/23 (£71,000 compared to £79,000 in the previous year). Income to support the academy of £104,000 represented a small decrease compared to the previous year (£114,000) and income from functions and events totalled £183,000, which was significantly higher than in 2021/22 as the club hosted significantly more events in 2022/23 and several organisations began using Broadhurst Park as a regular venue.

In addition, there were some important one-off income streams that weren't budgeted for. Prize money increased substantially in 2022/23 to £12,000 largely as a result of the women's team making it through to the first round proper of the Women's FA Cup and the increased prize money in the women's game following the England team's success in the Euros in 2022. Meanwhile, income from player transfers was £7,500 following the transfer of star striker Regan Linney to Altrincham.

The club's total costs of £1.4m in 2022/23 comprised 'cost of sales' of £751,000 – the costs incurred by the club in selling goods and services – and £643,000 of 'administrative expenses', which includes the day-to-day costs of running the club such as office staff pay costs, utilities, insurances, bank charges and the depreciation of fixed assets.

The single biggest cost was the £205,000 spent on paying players, coaching staff and other backroom staff, which included employers' national insurance and pension contributions. Interestingly, this was only 1.8 per cent higher than the sum spent on players and management staff five years before, which reflects the prudent approach that the club has taken to managing its football budget over the last few years in contrast with the 'boom and bust' approach adopted by many other clubs as they chase success.

Administrative expenses totalled £722,000 and included: office staff pay costs of £120,000, which included the costs of the chief executive, club and company secretary, commercial manager and finance manager; utilities costs (for gas, electricity and water) of £82,000; and the depreciation of the club's fixed assets which totalled £165,000.

Staff costs were, not surprisingly, the club's single biggest cost line and feature in both the cost of sales and administrative expenses and totalled £627,000 in 2022/23, which was 2.3 per cent less than the previous year and reflected the careful approach the club had taken to managing staff costs in the first year of its business plan.

It's useful to note here that in addition to our paid staff the club is also very reliant on a team of unpaid volunteers who perform a whole range of matchday and non-matchday tasks. According to our most recent estimate, this volunteer contribution totals around 11,000 hours per year and was conservatively valued at more than £200,000.

* * *

So how do FC United's finances compare to other clubs, particularly those that are also fan-owned? Perhaps closest to us in terms of size, structure and finances are Lewes FC who are wholly supporter-owned (with 2,178 members in 2021/22) and also compete in the seventh tier, in the Isthmian Premier League. They also entered the Fenix Trophy for the first time this season.

Lewes's most recently published accounts reveal that they made an operating loss (before interest and taxation) of £100,000 in the 2021/22 financial year from a turnover of nearly £1.5m. So, despite the loss, they performed significantly better than us in 2021/22 when we incurred a loss of £345,000. They don't share as much detail as FC in their accounts but staff costs totalled nearly £1.1m or 71 per cent of their turnover, which was significantly higher than us, and the notes to the accounts recorded that a club director loaned £600,000 during 2021/22 'to assist cash flow'.

It appears that none of this loan was repaid in-year and it was written off at the year end.

Scarborough Athletic FC are also wholly fan-owned (with 1,315 members in 2022/23) and are familiar to us having won promotion from the Northern Premier League to the sixth tier in 2021/22. Their accounts for the 2022/23 financial year – which covered their first season in National League North – reveal that they made an operating profit (before interest and taxation) of £81,000 from a turnover of £731,000. Their 'first team costs' in their promotion season were £211,000 but they rose by 69 per cent to £357,000 in their first season in National League North, which they were able to afford on the back of substantial increases in matchday and commercial income.

Although they are not supporter-owned, the annual accounts of local rivals Curzon Ashton, who are also a community benefit society, can also be viewed on the Mutuals Public Register and their most recently published accounts for 2021/22, covering a season in which they finished in a mid-table position in National League North, reveal that they made an operating loss of £63,000 from a turnover of £753,000.

Interestingly, their expenditure breakdown identified total 'players' wages and expenses' of £210,000, which was similar to the amount that FC United spent on players, management and medical staff in the same year (£202,000) but direct comparisons are difficult as it's unclear where the pay costs of management and backroom staff are included in Curzon's accounts. That said, their wage bill in 2021/22 is substantially lower than that of Scarborough in their first season in National League North in 2022/23 when their 'first team costs' were £357,000.

I did some further digging around on the Companies House website and managed to find accounts for either 2022/23 or 2021/22 for 16 of the 22 clubs in the Northern Premier League, which revealed that only three – Marine, Ilkeston Town and Basford United – reported a profit in their latest figures. The most profitable, by some distance, was Ilkeston Town whose finances were buoyed by a two-year 'six-figure sponsorship deal' with a local transport software logistics firm in 2022.

And how about Workington, whose win at Broadhurst Park in March prompted the 'where does all the money go' question? A glance at their balance sheet at the end of 2022/23 indicates that they made a loss of £35,000 but, as with almost all other clubs in this division, there were few other indicators of the financial health of the club.

What was also noticeable in all of this is that FC United is, by some distance, the most financially transparent club in this division – the only one to submit comprehensive financial statements for the 2022/23 financial year which also included a profit and loss account. All the other 15 clubs for which annual accounts information was available submitted only balance sheet information as they are allowed to do.

Finally, in terms of comparisons, on what feels like a different planet but is actually just across town, Manchester United reported a £42m loss in 2022/23 despite a Premier League record revenue figure of £648m, which was up by 11 per cent on the previous year. To put that into perspective, it means that, on average, it took Manchester United a mere 15 hours and 53 minutes to generate the same level of revenue that we grafted all year for at FC United.

Meanwhile, it was reported that United's highest paid player in 2022/23, Casemiro – apparently on £350,000 per week – cost the club around £24.7m over the year including national insurance contributions, bonuses and image rights. Which means that FC United's annual turnover equates to little more than three weeks of Casemiro.

Finally, to come back to the original question of where FC United's money goes, for each £1 of revenue that the club generated in 2022/23:

- 15p was spent on players, coaching and backroom staff and this also included not only wages but the employer's national insurance and pension contributions too.
- 15p was spent on making matchdays an enjoyable experience for all including bar staff, stewards and security staff, food and drink, the costs of broadcasting matches and the matchday programme.

- 9p was spent on the facilities staff who look after our Broadhurst Park ground and facilities and included employers' national insurance and pension contributions.
- 9p was spent on functions and events including the staff who ensure that the functions and events that we host at Broadhurst Park provide an enjoyable experience for all and also the costs of food and drink.
- 8p was spent on our academy including staff, travel and kit.
- 8p was spent on the office staff who are responsible for the day-to-day running of the club including the chief executive officer, club and company secretary, commercial manager and finance manager; again, this included employer's national insurance and pension contributions.
- 6p was spent on utilities such as gas, electricity and water.
- 5p was spent on other overheads such as insurances, bank charges, information technology, audit and accountancy fees and legal fees.
- 4p was spent on interest payments.
- 4p was spent on pitch and general maintenance.
- 3p was spent on merchandise for the club shop.
- 2p was spent on the club's community programme including community staff and grant costs.
- 1p was spent on administering the Development Fund including the Holiday Draw and Development Fund events.
- 11p was accounted for by depreciation of the club's fixed assets which mainly comprises our ground.
- 0p was spent on repaying the club's debt but from 2024/25 onwards this will change (and we'll come back to this later in the book).

11

What are they singing now?

IT'S RARELY a good sign when your manager ends up arguing with one of the team's own supporters at the final whistle and one of Neil Reynolds's coaching team ought to have steered him away from a heated exchange with an FC fan as the team were, as ever, applauded off at the end of the 2-0 defeat at home to in-form Ashton United on Easter Monday. Ashton were worthy winners and now sit just outside the play-off places with a couple of games in hand on their nearest rivals.

It felt light years away from Easter Monday last year when we had romped to a 5-0 win against Ashton at Hurst Cross as we finished the season on a good run of form. Despite their promotion push and this being a local derby, the visitors brought about 50 fans, who mostly congregated behind the goal at the Lightbowne Road End.

Aside from the opening few minutes when we played with urgency and should have taken the lead, it was a limp performance on a pudding of a pitch against a side, in contrast, that looked confident and played some incisive attacking football. It was no surprise when ex-FC striker Jason Gilchrist gave them the lead after half an hour – the ball trickling across the line after a defensive mix-up.

The highlight of the day was perhaps the FC fans singing 'we paid for your tan' at the bronzed ex-Broadhurst Park midfielder Nathan Lowe, who shortly after this prematurely celebrated what he thought was Ashton's second goal – with arms outstretched in front of the home fans at the St Mary's End – only to spot the linesman's raised flag. Small pleasures.

The post-match mood on The Soul is One was gloomy and, again, there were calls for a change of manager. 'I've already bought my season ticket for next season and I've always backed Reno but I would like to see a fresh appointment,' reckoned one poster. 'First time ever that I didn't want to bother going … dragged myself to the ground last minute. Everyone I go with couldn't be bothered,' wrote another.

'I love Reno and this group of players but we're three or four signings short of really competing in this league. Our problem is that the players we need won't come cheap. Unless we find the budget to get some of them in then we will rinse and repeat for next season' was another measured response.

And another poster reckoned that the board was guilty of 'misjudging the mood' of the fans when awarding Neil a two-year contract extension earlier this year. 'The mood among the fans is definitely swinging against Neil,' said another.

* * *

A couple of days later the club announced that we've sold 100 season tickets and ten match ticket books for next season in the first couple of weeks of the season ticket campaign, which means that we're roughly about two weeks ahead of last year's campaign which commenced on 11 April and by the end of the first week had sold 106 tickets.

Meanwhile, the *Manchester Evening News*, never afraid to chase clicks, published CCTV images of 'the 13 people police want to speak to after violence erupts at FC United match' on its website – the match in question being against Workington at the beginning of March – and appealed for 'anyone with information that may assist officers with their enquiries' to get in touch with the police. The *Manchester Evening News* had also invited football fans to grass on fellow supporters after the protests in 2021 that forced the postponement of the match between Manchester United and Liverpool at Old Trafford.

The club issued a statement saying that it 'condemns all forms of violence' and added, 'We are a community football club and any behaviour that endangers the safety of our staff and supporters is completely unacceptable.' No further comment was possible at this stage due to the ongoing police investigation.

* * *

FC's women's team beat Leeds United Women 5-4 in a Thursday night thriller at Broadhurst Park watched by a crowd of 152. FC trailed three times but goals from Sacha Lewis, skipper Shaunna Jein and substitute Naomi Lawrence in the final 20 minutes put us 5-3 up going into injury time only for a late fourth goal for the visitors to mean a tense finish. It was a tremendous fightback and a richly deserved three points. 'I'm in agony. What a second half. Hopefully that'll be the springboard to push us on to avoid relegation,' said manager Jennie Swarbrick at the end.

It's only the team's second win of the season – the other was also 5-4, against Chester-le-Street Town Ladies in September – and we still sit bottom of the table with eight points from 20 matches. With our massively inferior goal difference to our rivals we would almost certainly have been relegated had we lost against Leeds. But it's possible that four points from our final two games might be enough to keep us up. The great escape might still be on.

Regardless of which division the women's team end up in next season, chair Nick Boom had mentioned at March's board meeting the need for the club to set out its ambitions for women's and girls' football. He noted that there has been a step change in the level of commercial interest in women's football over the last two years – something we've seen with PrettyLittleThing's substantial sponsorship last year – and it's clear from conversations the club has been having with potential sponsors for next season that some businesses are more interested in the women's team than the men's.

FC's women's team don't currently get paid for playing but even if we are relegated back to the North West Women's Regional League, the likelihood is that we will be competing against some teams that are able to pay their players. We've already seen with the loss of so many players to Wythenshawe Women – who currently play in the sixth tier but could be in the same division as FC next season – the difference this makes to the calibre of players who clubs are able to attract. Only in the last few weeks, the FC United captain Chaneece Reeves dropped down two divisions to join Wythenshawe.

* * *

'Darren, we don't want to go to Dane Bank.' I've arrived at Hyde bus station and an out-of-breath Darren has just been informed that he's scampered for the wrong bus. I made a similar mistake on Piccadilly less than an hour ago – boarding the 202 after just missing the 201, which was a schoolboy error as the 202 takes 15 minutes longer to get to Hyde. Still, at least I got to see Haughton Green.

Hyde is a town, like many that ring Manchester, that boomed on the back of the cotton industry in the 19th century when there were as many as 40 working mills locally. There's not much evidence of these boom times nowadays as I stroll along the main shopping street on my way to Ewen Fields past a bookies ('Bruno Fernandes to score anytime 11/2'), a store selling soft furnishings ('come and see the Paloma Faith collection'), another bookies, a charity shop, a Greggs, a pub – a line-up familiar to the run-down high streets of so many northern towns.

There's meant to be 'soft segregation' in place – the two sets of fans encouraged to enter the ground via separate turnstiles – but by the time I arrive a few minutes after kick-off, everyone seems to be heading through the same set of turnstiles anyway and once inside the ground supporters are free to mix as they please. It must have sounded like a good idea to someone.

I take up a position near the halfway line behind a bloke in a denim jacket with sewn-on badges reading 'Hyde United' and 'Supporters Club' encircling another badge on which is displayed a picture of a tiger – Hyde are known as 'the Tigers'. 'Come on, Hyde, these are shit,' shouts the tiger-clad one and, shortly after, FC take the lead as an unmarked Charlie Oliver meets a free kick from the right with a simple header. It's a soft goal to concede for the home side who currently sit in the last of the four play-off places.

A combination of a fierce crosswind and an artificial surface on which the ball occasionally bounces higher than Zebedee makes for a poor spectacle. The morning weather forecast warned of Storm Kathleen passing through and gusts of up to 50 miles per hour but thankfully there's been little precipitation – aside from the gusts, it's another warm Saturday afternoon.

Shortly after taking the lead there's a defensive mix-up by FC and the ball trickles into the net with no one entirely sure who had the last touch. For the second time this week FC have gifted the opposition their opening goal.

In 2010 Hyde United signed a deal with Manchester City that allowed the Premier League club to stage reserve and youth team fixtures at Ewen Fields while a new venue was being built on the Etihad Campus. The Abu Dhabi money allowed the club to clear debts of £250,000 and in return it underwent a complete makeover. The ground got a blue paint job, 'United' was dropped from the club's name and the kit became blue and white rather than red and white, City's crest appeared besides Hyde's on the main stand and the only advertising at the ground was for the Etihad. The deal ended in 2015 and the club became fan-owned after being taken over by the Hyde Supporters' Trust, who sought the advice of FC United.

For the second half I move behind the goal where most of the FC fans are softly segregated and singing non-stop throughout. Hyde take the lead midway through the half with a well-taken goal but still the songs keep coming. 'Why are you still singing?' enquires one of the young Hyde supporters who have located themselves close to the FC fans and are very much enjoying informing us that we are losing 2-1. There's a youthful feel to Hyde's support that is admirable even if their songs lack originality.

We don't come close to scoring an equaliser and that's that. At the final whistle FC's official X account rather churlishly refers to FC being beaten by 'an average-looking Hyde side'. I thought they were full value for their three points and still have a sniff of a play-off place although their

Tameside rivals Ashton United appear to be in the box seat with games in hand.

Later, as the 202 meanders back into town, Haughton Green basks in warm evening sunshine.

* * *

It's full speed ahead to Desenzano del Garda, as Clive Tyldesley might have said, as FC thump Vinsky 4-0 on 10 April in our final group match to secure a place in this season's Fenix Final 4. The goals are shared by Dec McLoughlin, Charlie Ennis, Lewis Gilboy and Josh Askew. Meanwhile, two of the academy lads – Alfie Henstock and Elliot Wilkinson – come on in the second half and make their first-team debuts, with Henstock claiming an assist for the final goal.

Only a few FC fans make our first trip to France since competing in a futsal tournament in Lille in the summer of 2017 – some travel to Magnanville via Paris while others fly to Beauvais – and in keeping with the spirit of the Fenix Trophy they're made very welcome by the hosts. For those watching on at home, the live stream of the match – viewed by an audience of around 240 – breaks down midway through the second half.

On the same afternoon the academy team thrash Eccleshill United 7-0 and now need only three points from their final four league matches to clinch their divisional title in the National League U19 Alliance. Only Stockport County and Buxton could possibly finish above us at this stage.

* * *

In our penultimate home match of the season on 13 April, FC beat Bamber Bridge 3-0 after the visitors' goalkeeper Aidan Hunt was sent off in the first half for a terrible challenge on the edge of the penalty area from which Charlie Munro curled his free kick around the wall to open the scoring. Aaron Bennett and Lewis Gilboy scored in the second half to give FC perhaps their most comfortable home win of the season. We remain in 14th place with two games left. It's Brig's sixth consecutive defeat.

It's notable that only three FC players in today's starting 11, Guy Hall, Curtis Jones and Dontai Gabidon, played in the same match last year – with two of last year's starting 11, Mike Potts and Adam Dodd having joined Bamber Bridge in the close season.

Elsewhere, Radcliffe clinched the title with a 2-1 win at Whitby while Warrington Rylands, Macclesfield and Marine are pretty much nailed on to be in the play-offs and will be joined by one of Hyde United or Ashton United. Radcliffe have been worthy winners – ever since their turbocharged start to the season they've looked like the team to beat.

* * *

Monday, 15 April marks the 35th anniversary of the Hillsborough disaster which resulted in the deaths of 97 Liverpool supporters in a crush caused by severe overcrowding on the Leppings Lane terrace at the Sheffield stadium during the FA Cup semi-final between Liverpool and Nottingham Forest. After a long and courageous fight by the families of those who lost their lives and survivors of the disaster, the Hillsborough Independent Panel's report published in September 2012 resulted in the previous finding of accidental death being quashed and a new coroner's inquest was launched in 2014.

This second coroner's inquest eventually concluded in 2016 that the supporters were unlawfully killed owing to grossly negligent failures by police and ambulance services and also found that the design of the ground contributed to the crush and that supporters were not to blame for the dangerous conditions.

None of this would have been any surprise whatsoever to the more than 15,000 Manchester United supporters – some of whom, including me, now follow FC United – who had also crammed on to the Leppings Lane terrace for a league match against Sheffield Wednesday only nine weeks before the disaster in February 1989 when the central pens of the terrace had also become overcrowded and some supporters were escorted to less congested areas of the terrace.

Following the publication of the panel's report I'd written a piece on my blog which recounted my experience that day; the article was subsequently published in FC United's matchday programme to show solidarity with those campaigning for justice for the victims of the disaster.

The Hillsborough disaster could have occurred to the supporters of several clubs, including United, who played in high-profile matches at the stadium in the 70s and 80s – it's no exaggeration to say that the design of the ground and incompetent policing made it a disaster waiting to happen.

Shamefully, a year earlier several FC United supporters had been ejected from a match at Marine for what is known as 'tragedy chanting' after chants relating to the Hillsborough disaster. The club issued a statement to co-owners, in the strongest possible terms, condemning any behaviour which seeks to make light of the deaths of fellow football supporters. The Merseyside and Greater Manchester police forces investigated the incident.

The disaster changed football for ever as is brilliantly chronicled in Hillsborough survivor Adrian Tempany's book *And the Sun Shines Now*. And it was also the beginning of a timeline that led to the formation of FC United in 2005. The flotation of Manchester United on the stock exchange in 1991 ultimately provided the opportunity for a hostile takeover by the likes of the Glazers. But the chief purpose of the 1991 flotation was to raise funds to redevelop the Stretford End into what would become an all-seater Old Trafford, which was a requirement laid out by the Taylor Report following the Hillsborough disaster.

* * *

The biggest crowd of the season flocked to Broadhurst Park on Tuesday, 16 April as more than 3,500 spectators watched Bury take on Padiham, giving our cash flow an unexpected boost. We had agreed to host the match after it was postponed the Saturday before as the Gigg Lane pitch was waterlogged. With the North West Counties League season due to finish next Saturday, Bury were forced to look for an alternative venue and we were keen to step in and help out a fellow fan-owned club.

It's great to see us doing this and there's a positive reaction from Bury fans on social media. 'It's nice of FC United to remember we helped them out when they first started out,' posted one. There's an interesting historical coincidence here too as Padiham were also the opposition for FC United's first match at Gigg Lane in August 2005.

Despite the recent monsoon-like conditions in Manchester, our groundsman is confident that hosting this fixture will not affect the preparations for our final home match of the season on Saturday, 27 April against Lancaster City, particularly as the weather forecast is predicting largely dry weather, for a change, for the next week or so.

193

* * *

Five years ago FA Cup replays were removed from the fifth round onwards and now, with grim inevitability, the FA announces that it is scrapping replays from the first round onwards from the 2024/25 season 'in light of changes to the calendar driven by the expanded UEFA competitions', which will see an expansion in the Champions League group stage and an expanded Club World Cup from 2025.

Had they done this a quarter of a century ago it would have denied many of us the opportunity to watch Manchester United's FA Cup semi-final replay with Arsenal at Villa Park in 1999, which remains the best match I've ever attended – the two best teams in the land tearing into each other in what was possibly the greatest FA Cup tie ever. Ryan Giggs's stunning solo goal – and the subsequent pitch invasion – in extra time is one of my most vivid football memories. It was the last FA Cup semi-final to go to a replay.

Predictably, the announcement was met with a fierce backlash from EFL and non-league clubs and a steady stream of statements followed over the next day or so including one from FC United which remarked that we are 'dismayed' by the decision to scrap replays and added, 'We fail to see how this decision does anything other than benefit the top three per cent of clubs at the expense of the other 97 per cent who proudly take part in the FA Cup each year.' More than 700 clubs take part in the FA Cup every season but it's the views of the 20 in the uppermost tier of the pyramid that seem to matter most to the FA. The statement also went on to point out, 'At a time when so many non-league clubs are struggling to make ends meet during this cost of living crisis, we are once again an afterthought as the big clubs are handed yet another advantage.'

The only time that FC have been involved in a replay in the FA Cup first round or beyond was in 2010 when we took Brighton to a second-round replay. After the famous win at Rochdale, it was the toughest possible second-round draw as the Seagulls were flying high at the top of League One at the time (and were ultimately promoted as champions that season), but after a first-half goal by Nicky Platt put FC ahead we eventually clung on for a 1-1 draw at the Withdean Stadium after a late penalty save by keeper Sam Ashton.

This was Brighton's penultimate FA Cup tie at the Withdean prior to them moving to a new stadium and many of their supporters described the atmosphere generated by FC United fans that day as the best by any set of away followers at the 'theatre of trees' – not the easiest of grounds to crank up the decibels with its open away end and an athletics track circling the pitch. Some also praised us for refraining from the tiresome homophobic chants that they tend to hear from away fans at every home match. Meanwhile, Sussex Police reckoned that we were 'the best fans to ever visit the Withdean'.

FC United lost the replay 4-0 on a freezing night at Gigg Lane in front of a crowd of 6,731, which remains a club record nearly a decade and a half later. The match was televised by ESPN and probably wouldn't have gone ahead but for the broadcasters paying for heated covers to thaw out the pitch. Jake Cottrell missed a second-half penalty but the Reds were well beaten as the 113 league places separating the sides really showed. Despite the result, that replay created memories to last a lifetime and remains the furthest we have progressed in England's premier cup competition.

Meanwhile, the body that represents supporters, the Football Supporters' Association, released a brief statement describing how the announcement of the scrapping of replays 'has not gone down well with a lot of fans up and down the country'. Many questioned why the body that's meant to represent supporters wasn't being more critical of this decision. 'Aren't you supposed to be a more strident campaigning voice for the little guy?' replied @ supersilverfox on X. 'Weak as piss,' said others.

* * *

The following day the club receive a call from the BBC asking if it would be possible to talk to someone about the escalating FA Cup replay story for a piece that they're going to broadcast on Friday evening.

Later, we post on X that the club contacted the FSA regarding its statement yesterday and highlighted the 'overwhelming negative reaction from supporters up and down the country' and urging the supporters' body to 'speak out strongly on this issue'. The club had written to them to express its disappointment at yesterday's response by the FSA, and adding, 'To put out a bland statement with no criticism of the decision of the removal of FA Cup replays was a very big missed opportunity.'

In addition, the club informed its co-owners that it will be writing to the Northern Premier League 'to make our views clear and encourage the league to take a strong stance against this decision'. While none of the leagues at this level were consulted on this change it's important that the Northern Premier League 'acts as an effective lobby group and a voice for non-league on behalf of its 81 member clubs'.

Why does all this matter to a club that's only been involved in one replay beyond the FA Cup first round in its entire history? Well, we were formed to show that there is a better way for football that prioritises the concerns of supporters and the club's local community over greed and profit and, just like the failed plans to establish a European Super League in 2021, this represents another attempt by the wealthiest clubs in the land to boost their finances at the expense of lower-league clubs for whom FA Cup replays can be life-changing. It's something that all supporters, not just those of clubs in the lower tiers, should be concerned about and speak out against.

As the club's letter to the FSA said, 'We believe it is time for change in how the game is governed and for supporters to be given a real voice as they are at FC United. Supporters are the lifeblood of the game, not just a prop for the governing body to roll out when it is convenient for them. The sooner an independent regulator is installed the better.'

* * *

Our final away trip of the season saw us cross the Pennines to take on Guiseley and, in another match that won't live long in the memory, we were beaten 3-1 in front of a crowd of 1,180 at Nethermoor Park. It was a comfortable win for the home side whose form had dipped in recent weeks after looking like they might make it into the play-offs earlier this year. The Lions roared into a 2-0 lead just after the half-hour mark before Charlie Ennis pulled a goal back after we were awarded a soft-looking penalty. But there was still time for the home side to grab a third right at the end of the first half – Kallan Murphy with a smart overhead finish that was the best goal of the match.

FC only created one decent scoring chance in the second half, which was well saved by the Guiseley goalie. But the singing went on for the full 90 minutes. 'What are they singing now?' asked a nearby steward as the FC fans chorused 'Won't pay Glazer or work for Sky ...' to the tune of 'Spirit in the Sky' made famous by Doctor and the Medics' 80s cover version. The FC songbook tends to eschew the generic songs that soundtrack almost all EFL and Premier League matches these days, which makes it trickier for casual observers to decipher lyrics.

There was some mither at the end of the match as a group of young, local wannabe hoolies seemed intent on causing trouble as the two sets of fans left the ground. 'About 30 kids. Pure *Green Street* cosplay but enough to draw blood from a lad on one of the FC minibuses,' observed a poster on The Soul is One who also wondered, 'At what point is self-defence legitimate when the aggressors aren't old enough to buy fags?' Later, several Guiseley fans posted on their own forum that they were annoyed, but not surprised, by the antics of these kids, referring to 'mindless idiots who are hell bent on tarnishing Guiseley's reputation' and also, sadly, 'repeated sick chants about the Munich air disaster'.

Meanwhile, on The Soul is One, a regular contributor posted, 'It was a poor result but I had a fantastic day out. Great weather, top sing song and a good away following.' Aside from the weather, that's an apt summation of most away days this season.

Post-match, a few FC fans completed the second leg of a Yorkshire double-header by making the relatively short trip to Doncaster to watch the women's team take on Doncaster Belles in a 7pm kick-off. The women needed to win to give themselves any chance of avoiding relegation going into their final match of the season, against Hull City. FC began brightly and had a goal disallowed but Doncaster ran out 3-0 winners to confirm our relegation back to the fifth tier next season.

'Despite the challenging start to our season, I am disappointed with being relegated. We have worked tirelessly this season to recruit new players and staff, as well as to drive standards and performances. I feel that if we had a few more games left in the season, we might have been able to pick up the points needed to stay up!' reflected manager Jennie Swarbrick.

* * *

'Join thousands of passionate Manchester United fans at the largest outdoor fan park extravaganza ever witnessed!'

Following Manchester United's semi-final victory against Coventry City, FC United have partnered with Red Square to screen the FA Cup Final – for Red Devils fans only – at Broadhurst Park on Saturday, 25 May. Red Square bill themselves as 'the ultimate unofficial Manchester United fanzone' and have been screening United matches – along with beer, food and music – for several years now in the Victoria Warehouse close to Old Trafford so they're experienced in putting on this type of event.

Meanwhile, over on the Bluemoon forum the inflatable banana wavers aren't quite so enamoured by this Mancunian 'extravaganza'. 'And there we have it folks … the community club, for the people … funded by Manchester City Council – putting on an event and stating Man United fans only. The fuckers need challenging over this ruling,' screamed one poster, before later going on to add, without a trace of irony, that City should do something similar and open their council-owned stadium for a cup final screening for City season ticket holders or members only.

* * *

FC's young reds beat Halifax Town 4-0 at Broadhurst Park on 24 April to clinch the Division H title in the National League U19 Alliance in some style with all four goals scored by Bob Jammeh. Last year we finished sixth in this division but we now go into our final league match six points clear of nearest challengers Stockport County.

* * *

Prague Raptors beat the Finnish side Gilla FC 3-1 to join FC United, Lewes and Enfield Town in the Fenix Final 4 in Italy next month. Along with FC the Czechs are the only club to appear in all three editions of the tournament so far – finishing runners-up in both of the previous two. The draw for the semi-finals will take place early next week.

Meanwhile, FC's board has approved our participation in next season's tournament following a recommendation from the club's Fenix Trophy lead, Adrian Seddon. Adrian had prepared a report for the board which reviewed the club's participation to date in this year's tournament and focused on finances, football and the wider value to the club in terms of its profile and fan and media engagement.

The disappointing attendances at both Fenix Trophy home games resulted in a small loss of £66 on the four group matches – when we subtract accommodation, travel costs and the cost of streaming matches from the revenue earned from hosting the fixtures – but it's anticipated that we will make a small profit on our participation in this year's tournament when we factor in the likely receipts from merchandise sales at next month's finals.

There are mixed views on the merits of the Fenix Trophy among supporters. While some see it as the closest thing non-league clubs will get to the Champions League and in keeping with Manchester United's, and now FC United's, long-standing tradition of playing in Europe, others view it as little more than a collection of glorified friendlies that risk disrupting our league campaigns. Interestingly, 86 per cent of co-owners who voted at the AGM in December 2024 backed a members' vote that 'subject to final approval by the board each season, co-owners are supportive of our continued involvement in the Fenix Trophy'.

On the football side, all the players, coaches and backroom staff were surveyed to get their views on entering next season's tournament and all 16 respondents to date had given it the thumbs-up. Adrian's report also noted that our Fenix participation is an asset when it comes to player recruitment and retention as 'while players may receive tempting offers from other clubs' the Fenix Trophy gives them, uniquely at this level of football, 'the chance to showcase their talents on the European stage'. While we may not always be able to match other clubs financially, participation in Europe adds to the club's distinctiveness in the non-league football landscape.

And a message from one of the players in the travelling party WhatsApp group the day after the team returned from Kraków summed this up: 'Thanks for a great trip once again for everybody who made it possible at the club; staff, fans and players etc. Special, special club … opportunity to experience things that just doesn't happen at this level or many levels of football.' There are some things you can't quantify on a spreadsheet.

This year's tournament has also given three players from the club's academy – Elliot Wilkinson, Dominic Doyle and Alfie Henstock – the opportunity to make their first-team debuts and another academy player, Bob Jammeh, also scored his first goal for the club in the 14-0 rout of Kraków Dragoons.

Despite FC racking up 26 goals in four group matches there is a general sense that the standard of football is improving each year and both Enfield Town and Lewes, who are enjoying better league campaigns than us in the seventh tier, have enjoyed some tough contests in their first season in the competition, and last year's winners BK Skjold have failed to advance beyond the group stage this season.

Regular trips to Europe have been part of our supporter culture at Manchester United and now at FC United for donkey's years and tales of trips to the likes of Saint-Étienne, Rotterdam, Turin, Barcelona, Leipzig and Hamburg are the stuff of legend. Big United were, of course, the very first English club to play in the European Cup in 1956 and, more than six decades on from Matt Busby's European trailblazers, it's been fitting that FC United should create our own little bit of history as the first English team to compete in a new European football competition.

Ever since the trip to play Lokomotive Leipzig at the end of our first season in 2006 the 'Euro Away' has been a highlight for supporters, players and coaches and the Fenix Trophy continues that tradition in a competitive and more organised fashion. As Adrian's report notes, 'Travelling to different countries and witnessing matches abroad creates lasting memories and fosters a sense of camaraderie among fans,' and importantly it also gives younger supporters the chance to experience the type of European away trips that many older fans enjoyed, often several times a season, at Manchester United.

The media angle is important too as, while the bread and butter of the Northern Premier League rarely arouses interest beyond the *Non-League Paper*, we have benefited from increased exposure from playing in Europe with the likes of *France Football* and *FourFourTwo* magazines penning articles about our participation in this year's tournament, and ESPN will be sending journalists to cover the Fenix Final 4 in Desenzano del Garda next month.

* * *

Women's team manager Jennie Swarbrick reflects on a 'challenging season' with a statement on the club's website that describes relegation as 'a difficult pill to swallow' but thanks 'every player, staff member and fan who has stood by us' through a 'crazy' season.

She added that the team is committed to finishing the season on a positive note as it prepares for a County Cup Final against Mancunian Unity Women next Wednesday and our final league game of the season against Hull City Women on 5 May. Looking forward to next season, Jennie reminded us that 'the comeback is always stronger than the setback'.

* * *

'What ya doing for Lake Garda?' Saturday, 27 April was one of those days when there's not much at stake on the pitch and minds tend to wander elsewhere, with many supporters looking forward to another trip to Italy in early May.

Right from our first season in 2006 when we lost 1-0 to Great Harwood Town in front of a crowd of more than 6,000 at Gigg Lane, our final home game of the season has often served up a stinker but fortunately this wasn't one of those occasions as FC rounded off the season on a high by beating Lancaster City 4-3 in an entertaining contest watched by a crowd of 2,012 which was boosted by a decent turnout from Lancaster. The crowd included 874 spectators who paid on the day – up by nearly 400 on the number that had paid on the day at the previous home fixture – and resulted in bar takings which were nearly double the takings on a typical Saturday afternoon.

The three points were enough to secure 14th place in the final league table with 48 points from 40 matches. It's the lowest we've ever finished in ten full seasons in this division although it's not quite our worst points total as we only got 47 in 2009/10 but played two fewer matches that season. The only teams with a worse goal difference than us – we scored 55 goals and conceded 77 – were those that got relegated.

Lancaster's goalkeeper Tom Stewart was injured early on and was replaced by Paul Jarvis, one of the two visiting players making their final appearance for the Dolly Blues today. The other one, 43-year-old David Norris, gave the visitors the lead in the 25th minute and went on to score a hat-trick in his final game. Norris joined Lancaster in 2018 after making more than 400 appearances in the Football League, mostly at Plymouth Argyle and Ipswich Town.

A few minutes later the visitors were down to ten men as Charlie Barnes was sent off for a professional foul on Lewis Gilboy, which looked a harsh decision to me. Jordan Buckley equalised for FC soon after and Dontai Gabidon and Charlie Ennis also got on to the scoresheet – the latter scoring the winner in the 58th minute after a lovely move down the left. At that stage there was still half an hour to play but although both sides continued to create scoring opportunities, there were no further goals.

Post-match, the main stand bar was busy for the end-of-season awards for the men's, women's and academy teams. 'It's a long time since I've seen it that rammed, a great carnival atmosphere,' said chair Nick Boom. Left-back Guy Hall was the supporters' pick for the men's player of the season and Declan McLoughlin won the goal of the season award for his long-range thunderbolt against Stafford in December.

Meanwhile, goalkeeper Sophie Donald was the supporters' women's player of the season and Emily Walton won the goal of the season award for a superb finish from a tight angle against Durham in February. Sadly, Emily suffered an anterior cruciate ligament injury early the following season and, faced with a long wait for reconstructive surgery on the NHS, she was trying to raise funds to go private.

The academy side also got the chance to show off the silverware they won earlier in the week as they came on to the pitch after the match to receive the acclaim of the supporters. As did the women's team, and all three teams were photographed alongside each other in front of the St Mary's Road End in a nice display of togetherness.

After the awards, Jennie and Neil reflected on the season just gone. Earlier Neil had been stood with fans on the St Mary's Road End in the second half as he was unable to take his usual place in the dugout for this one due to suspension.

Members of Nobby Stiles's family were also at the game to present the Nobby Stiles Shield for the academy team's young player of the year. The Manchester United and England legend was born just down the road from Broadhurst Park in Collyhurst, and when a street there was renamed Nobby Stiles Drive in his honour in 2016 FC United were invited to the unveiling ceremony, which was also attended by many of his former United team-mates including Denis Law and Bobby Charlton.

Later, FC had discussed with Nobby's family how best the club could pay its respects to a local legend and it was agreed that naming the award for the academy player of the year the Nobby Stiles Shield would represent a fitting tribute, particularly as Nobby went on to be a youth team coach at United in the early 90s where he played a key role in the development of the likes of Ryan Giggs, David Beckham, Nicky Butt, Paul Scholes and the Neville brothers. And he remains the only Mancunian to hold league championship, European Cup and World Cup winners' medals.

Prior to the match the final Course You Can Malcolm of the season was a gem. First, up Manchester comedians Eryn Tett and Cameron Jones brought their Global Megacorp Institute of Manchester (GMIM) show to Moston – a funny take on the modern-day phenomenon of cryptocurrency, marketing, and wellness and life coaching which, among other things, urged us to 'escape the algorithm and live your best life'. Amen to that. And then Manchester-based three piece The Cutter, who'd released their debut single 'Pulling Me In' the day before, played a superb set of dark electronica that resulted in some of us missing the first few minutes of the match.

* * *

Non-league football's popularity has risen substantially in recent years as the top-flight game has increasingly become unaffordable for many fans, but FC United's crowds have declined. A decade ago our average attendance was 1,969 and we were the tenth-best supported club in the whole of non-league football, bettered only by an assortment of big ex-league teams which included Luton Town. The 2013/14 season was our last at Gigg Lane and saw a titanic struggle with Chorley for the league title but we struggled to attract more than 2,000 to a home game until the latter stages.

But in the campaign just gone that average had fallen to 1,681 which was around three per cent down on last season's average. A downward trend has been apparent since Covid restrictions were lifted – our average crowd is down from around 1,800 in 2021/22 to nearly 1,700 now. And viewed across a lengthier time frame our crowds have fallen by 15 per cent compared to a decade ago while, in marked contrast, the overall average for the Northern Premier League's Premier Division doubled from 405 ten years ago to 807 last season.

Marine have seen the biggest increase – up by 248 per cent from an average of 359 in 2013/14 to 1,250 this season – while Matlock Town and Worksop Town saw increases of more than 100 per cent. The last few times we've been to Matlock, for instance, it's been noticeable that not only have their crowds swelled but there appear to be a lot more younger supporters at their games than there were a decade ago.

So we are very much an outlier when it comes to attendances over the last decade and despite blaming some of this on the recent cost of living crisis it highlights that we have a more serious problem that perhaps shows our over-reliance on social media to promote matches at the expense of planting a seed with those in easy reach of the ground.

With this in mind, April's board meeting included an update on the club's mission to grow attendances at men's and women's matches over the next few years. While we've tended to rely heavily on digital marketing of matches, Nick felt 'it's crucial that we engage with our local community directly' when it comes to promoting matches. 'I've always felt that we haven't done enough to foster a sense of place and belonging among local people and businesses,' he added.

Nick suggested that ways of boosting attendances could include: engaging with local schools through football coaching, player visits, school assembly talks and offering free tickets to pupils for both men's and women's matches; better and more engaging promotion of FC United matches – for instance by increasing our use of video on social media; and establishing a team of volunteers to promote FC United matches by distributing posters and flyers across the local area and further afield and also posting on social media.

In addition, we will be looking to potentially host six community day events next season – each with a different focus – where we will distribute promotional tickets to local residents, schools or grassroots clubs, similar to last month's community day against Basford United.

Warren Heppolette felt that this mission to grow attendances, particularly through community engagement, is crucial to improving the club's financial performance over the next few years – we saw what a difference it can make at the Basford match when a bumper attendance resulted in matchday revenue that was up by around £3,500 on a typical Saturday afternoon.

12

A totemic importance

DESPITE RELEGATION, FC's women's team had the chance to claim some silverware as they lined up against Mancunian Unity in the final of the Manchester FA Women's Challenge Cup at Rochdale's Crown Oil Arena on 1 May. It was always going to be a tough match as Unity had won the North West Women's Regional League North Division with a 100 per cent record – winning all 22 matches and scoring 110 goals in the process – a tremendous achievement in their first season at this level of football. So it was no surprise to see them on the attack in the early stages of the final but FC stood firm and created chances of our own, particularly in the second half, but the match finished goalless and went to a titanic penalty shoot-out which we eventually won 9-8 after keeper Sophie Donald saved Unity's ninth penalty.

Despite Sophie's heroics, Isabella Kershaw was chosen as the player of the match by the Manchester FA and afterwards she told women's match reporter Valentina Vettore how happy she was, adding, 'I think collectively as a squad we deserved this. We set this as a goal at the beginning of the season to win the cup and we did just that.'

Sophie, who is due to take her A levels shortly, had managed to get a hand to a few of the earlier Unity penalties to no avail but described how 'as the last taker jogged up, seemingly in a rush, I slowed things down and felt confident to make the save'. And Isabella said, 'This season Soph has been a massive asset to the squad helping us in crucial moments,' so when she saved the penalty 'it was pure scenes'.

* * *

The following Sunday the women's team were beaten 6-1 by champions Hull City Ladies in their final league match of the season and finished the season firmly rooted to the bottom of the table with only eight points from their 22 games.

The latest operational report, presented to the board at April's board meeting, noted that just as we're witnessing serious wage inflation in men's semi-professional football, substantial investment in women's football over the past couple of years has also swiftly altered the landscape, with clubs like Middlesbrough offering their players wages of up to £1,000 per month and even teams in lower leagues beginning to pay their players, a trend that is expected to persist. Up to now we haven't paid our players but even playing at a lower level next season we will be competing against some clubs, such as newly promoted Wythenshawe, who already do.

* * *

On the same afternoon that a corner of Old Trafford briefly rivalled Cautley Spout as one of England's tallest waterfalls – and highlighted again the neglect of the parasitic Glazer regime – FC United won the Fenix Trophy for the second time in three seasons in Desenzano del Garda in northern Italy. In doing so they became the only English club to win a European trophy this season, one for pub quiz contestants to mull over in a few years' time.

A huge storm had begun during the final moments of Manchester United's 1-0 defeat at home to Arsenal and the combination of a leaking roof and the sheer volume of water deposited – more rain fell in a two-hour period than had fallen in the whole of last May – resulted in water cascading on to the seats below.

Meanwhile, on a gorgeous early summer afternoon on the shores of Italy's largest lake, FC beat Prague Raptors 4-0 in a one-sided final. The two clubs had also met in the first Fenix final in Rimini in 2022 which was a much more even contest and the Czech side have now been defeated in all three finals having been beaten by Danish side BK Skjold last year in the San Siro.

You couldn't quite see Lake Garda from the covered main stand of the Stadio Francesco Ghizzi but the distant Alpine foothills, bathed in a heat haze that made them look like they'd been added by a water colourist, provided a stunning backdrop that rivalled the view from behind the goal at Matlock Town. And the locals had even added a crane, in the foreground, to make those of us visiting from Manchester feel more at home.

And the town itself, adorned in pink bunting, looked resplendent as it geared up for hosting a stage of the Giro d'Italia the following weekend. It may be more accustomed to lycra-clad early risers heading into the mountains to 'do some sport' than hosting a football tournament but it's no surprise that many fans have described the trip to Desenzano as the best Fenix finals weekend so far and commended the organisers on the choice of venue.

The FC fans, as ever, created a decent atmosphere but the occasion felt a bit flat as FC dominated right from the off. The only surprise was that it took them until midway through the first half to take the lead as Curtis Jones nodded home a cross from the right. A superb through ball by Jordan Buckley gave Aaron Bennett the chance to round the keeper and put FC two goals in front just before half-time and, by that stage, a victory felt inevitable. Dontai Gabidon and Lewis Gilboy added further goals in the second half and that was that. The Raptors barely had a sniff of a goal.

'We've got our trophy back,' sang the travelling Reds, but you hope for the long-term good of the tournament that FC don't come to dominate the Fenix Trophy like Real Madrid did the European Cup in its early years. This year's tournament has felt more competitive overall but this was the most one-sided final to date.

Picture the scene. A pub, somewhere in England, on a Sunday evening in 2034. There's a quiz on and they're halfway through the sports round. 'Which football club from the north-west was the only English team to win a European trophy in 2024?'

A couple of nights earlier FC had beaten Lewes 1-0 in the first semi-final, a tense contest between two evenly matched teams which was settled by a fine strike from the edge of the penalty area by marauding full-back Joe Ferguson early in the second half – a goal worthy of winning a European trophy semi-final. And it provided one of the best goal celebrations of the entire season for the hundreds of travelling Reds gathered in the main stand.

The Rooks fought hard for an equaliser in the last half an hour but FC defended well – bodies-on-the-line stuff at times – and when the referee eventually blew the final whistle you could see how much the victory meant to Neil Reynolds and his players. They weren't here for a piss-up in the sun, that was clear. The post-match celebrations went on for quite a while on the running track in front of FC's travelling support, while the Enfield Town and Prague Raptors players warmed up for the second semi-final.

The Lewes Supporters Club X account wasn't quite so thrilled with FC's victory as it posted that 'FC United have absolutely shithoused their way to victory here' and also accused us of being 'not afraid to leave a foot in'. Midway through the first half, Lewes's Paul Rooney had been stretchered off after an innocuous-looking challenge by Guy Hall. Meanwhile, on the unofficial Lewes FC forum, one fan lamented, 'It was much the same all season. Loads of possession ... but not enough chances created and an unwillingness to shoot.' There were also complaints about a 'slow build-up'. This reads uncannily like a copy and paste job from FC United's unofficial forum after any number of matches this season.

Given the league season we've just endured, many FC fans weren't optimistic about making it to the final – particularly as Lewes had finished higher in their league and had performed well in their first season in Europe against tougher opposition than we had faced in the group phase. But if FC beating Lewes was unexpected, then Prague Raptors defeating Enfield on penalties in the other semi-final after the match finished goalless after 90 minutes was probably the biggest shock of this year's tournament. The Londoners were riding high after a play-off victory had secured promotion to English football's sixth tier a few days earlier so were hot favourites to progress to the final, having twice beaten last year's winners BK Skjold in the group stage.

Perhaps they'd overindulged after securing promotion and who can blame them. The Raptors received the support of those FC fans who stayed for the second semi-final – 'We're extinct but we're louder than you' they chorused – and a long penalty shoot-out eventually concluded after 11pm with the Prague side winning 13-12. The cheers as the final Enfield penalty was saved could be heard a mile away as some of us walked up the hill to the railway station from the Pit Stop bar, where FC fans had been clustered round mobile phones watching the shoot-out.

The long queues for beer at the ground on Friday evening also prompted some moans among the travelling fans, particularly as, at first, we were unable to take drinks into the stands, until common sense eventually prevailed. And the presence of officers from three different police forces raised eyebrows too but there wasn't a hint of trouble.

The Fenix Trophy is a UEFA-accredited tournament so it's inevitable there will be some rules that can feel overly officious compared to the Northern Premier League. And any inconvenience was, to be fair, negligible in comparison to the police baton charges and tear gas that often greeted Manchester United fans on their regular European trips back in the day.

Before Sunday's trophy presentation Neil Reynolds addressed the crowd and spoke of how delighted he was to win the trophy again; he also thanked the fans for travelling in such good numbers after a disappointing season. Neil also pointed out that this was a great way to celebrate Elliot Wilkinson's 18th birthday. Elliot came on as a substitute late in the game and is one of four academy players to make their first-team debuts this season. 'We've been shit this season,' said Aaron Bennett as he picked up the award for the player of the tournament, but he hoped that this win made up for it a little.

The aperitif-fuelled celebrations went on long into the night in the lakeside resort, and amid numerous trophy lifts by players and fans for the cameras the silverware ended up on the floor at one point after being dropped by, of all people, on-loan goalkeeper George Murray-Jones. Shortly after his return to Manchester City, George was sold to Premier League club Nottingham Forest for a fee of up to £1.1m.

Later on, FC United posted its thanks to Leo Aleotti and the Fenix Trophy team for organising this year's tournament and added, 'Something very special has been created and we're proud to be part of it.'

*   *   *

A fortnight ahead of the general meeting the board shared the club's business plan for 2024/25 – along with the budgets for the next three years – on the members' forum. It stressed, again, that 'we stand firm in our commitment to the sustainable supporter ownership model' and 'will never put the future of the club at risk to chase glory'.

And it acknowledged that 'football alone doesn't generate anywhere near enough revenue to cover the club's costs' so there is a need 'to focus on wider income generation – through commercial activity, merchandising, events and hospitality'. And, in turn, the growth of our non-football income will enable us to increase our playing budget.

The budget for 2024/25 predicts an operating profit of £83,000 on the club's core trading activities, which would represent a substantial improvement on the £6,000 operating loss that we're currently predicting for 2023/24.

* * *

For the second year in a row FC hosted a charity match, on Saturday, 18 May, to raise funds for the campaign to build a statue to celebrate local boxing hero Len Johnson, whose largely forgotten story resurfaced during the Black Lives Matter protests in 2020. Len was born in Manchester and was regarded as one of the best boxers of his era – beating some of the biggest names in Britain and Europe in the 1920s – but was prevented from fighting for any titles purely due to his skin colour. The British Boxing Board of Control's racist 'colour bar' meant that in order to fight for a championship a boxer must have two white parents. Len's mother was of Irish descent and his father was from Sierra Leone. Later, after quitting boxing in the early 30s, he went on to become a civil rights activist and played an important part in overturning the colour bar in 1947.

Last year's match, between an FC United legends team and a team of celebrities wearing the colours of Sierra Leone – which included mayor of Greater Manchester Andy Burnham – had been watched by a crowd of more than 1,000 and had raised over £10,000 for the campaign. This year's game attracted a crowd of around 1,600 and, as last year, it was significantly younger and more diverse than for a typical FC United match.

One poster on The Soul is One reckoned, 'Looking around and seeing loads of young Asian and black faces in a football ground was refreshing and it encapsulated modern Manchester pretty well.' Many youngsters were also excited to see the 'popular gaming streamer and content creator' Angry Ginge at Broadhurst Park. The United-supporting ginger lad has more than a million followers across his various social media accounts.

Although others weren't happy with the way some fans behaved – particularly those who invaded the pitch – and one poster, who left before the second half, described the 'prominent appearance of pro-Gaza/anti-Israel banners' as 'quite divisive and inappropriate' and 'notably something that doesn't happen at scale on our own matchdays'. It offered a reminder that in our mission to increase attendances at Broadhurst Park, many of the 'new' fans that we are hoping to lure from across north Manchester and beyond will probably not look or sound like the majority of our current match-going fanbase.

The event was organised, as last year, by the local actor, activist and FC supporter Lamin Touray, who explained, 'It means so much to us to be able to raise more crucial funds for the statue and massively increase awareness of the remarkable story of Len – Manchester's uncrowned boxing champion. We want to celebrate his successes and highlight the struggle he went through.'

* * *

On another damp Manchester evening, around 50 co-owners attended FC's 2024 general meeting in the function room at Broadhurst Park on 23 May with a further 60 or so joining online. The main purpose of this general meeting was for co-owners to approve the business plan for the forthcoming financial year and also vote on any resolutions or members' votes proposed by the board or co-owners.

There were only two members' votes at this meeting with one proposing that the club should establish a donation scheme to raise money which would be earmarked for the playing budget for the men's first team and the other vote proposing the same for the women's first team.

Warren Heppolette presented the club's business plan and budget for 2024/25 and the next two years up to 2026/27. The 2024/25 financial year is the final one of the original three-year business plan that was approved by co-owners in 2022. Warren emphasised that the budget for 2024/25 had been built on 'cautious revenue growth and cost discipline' and it is expected to deliver an operating profit of £83,000.

The main goals of the next three years include the men's team challenging for promotion to National League North by the 2026/27 season and the women's team securing promotion straight back to the National League at the end of next season. The playing budget for the men's first team will increase by £20,000 to £240,000 for next season with the intention to implement a larger increase the following season. In addition, we will also introduce a modest playing budget for the women's team next season, reflecting the norm even at the level they will be playing. The business plan was approved by a show of hands from those in the room and online.

The board particularly wanted to focus on its mission to develop an integrated football strategy at this meeting and Paul Hurst began by highlighting that almost on a daily basis at the moment there are reports in the media of non-league football clubs in financial difficulty or announcing major new investment. In the 24 hours following the general meeting, Coalville Town became the latest financial casualty, announcing their resignation from the Southern League Central Premier Division following their chairman's admission that he could no longer afford to subsidise the club.

Paul added that following the conversations we have with officials from other clubs over the course of the season, we reckon that weekly first-team wage bills vary from £3,000 to £15,000 in this division and FC United probably sit about three quarters of the way down this scale. He said there is an argument that last season, in finishing in 14th position, we slightly over-performed relative to our playing budget.

Our playing budget has actually fallen in real terms compared to 2017/18 and, interestingly, the amount that we spend on players and backroom staff as a proportion of our total revenue (18 per cent in 2022/23) is lower than any other club that we've been able to compare our finances to. When I shared this detail with the football finance expert Kieran Maguire, he responded that he'd 'not seen a wages to revenue percentage as low as yours'.

Nick Boom said that it's clear that we need to change our approach to remain competitive and that's why we're developing a new club-wide football strategy. In nearly 20 years as a football club, we've never had one – we've effectively been hoping for the best on the pitch. And while that might have worked in the past, the increased financial competition at this level means we're now struggling to keep up. Therefore, we must explore other ways to compete effectively and that's the purpose of our football strategy.

Nick explained that each season we are finding it increasingly difficult to recruit players of the standard we desire. The once strong pull of the club's brand, stadium and facilities and our loyal supporters is no longer as influential, as financial considerations have become more significant. Playing at this level has become the primary source of income for many younger players – evidenced by the frequent requests we receive to verify mortgage applications – when once it was a nice bonus on top of the day job.

Indeed, there's a case for dropping the term 'semi-professional football' as the game is becoming professional for many players at this level. As a result, when we're recruiting players in the close season, we often have to overlook our top five targets in each position and are fortunate if we secure anyone within our top ten. 'Does the NPL need its own version of financial fair play?' pondered a poster on The Soul is One a few days earlier.

We can either bemoan our luck and become victims of the changing face of non-league football, or we can adapt to this new environment in our own way. We will therefore seek to recruit and develop players by establishing a dedicated player recruitment department, developing a wider scouting network and using the dual registration system to aid the development of young players. Through our community football programme we are also linking up with local grassroots clubs and, in addition, we will introduce new teams for under-17s and under-21s to bridge the gap between our academy players and the first team.

Neil Reynolds said he's excited by the club's football strategy and added that he's aiming to build a team for next season that supporters will be proud of. We'll have more players on contracts and this should ensure a more settled squad and build a 'band of brothers' similar to the squad we had in 2019/20, which was strong and settled in all its key positions.

However, Neil said that the increase in the playing budget, albeit relatively modest, should allow us to strengthen in key areas such as more support for Jordan Buckley up front. Interestingly, ex-Premier League striker Adam Le Fondre has been training with the squad while looking for another club – having been invited to FC by his close friend Charlie Ennis – although ALF isn't expected to still be around come the start of the 2024/25 season.

There were a few questions from co-owners for Neil which included the perennial one of 'where are the goals going to come from?' next season. Neil explained that a 25-goal-a-season striker at this level would currently expect to be paid at least £600 to £700 per week which is significantly more than we can currently afford, but he added that we've recruited a couple of younger forwards from teams below us in the pyramid and he remains in discussions with some more experienced frontmen who may still join us. He also added that the likes of Callum Gribbin and Jay Fitzmartin coming back into the squad after long-term absences should also make a big difference when it comes to bagging goals.

There were also questions for the board including one asking 'what does success on the pitch look like next season?' and Nick explained that the board will be holding a closed session ahead of next week's board meeting that will assess the 2023/24 season and establish goals for the upcoming campaign which will subsequently be discussed with Neil in a separate session. He underscored the significance of setting objectives collectively as a board, ensuring fairness while considering the resources at the club's disposal and emphasised the importance of holding Neil to account for his performance against these objectives.

Despite some minor sound-quality issues, feedback from co-owners on how the meeting went was largely positive. And the fact that a seventh-tier semi-professional club is able to allow co-owners to watch formal meetings from the comfort of their living rooms is something to be proud of.

The results of the votes were announced a few days later with a total of 585 votes (575 online and ten by post), after voting had closed and a vote count, in the presence of a scrutiniser from Co-operatives UK, had taken place at Broadhurst Park. This represented a turnout of nearly 30 per cent of the 1,955 members who were eligible to vote and is comparable to the turnout in the ten mayoral elections that took place across England at the beginning of May.

Both members' votes received support from more than 85 per cent of the co-owners who voted – and were therefore passed – and the resolution to reappoint the club's auditors was also passed with 96.9 per cent of co-owners supporting it.

* * *

Around 2,000 Manchester United fans watched United beat City 2-1 in the FA Cup Final on Saturday, 25 May on a large screen at Broadhurst Park and many piled on to the pitch to celebrate at the final whistle. It was our first time hosting an event like this and despite a few complaints about the distance from the screen and queues for the bars it was a successful afternoon.

There's plenty for us to learn from when it comes to hosting events of this kind in future – we could probably have doubled bar sales with more bar staff and bars and we could clearly do with publicising rules around smoking and not going on the pitch a bit better. But it was generally good-natured stuff from a youthful crowd and no doubt the result helped. The *Manchester Evening News* posted a video of the celebrating United fans on its website and a poster on The Soul is One said, 'This fills me with pride, fellow Reds celebrating at our football ground.'

Adrian Seddon posted that he's 'never seen the bars so busy before' with supporters queuing out of the doors of the St Mary's Road End from an hour before kick-off to the final whistle. And he felt that around three quarters of those in attendance had probably never been to Broadhurst Park before and there was plenty of advertising for FC's pre-season friendly against Salford City that will hopefully attract a few to come back for a match.

* * *

Nick Boom kicked off the board meeting on Monday, 27 May by announcing that co-owner Paul Haworth has been appointed as the club's full-time commercial manager with effect from the beginning of July. Paul has been working as the club's part-time business development manager since January and is a qualified professional with over 25 years' experience in marketing, brands and communications. He's also a founder member of FC and since 2010 has regularly volunteered to assist the club with its marketing and communications. In 2018 he was co-opted on to the board for six months to oversee the club's income generation.

The role of commercial manager has a broad remit and Paul will be responsible for all the club's income streams including season tickets and membership, matchday income, merchandise, functions and events and sponsorship and advertising. It's the first time since the departure of former CEO Natalie Atkinson last summer that we've had a full-time commercial manager and the consensus among the board and management team is that this will make a significant difference to our commercial revenue going forward.

The latest finance report and management accounts reported an operating profit of £13,000 in April and meant that we were able to report a cumulative operating profit of £7,000 in the first ten months of 2023/24. It's well below the operating profit of £77,000 we had originally budgeted for at this point in the year but it's impressive nonetheless, in the current financial climate, to be making any sort of profit; it's possible that we may be able to report a small operating profit come the year end when we factor in the likely financial benefit of hosting the FA Cup Final screening.

The board deliberately left some time towards the end of May's meeting to discuss a marketing and commercial strategy for the 2024/25 season prepared by Paul Haworth. The strategy paper entitled 'A Cause For Celebration' proposes a year-long series of events to mark the club's 20th anniversary in 2025 (and also ten years since we moved into Broadhurst Park), which will also raise the club's profile, drive an increase in attendances and commercial revenue and enable us to deliver the 2024/25 budget that co-owners approved at last week's general meeting.

The feedback from the board was positive with Nick Boom describing this commercial strategy as what 'we have been crying out for' for some time and Bhavna Mistry felt it was 'ambitious but doable' but added that its success will ultimately depend on how well we're able to deliver the events. Nevertheless, the recent *Early Doors* event had been a success and should provide a template for how we host such events in future. Paul Hurst reckoned that supporters would buy into the DIY ethos of this strategy as it provides an opportunity for everyone at the club to get involved in our anniversary celebrations.

* * *

Later in the week, board members Dave Ashurst and Matthew Haley held a video call with Kevin Miles, the chief executive of the Football Supporters' Association, along with Nick Duckett, FC United's FSA representative, to discuss strengthening the voice of supporter-owned clubs and how FC United could play a leading role in this. The FSA describe themselves as 'the leading advocates for supporter ownership' but since the merger of Supporters Direct and the Football Supporters' Federation in 2018 it's often felt like its voice hasn't been as strong as it could be and its tepid response to the recent axing of FA Cup replays typified this.

Changes at the elite level of football, driven by the greed of Premier League clubs, have increasingly sidelined supporters' interests and views and it's more important than ever that our collective voice is heard. Supporter-owned clubs are at the forefront of prioritising fans' interests, and we must ensure that this perspective is not lost amid the noise of big-money football.

Effectively we're asking the FSA to help organise supporter-owned clubs into an effective lobby group to ensure that our voices are heard in the corridors of power and the wider football world. With our social media reach of more than one million followers across all platforms we feel that we can provide effective support to the FSA in getting important messages out.

Kevin welcomed any input from FC United in renewing the supporter-owned network's campaigning zeal, particularly as he was aware of the huge demands that running supporter-owned clubs places on the representatives of those clubs. He felt that FC have 'a totemic importance' that people recognise and added that he would love to help us use this status in a more influential way. He said that the FSA only has a small team of staff and it's therefore important that it works closely with club representatives to expand what the FSA can do on a day-to-day basis.

Dave also used the meeting as an opportunity to highlight that the Football Governance Bill, currently paused prior to the general election, only mentions the distribution of monies as far as step two of non-league and he stressed that FC United is keen for the levels below to be included. Step three – the level at which FC's men's team currently play – and below falls awkwardly between the professional game and grassroots football so often loses out.

The Tory MP and former sports minister Tracey Crouch, who had initiated and chaired the 'fan-led review' whose recommendations formed the basis of the Football Governance Bill, had visited Broadhurst Park in 2021 – and during the visit the chair at the time, Adrian Seddon, expressed the club's concern that any proposed restructuring of the game appeared to end at the National League.

13

A team we can
really get behind

THE FIRST week in June is Volunteers' Week, an annual celebration of the contribution that volunteers make to communities and organisations across the UK, including non-league football clubs like FC United. The business plan for 2024/25 highlights that volunteers at FC collectively work nearly 11,000 hours each year and this is conservatively estimated to save the club more than £200,000 annually. Interestingly, 17 per cent of co-owners who took part in the 2021 survey said that they volunteered for the club and this is broadly in line with the results of the Community Life Survey in 2021/22 which identified that 16 per cent of adults in England took part in formal volunteering – providing unpaid help to groups or clubs – at least once a month.

Much of FC United's volunteering effort takes place quietly behind the scenes and encompasses a whole host of tasks including helping out in the office; organising fundraising events; attending board meetings; offering expertise through one of the club's committees; keeping members and supporters up to date with goings-on at the club; reviewing the club's business plan and how it's communicated to co-owners.

I've been volunteering for the comms team since 2016 after some mithering from Paul Haworth about helping out with the club's communications – particularly in writing feature-length stuff for the website. It was around the time that a new board was elected in the aftermath of our annus horribilis and there was a call to arms when it came to the day-to-day running of the club. I'd been writing about FC United on my personal blog, and also for *A Fine Lung* fanzine and the matchday programme, for several years so my volunteering grew from that.

A few weeks later Adrian Seddon, one of the newly elected board members, mentioned that the new board was looking to improve transparency around its decision-making by issuing a report to co-owners within a few days of each board meeting that would summarise that meeting's discussions (something that the Dons Trust, the majority owners of AFC Wimbledon, had already been doing for several years) and he asked if there was anyone in the communications team who fancied being the board summariser. I offered to give it a go – if no one else was interested – but with some trepidation as I was living in London at the time and wasn't sure how travelling up to Manchester once a month for a midweek board meeting would work out. Eight years later I've attended more than 80 board meetings and scribbled nearly half a million words.

Writing the monthly board summary report generally takes around 15 to 20 hours to complete and involves me taking a day off work so that I can get stuck into it. Until I moved to Manchester in 2020 it also involved me getting trains to and from London to Manchester and an overnight hotel stay (all out of my own pocket) in order to attend midweek meetings – something which feels a bit daft now as only a few weeks after I moved back up north Covid rocked up and meetings ended up being held online.

Most of the 'summary' reports tend to be somewhere between 5,000 and 8,000 words in length and it's still a source of pride that we almost always share it with co-owners within three or four working days of the board meeting happening. Last year we also began emailing the report to co-owners so that they can access it through their inbox via a single click rather than having to log in to the members' forum (something which some co-owners find problematic). I don't think there are any other supporters in the country who are as well informed about the running of their club.

When we introduced the summary report in 2016 we envisaged it as perhaps a two- or three-page summary of the main points covered in the meeting – similar to the one that the Dons Trust produced, which is where we got the idea from in the first place. But it quickly became apparent to me that something of that size didn't do justice to the huge amount of work that the likes of Adrian Seddon, Sam Mullock and Tim Worrall were putting in at the time trying to keep the club afloat. Somehow a few bullet points didn't feel adequate. And this is how I've approached writing the board report ever since – the need to do justice to the incredible amount of work that goes on behind the scenes at this football club has been foremost in my mind.

More recently we've also introduced a regular blog which aims to give co-owners an insight into the board's thinking on the key issues of the moment and is emailed directly to co-owners upon publication. That the board is able to call on others to help with tasks such as this is one of the benefits of the committee structure.

What's it like being a volunteer? Des Gallagher, who helps out in the office at Broadhurst Park, describes how FC United has given him some great memories and he feels that he 'needed to repay the club for that'. He adds, 'To own your own football club and volunteer for it is tremendously rewarding and I'd recommend volunteering to anyone.' And I can't put it any better than that. I'd also add that it can be bloody hard work as well – it can often feel like having two full-time jobs at the same time.

But volunteering isn't just a one-way process. Working alongside an experienced comms professional like Helen Johnston I've learned loads about how to write formal communications and press releases. And also, as someone who has very much been an NHS 'lifer' in my day job, working with people whose background is in the commercial sector – often at a very high level – has provided an insight into different thought processes and ways of working that I've taken back into my NHS role.

Are there any downsides to the club being so reliant on volunteers? Yes, of course. Many of us have day jobs that limit the amount of time we can devote to club tasks so it's not always easy to respond to urgent demands. And Jake Worrall mentioned that one thing that he had found from his work implementing new systems was that some volunteers can often be resistant to change, which can make things tricky when trying to professionalise the way that the club operates. There can be an element of 'We've done it this way for years so why do we have to change', he says.

* * *

With the start of Euro 2024 only a week away, 'England – yes or no?' enquires a poster on The Soul is One. It's an old favourite that crops up each time there's a major international tournament on but this time there's an added dimension as there's been some talk of screening England's matches at Broadhurst Park, following the success of the recent FA Cup Final screening.

The ridiculous over-reaction of the ABU ('anyone but United') nation to David Beckham's sending off against Argentina in the 1998 World Cup altered many United fans' relationship with the national team, mine included, and quarter of a century on I still care little for the 'Three Lions'.

During FC's trip to play a pre-season friendly in Salzburg in the summer of 2018, however, I was reminded that there are plenty of FC United supporters, particularly younger ones, for whom the ABU tit for tat of the late 90s means little. And equally there are some among our support who have followed England home and away for years. So it shouldn't have been a surprise that so many FC fans celebrated England's victory over Sweden in the quarter-finals of the World Cup by singing 'Football's Coming Home' at regular intervals during our match, later the same day, against fellow fan-owned side Austria Salzburg.

One poster reckoned that while 'it was great fun winding up the Little Englanders with the Argentina chants' after the treatment dished out to Beckham following his sending off in 1998, 'I do quite like the sense of occasion that a big England match brings … if they do reach the final maybe it would be an opportunity to put some coin in our coffers by broadcasting the match at Broadhurst Park?'

* * *

On yet another unseasonably wet and windy evening the all-female Manchester punk band Loose Articles, who had played at Course You Can Malcolm in 2020, supported Foo

Fighters in a sold-out gig at the Old Trafford cricket ground on 13 June, less than a week after releasing their long-awaited debut album *Scream If You Wanna Go Faster*. There were four different versions of the CD release, including one paying tribute to FC United.

The band posts on Instagram that it is 'dedicated to our favourite local team who have been massive supporters of the band since we played before one of their matches in February 2020'. And they describe the club as 'a team we can really get behind due to the fact they're a not-for-profit, community football club who are committed to delivering affordable football to as many people as possible'. From Course You Can Malcolm to a stadium gig supporting one of the biggest bands on the planet, Loose Articles follow in the footsteps of the likes of Slow Readers Club and Shame as CYCM alumni that have gone on to much bigger things.

* * *

'We are officially 19 years old today,' posts the club on its social media channels along with a video of some of the highlights from those 19 years set to a soundtrack of the Courteeners' hit 'Not Nineteen Forever'.

The anniversary date of 14 June had been chosen by co-owners at the annual general meeting in November 2014 as the club approached its tenth anniversary. There had been nine dates to choose from spanning a three-month period from 12 May – the infamous date of Malcolm Glazer's takeover of Manchester United in 2005 – to 13 August which was the date we played our first competitive match, against Leek County School Old Boys.

Instead, 14 June 2005 was listed, somewhat dryly, as the date of 'the legal incorporation of the club' on the voting papers but in reality it was also the date that Football

Club United of Manchester was born. The original choice of FC United was deemed 'too generic' by the Football Association so four options were put to the vote by those of us who had pledged money to the club which, by this stage, already numbered more than 2,600 supporters: FC United of Manchester, FC Manchester Central, AFC Manchester 1878, and Newton Heath United FC. After voting had concluded, the steering group, set up to get the football club up and running, announced on 14 June that FC United of Manchester was the preferred choice.

A few days later on 18 June FC United were accepted into the North West Counties Football League after the steering group had presented a comprehensive business plan and structure of the club at the league's annual general meeting.

My first real-life encounter with FC was at the meeting at the Apollo on 30 May 2005 (one of the other possible dates for the club's anniversary that we voted on) which was attended by around 2,000 United fans. I'd gone along to the Apollo – a venue more used to hosting famous musicians than disgruntled football fans – primarily to find out what the plans were for the next stage of the fight to get rid of the Glazers.

That afternoon was a game-changer for me, though, and by the time I emerged into the sunshine of Ardwick Green I'd pledged my support to FC United – both in the form of a financial donation and in an offer of help to get the club up and running. Maybe it was hearing Kris Stewart from AFC Wimbledon describe forming your own football club as 'the best thing you will ever do'. Or maybe it was re-reading the photocopies of that stirring 'think about the future' article about FC United that had appeared in *Red Issue* back in February 2005 as the Glazer takeover loomed large.

There were some nice replies to the club's anniversary post on X from United fans. 'I remember being at the IMUSA [Independent Manchester United Supporters Association] meeting in Stretford when it was first mooted that we supporters start our own club. I admit to being sceptical at the time and own up to never having been to a UoM match, but fantastic, well done to all and best of luck for the future,' wrote one, while another said, 'Visionary club! Spotted the issues that nobody noticed or believed in 2005. Wishing you nothing but the best for your future.' Kris Stewart, who provided FC with so much support in the early days, replied with a simple 'happy birthday'.

Meanwhile, on the members' forum, Graham Voaden posted that the video 'has had me in floods' and added, 'I honestly don't know what I'd have done if it weren't for FC this past 19 years.' In a similar vein, another co-owner posted, 'The hairs were standing up on the back of my neck (well they would be if I had any).'

* * *

The club announced on 19 June that Jennie Swarbrick had signed a new two-year contract as women's team manager which is great news as Jennie is well respected in the women's game and has a good record of developing players. Jennie said she was delighted to commit for a further two years and added, 'We built some momentum towards the end of last season, particularly in winning the Manchester FA Challenge Cup trophy, and I'm very much looking forward to strengthening our talented young squad over the summer and pushing on next season and also continuing to lead the club on its journey to developing women's and girls' football.'

* * *

If you were an artist a decade ago, trying to create an impression of what FC United's Broadhurst Park ground might look like out of season, then the end product might have been pretty close to the scene around the ground on the warm summer evening of Monday, 24 June 2024.

The 3G pitch adjacent to the ground was alive with kids playing football while a gentle breeze rustled the leaves on the surrounding trees. Meanwhile, parents and relatives were either watching on or perched on the boardwalk wall fiddling with their phones. Behind the St Mary's Road End terrace a learner driver manoeuvred a small car into a parking space under the watchful eye of a driving instructor. A football club providing a source of recreation and learning for its local community and a reminder why in 1878, barely a mile from here, a group of Lancashire and Yorkshire Railway workers formed their own club, Newton Heath FC, which subsequently became the 20-times champions of England, Manchester United.

As a few of us waited in the lobby for FC United's final board meeting of the 2023/24 year to begin, people were also arriving for a Football Association meeting upstairs in the function room. Meanwhile, as the doors to the dressing rooms occasionally opened as staff went about their business, we got a glimpse of the pitch, which now, unlike a few weeks ago, had grass on it. New drains had been installed, it had been renovated and seeded and some welcome sunshine had provided decent growing conditions. We'd gone from brownfield to greenfield in barely a month.

Once the board meeting had kicked off we learned, among other things, about the steps the club has been taking over the last few weeks to implement its ambitious football strategy that was unveiled to co-owners at May's general meeting.

The trials for the new under-21 development team were over-subscribed and there has also been plenty of interest in the new under-17s team. A new recruitment department is up and running and we already have 12 scouts who are focused on recruiting talented young footballers from across Greater Manchester. The aim is to develop a pipeline of homegrown talent that can feed the men's and women's first teams in keeping with the tradition of red-shirted Manchester football clubs.

One of our aspirations through our schools and grassroots engagement programme is to become an umbrella operation for local grassroots football clubs and the feedback received so far has been encouraging. The parents of a member of the Prestwich Marauders girls' team recently recounted how when the players were invited to Broadhurst Park for a match last season they were particularly impressed with how Jennie Swarbrick engaged with all the girls and made them feel special and valued. The parents described their visit to the club as 'not just enjoyable but also memorable' and something which had left a lasting impression on the entire team.

We also learned at June's board meeting that Barrow AFC have invested a substantial sum to improve the grass pitches adjacent to the 3G pitch since they began using Broadhurst Park as their training base during the week. And this investment has benefited not only FC United but also the club's junior football partners, Moston Juniors, whose teams use these pitches throughout the year and have long struggled with poor drainage. Moston Juniors currently run 15 teams for more than 200 children aged five to 16 years old from Moston and the surrounding area.

The meeting also focused, among other things, on the more mundane work to update the club's rules to reflect its status as a community benefit society rather than the industrial and provident society that we were initially set up as in 2005. Two members of the finance and risk committee – Jo Purcell and Will Jacques – have been leading this process, which chair Nick Boom described as 'a mammoth task', and Jo had been invited to this month's meeting to update the board on progress to date.

She explained that the work involves eight phases which, all being well, will culminate in the rules being approved by co-owners at this year's AGM in November. Jo said that currently we're at phase two with a set of draft new rules having been shared with the board for review. She said that, on the whole, the rules are not hugely different to our current industrial and provident society rules but are better written and clearer. The work so far had involved Will going back through all the resolutions that have been approved by co-owners down the years to ensure that they are incorporated into the new rules. Ultimately, Jo said, we would like to have a robust set of rules that cover everything and are supported by detailed policies where necessary.

Warren added that once the board have signed off the draft rules we will move on to the third phase which involves engaging with co-owners regarding the rule changes ahead of a vote at November's AGM. The changes must be voted on by no less than 25 per cent of the club's membership with at least 75 per cent of the electorate voting in support of the changes – so the engagement of members is critical to the success of these rule changes.

The board was comfortable with the draft new rules and it was also keen to use this as an opportunity to tidy up or fix any issues with the club's rules that have previously been flagged, including those around co-opting board members and the current two-year term for board members.

Nick said that ultimately it's crucial that the board is able to govern effectively and he felt that, at present, we need a full quota of seven board members to be able to operate effectively and while the club's current rules talk about casual vacancies we've often referred to filling these vacancies by 'co-option' in the past which has confused matters. The updated rules should seek to draw that distinction more clearly.

Later in the meeting, the club's assistant accountant Jason Chan updated the board that we reported a small operating loss of £200 in May – £18,400 worse than budget – which meant that we reported a year-to-date operating profit of £7,200 after the first 11 months of the 2023/24 financial year which was £87,800 worse than the operating profit of £95,000 we budgeted for.

As the meeting drew to a close, and those observing the open session had chance to comment, a relatively new co-owner, observing a board meeting for the first time, explained that he is a long-standing Manchester United fan who left Old Trafford, and fell out of love with football, when the Glazers took over in 2005 and only began following FC United after being mithered to come along to a match by some of his mates who are FC fans. Since then he has fallen in love with the club and is excited for the future. Proof that, even nearly two decades on, we can still offer a refuge for United fans fed up with top-flight football.

* * *

A couple of days later the club launched an online suggestion box to make it easier for co-owners and supporters to share ideas, to provide feedback and help improve the running of the club – 'Every voice matters at FC United' declared a post on the members' forum which, again, highlights the collective strength of the club. A club with more than 2,300 co-owners ought to be capable of generating some decent ideas and Nick Boom reckons it will be a useful way for the board to prioritise issues.

And for those who don't use the internet a physical suggestion box will be available on the membership stall at matches next season for supporters to drop ideas into. The boxes will be monitored by the co-ownership committee which, together with the board, will prioritise ideas and make sure that they are shared with the right people at the club.

Michael Wehner, who lives in Detroit in the USA, will monitor the online suggestion box. And Lynette Cawthra noted that Michael has been the most regular attender at meetings of the co-ownership committee to date and provides proof that it's possible for co-owners who live far away from Broadhurst Park to get involved in the day-to-day life of the club.

Lynette felt that while the introduction of online voting had been a big win for the co-ownership committee, the committee's remit, as things stand, feels too broad, particularly as it includes fundraising for the Development Fund, which ought to sit elsewhere. She also felt that the committees haven't worked well together yet but envisaged that things should improve now that the work plan of each committee is incorporated into the board's forward plan.

Later in the week the club also advertised for a non-executive board member with community development experience to fill a gap in the board's knowledge and expertise regarding community work. 'The ideal candidate will have significant experience in community engagement and development, and a commitment to enhancing the club's impact within the local community,' the post read.

The club's founding manifesto states that it will 'develop strong links with the local community' and there have been plenty of examples down the years of it doing just that. However, it's significantly under-performed this year when it comes to bringing in grant income to support its community work which is one of the main reasons why we are likely to miss our original budgeted operating profit by more than £100,000. Bringing in someone at board level with the right experience should help address this.

* * *

As the 2023/24 year drew to a close there was an interesting board and management team discussion about the democratic health of the club. The level of access to information regarding the running of the club is perhaps unique in British football with summaries of board meetings emailed to co-owners within a few working days of each meeting. And there is opportunity to observe board meetings either in the boardroom or online and also ask questions direct to the board, and have a say in discussions of key issues, on the online members' forum.

The board summary reports emailed to co-owners in 2023/24 were viewed, on average, by 248 co-owners per month which equates to around one in seven of those who subscribed to receive emails from the club. Meanwhile, the 11 board meetings in 2023/24 were observed by a total of 22 co-owners which represented an increase of nearly 47 per cent compared to the total of 15 observers in 2022/23. Being able to join the meeting online has meant that, over the last year, co-owners have been able to observe board meetings from as far afield as the USA, the Netherlands, Cornwall and Sussex.

Helen Johnston felt, however, that we are 'failing co-owners' by not making it easier for them to access important information on the members' forum. Some co-owners have reported problems logging into the forum down the years and have been unable to access the reports and other documents that are shared on there or contribute to forum discussions of key issues. We've known about this for a long time now but not really addressed it.

While the monthly board summary report is emailed directly to co-owners, the rest of the reports presented at the board meeting – including finance reports – can only be accessed via the forum and Helen reckoned, 'It would be fair for some to question whether we are truly democratic when so many co-owners can't get in to view important documents and participate in co-owner discussions.'

Warren Heppolette felt that it's important to consider how we measure the democratic health of the club. Things like membership numbers, attendance at general meetings and voter turnout are obvious 'measures of democratic health' and the level of engagement with the board summary report ought to be a useful indicator too. We like to describe ourselves as a democratically run football club but does the reality match up to the rhetoric? Is it OK, for instance, that only one in seven co-owners appear to take an interest in what the board is discussing at its monthly meetings?

Warren said that 'democratic participation and exchange is as much a measure of the health of the club as financial, community and football performance' and we should take the opportunity to increase participation wherever we can. This should include: tackling the long-standing problems logging into the members' forum; reiteration and recirculation of content on key issues and the translation of board reports into bite-sized content that can be shared with co-owners through other channels.

He also felt that 'declining attention and participation is always a problem for a club like FC even when things are going well'. Although he recognised, 'It's entirely possible that general satisfaction with the direction and running of the club increases as democratic participation falls away.' And, likewise, participation may increase at times of conflict and challenge. The busiest time on the members' forum in more than a decade of its operation was in May 2021 shortly after the revelation that the club had received a donation from the Far East Consortium.

Another example of participation increasing during difficult times was the general meeting in Prestwich in May 2016 that, after an acrimonious period which had seen the resignation of the club's chief executive and seven board members, was attended by around 400 co-owners who discussed and voted on 23 resolutions and 13 members' votes over the course of more than four hours. Later, more than 820 co-owners voted on these motions – an impressive number considering this was long before we introduced online voting – which represented around 18 per cent of the club's adult membership at the time.

Helen added, 'We must not fall into the trap of being complacent around democratic participation and engagement if we want to fully achieve our ambition of being the leading fan-owned community football club.' Back in 2016 co-owner Mickey O'Farrell had eloquently described FC fans at the time as 'lazy utopians' – happy to sing the praises of supporter ownership but not to do the hard yards of actually making it work.

Another thing to consider here is the gap between the readership of the board reports (averaging fewer than 300 at the moment) and the turnouts we're now getting with online voting (typically around 600) and the importance of increasing readership of reports if we wish to have an informed electorate. The worry is that the gap in information, if we don't address it, is filled with rumour and conjecture on social media.

14

Come together

A FEW days before FC were due to travel to Southport on 3 August for their final friendly ahead of the 2024/25 season, a mass stabbing occurred at a dance class for children in the seaside town that shocked the nation. Three young girls were killed and ten other people were injured.

Southport cancelled their match the following evening against Morecambe but decided the game against FC the following Saturday would go ahead and all the money raised from a special 50/50 draw would be donated to the Alder Hey Children's Charity which supports the nearby hospital where victims of the attack were being treated.

On an emotional day, a delegation of FC United players, staff and board members visited the site of the tragic incident prior to the match to pay their respects and lay flowers to honour those who had lost their lives and also to show solidarity with the local community at a time of mourning. At one end of the road was a cluster of reporters and cameras but the FC group opted to avoid the media spotlight by taking another route. This was a day for solemn reflection rather than publicity seeking. Prior to kick-off the chairs of both clubs laid wreaths in the centre circle. Additionally, FC United's junior members had raised funds and donated 30 teddy bears to the dance studio where the senseless attack took place.

After the match one of Southport's directors, who has been involved with the club for more than 30 years, messaged FC United to say, 'Today we have found a bond with a club like no other. I hope this can be a friendship for many years to come. On behalf of my chairman and my fellow directors we thank you for your love and generosity.' As one FC board member put it, 'Today we all came together and showcased our club, team and supporters at our best.'

It was important to demonstrate solidarity with the residents of Southport in the aftermath, not only with regard to the tragic loss of three young lives but also the mindless violence which followed in towns and cities across England, including Southport and Manchester. As rumours circulated on the internet that the suspect arrested following the stabbings was a Muslim asylum seeker, violent protests by far-right thugs took place across the country over the next few days which targeted mosques and hotels where asylum seekers were living.

One such incident occurred only a couple of miles down the road from Broadhurst Park when a group, some draped in England flags, gathered outside the Holiday Inn on Oldham Road in Newton Heath and shouted abuse at asylum seekers living there. Later, some people threw missiles and the riot police were called in after trouble spilled out on to the busy main road, and two men were arrested for violent disorder.

A few days after the 'protest', two members of FC United's staff delivered 50 free tickets for FC's first home match of the season the following Tuesday evening to the Holiday Inn. Sadly, none of the tickets were used. No surprise given the threatening nature of the protests would probably mean that people wouldn't feel safe making the journey to and from the ground after dark.

It was an admirable gesture by the club, designed to demonstrate solidarity with some of the most vulnerable members of its local community. But we need to give more thought to how we can build a relationship with the hotel and its residents that allows those who would like to play and/or watch football the opportunity to do just that at FC United. Football – either watching or playing – is something that can often break down cultural and linguistic barriers and those arriving in this country seeking asylum are often football fans familiar with the Premier League. We should always offer a warm welcome to people who are new to Manchester but do it in a way that recognises that people seeking asylum are unlikely to be able to afford the cost of admission or indeed very much at all inside the ground – a derisory weekly payment of £8.86 to cover the costs of clothes, medicines and travel doesn't stretch far.

* * *

In early September Jennie Swarbrick resigned as women's team manager but the club, with Jennie's help, moved quickly to appoint Sam Irvine as her replacement. Sam joined us after managing Tranmere Rovers' women's team for the last two seasons. As last summer, the timing of the change was far from perfect with the new season about to commence. Two weeks later Jennie also resigned as the club's community manager to pursue a teaching career.

Meanwhile, the men's team endured a desperately poor start to the 2024/25 season, winning only one of its opening ten matches – a 1-0 win at Morpeth on the opening day.

Adam Le Fondre scored the winner that day and while his signing was a boost for the club, the loss of several key contracted players – Curtis Jones, Michael Donohue and new goalkeeper Ollie Byrne – to injury in the first few weeks of the season was tough. Michael Donohue, a talented midfielder who'd suffered several injuries in recent seasons, decided to take a short break from football to focus on his physical and mental health. He also, very generously, made it clear that, despite being on a contract, he didn't wish to be paid during this period of recuperation.

Barely a month into the season, manager Neil Reynolds was sacked. A 1-0 home defeat to Basford on 6 September – watched by a crowd of only 1,350 – had been the final straw for many fans and in a post-match interview Reno looked and sounded like a beaten man. We needed a good performance and a win away at Warrington Rylands the following Tuesday night but a 1-1 draw was only rescued with a late equaliser. The board had agreed to meet early the following morning to discuss Neil's future but as the match drew to a close Nick Boom felt it was in everyone's interests to speak to him on the night and at least allow him to say farewell to the players.

'I waited under the main stand to speak to Neil after the match,' recalled Nick. 'I was stood rather awkwardly near some toilets when an FC fan, who I didn't recognise, came up and started chatting to me, clearly thinking I was waiting to use the toilet. "We need to sack the manager," he told me. Little did he know that's precisely what I was waiting to do.' Neil eventually emerged. 'I gave him a hug and then we sat down and I told him we were terminating his contract,' Nick added. 'Both of us were in tears. It was emotional, as you'd expect it to be. Neil had been part of the fabric of this club for six years.'

Afterwards, Neil went into the dressing room and told the players he was leaving and reminded them what a special club FC United is and urged them to make the most of their time here. He also told the players he'd had fantastic support from the board in his time at FC. 'It was Neil at his best,' said Nick, but ultimately the results told the story and one win in ten games was nowhere near good enough.

'It was important that the club and Neil parted on amicable terms and that we did it in the right way,' added Nick. 'He's been a great ambassador for FC down the years and will be welcome back at Broadhurst Park anytime.'

And that included Neil's kids, Jack and Molly, for whom FC United has been a huge part of their lives over the last six years. Jack was only nine years old when his dad began his role so he's grown up as an FC United fan and attended the vast majority of our games in recent years, while Molly used to work behind the bar on matchdays. The board invited them both to the home match against Macclesfield a few days later so they could say their own goodbyes. It was another tearful occasion. As Adrian Seddon said on The Soul is One, 'Football can be a cut-throat business but I'm proud that our club can also be quite special at times like this.'

The board moved quickly to find a new manager and after an open recruitment process Mark Beesley was appointed less than two weeks after Neil's departure. Mark had, up until recently, managed Warrington Town who he'd led to promotion to National League North having moved into management after a 15-year playing career mostly at steps one and two of non-league.

There was some 'new manager bounce' as we won 3-2 at Hyde in Mark's first match in charge and then won 3-0 at high-flying Hebburn Town in the FA Trophy a week later, but FC were still in the relegation zone at the end of November and Mark acknowledged that we were in a relegation scrap.

Meanwhile, a few days after Neil's sacking a digital image bearing the legend 'Welcome to FC United of Manchester', below an arms-outstretched goal celebration by Dontai Gabidon, had greeted commuters and shoppers heading into town on a large billboard on Ashton Old Road – a cheeky twist on the infamous poster used by Manchester City when they signed Carlos Tevez following his time at Manchester United. It was designed by the Behaviours Agency at no cost to the club and even though it was only there for a day it didn't go unnoticed by those who frequent the nearby Etihad Stadium.

* * *

The club's audited annual accounts for 2023/24 were shared with co-owners prior to the AGM on 1 December and reported an operating loss of £156,000. However, if we exclude depreciation and amortisation, the club's core trading activities showed a small operating profit of £10,000, which represents a significant improvement on the loss of £63,000 recorded in 2022/23, and it's the first time we've reported an operating profit on our core activities in a year when our finances weren't boosted by Covid-related support, since 2015/16, our first season at Broadhurst Park.

While this impressive turnaround in the club's finances had been the result of a tremendous collective effort from staff, volunteers, players, co-owners and board members, it is also also worth highlighting the efforts of our finance team, who've been quietly working away behind the scenes. Jason Chan, the club's assistant accountant, only joined in

December 2023, and despite knowing little about football finances prior to coming on board he has brought a work ethic and curiosity to his new role that attracted the admiration of his line manager Danny Davis. 'I've never known anyone ask so many questions,' says Danny.

Jason has been supported by three experienced finance professionals from the club's membership – Amit Patel, Martin Potkins and Pete Cranmer – who are all members of the club's finance and risk committee. Amit is a founder member who heads the financial management team at an NHS trust with a budget in excess of £300m, Martin is a Norfolk-based co-owner who is a very senior finance professional at BUPA, and Pete Cranmer is familiar to many FC fans as a former board member and long-standing volunteer who is also an experienced finance professional. Both Amit and Martin responded to a call-out in club newsletter *The Pink* for co-owners with finance experience to assist the club in late 2022.

But there was no time for self-congratulation. Cash flow remained a worry and at the AGM co-owners were informed that some members of staff hadn't yet been paid for November and had agreed to delay their salary payment to assist with easing the situation. The clash of home fixtures with FA Trophy and FA Cup ties meant that in the 13 weeks between 21 September and Christmas the club had only played three times at home and it's estimated that this will cost us around £40,000 in lost income as a result of matches being rearranged for midweek nights. An online 'Missing Matches' fundraiser was set up which, by mid-December, had brought in more than £18,000 of much-needed income.

Chair Nick Boom described this as a 'make or break' period in the club's history and it's crucial that we break out of the cycle of regular cash flow problems to enable us to begin repaying the debt. As the business plan for 2024/25 points out, 'The inability to generate sufficient revenue across the club to sustain regular profitability has meant we've barely been able to pay the interest, let alone any of the actual debt, on the loans with Manchester City Council.' It seems a long time ago since we used to sing about being 'the only team in Manchester that's not in debt'; the amount owing to Manchester City Council currently totals £985,000 (including accrued interest amounting to £85,000).

An initial loan of £500,000 was provided by the council to cover rising construction costs during the building of Broadhurst Park, which were compounded by delays caused by a judicial review of the planning process and led to a £2m overspend on the project. In addition, the business plan for the club's early years in its new ground was overly ambitious and set unrealistic budgets. There were also ongoing financial challenges due to unforeseen expenses associated with an unfinished and inadequately constructed stadium, which forced the club to seek additional funding via loans, overdrafts, three-year season tickets and further support from the council consisting of a loan of £250,000 in 2019 and a further loan of £150,000 in 2022. These measures were taken primarily to address cash flow difficulties but were not sustainable in the long run.

The pressure of keeping the club afloat during this period resulted in conflicts, burnout and the resignation of board members, senior managers, staff and volunteers.

In the members' survey in 2021, 58 per cent of co-owners said that paying off the club's debts should be a financial priority, but we have consistently faced challenges in meeting our interest payment obligations, let alone making any progress in repaying the principal amount. Essentially, we have struggled to maintain even the status quo and have been treading water.

A members' meeting held in June 2023 had considered two options for restructuring the debt, and co-owners had supported the 'equal instalments in principal' option which means that a fixed amount is repaid each year against the capital debt only (with a variable amount repaying annual interest) and, as the capital debt reduces, the annual interest paid also falls, which means that total annual payments reduce over time. This option was deemed to be in the best interests of the club and safeguards its future.

The council was duly informed that co-owners supported this option and we also explained the club's community value across north Manchester which, while difficult to quantify precisely, was estimated at £305,000.

Eventually the council came back to us in early September 2024 with an offer to repay the debt over a 36-year period with a 'low start' payment profile which would require us to repay £30,000 in 2024/25, £75,000 in 2025/26 and then £91,000 per year. The lower repayment amounts in the early years provide some breathing space and allow us to realise the benefits of increased commercial activity and further cost reductions.

Importantly, this refinancing agreement with the council was approved by co-owners by a show of hands at the AGM along with a board proposal that the club should use the current funds raised by the Fund the Foundations donation scheme to make our symbolic first annual payment in 2025. Fund the Foundations is a fan-led initiative, launched in 2023, that encourages supporters to make monthly donations by direct debit, which will be used exclusively to repay the club's debt, and by October

2024 it had raised £30,000. The idea was that, a bit like overpaying on a mortgage, contributions to this scheme would significantly speed up the process of the club becoming debt-free.

Bringing in an outside investor is one possible alternative option but this would mean a dilution of our supporter ownership – similar to AFC Wimbledon and Exeter City – that would be unpalatable to many co-owners. The fact that we are 100 per cent supporter-owned is something we take great pride in. The board had also considered another community share offer but given that we have so far been unable to afford to repay our existing community shareholders this wasn't deemed a viable option either.

* * *

Each year supporters purchase season tickets and donate them back to the club to be distributed to local community groups and organisations thus allowing local residents the opportunity to come to games that they might otherwise find difficult to attend. This summer the club donated season tickets for 2024/25 to a host of organisations including: a dance group for young girls; a disability football group; an organisation that supports families struggling to put food on the table; a local boxing club; a local NHS trust that works with people with mental health conditions; and several local schools.

15

The people at the club

AFTER THE defeat at Guiseley in April, a poster on The Soul is One opined that 'the people at the club' need to understand that increasing our attendances – one of the board's five key missions – is largely dependent on us playing good football. But as a reply pointed out, we are all 'the people at the club'. FC United's organisational structure begins with the supporters at the top.

While fans of top-flight clubs are increasingly treated as passive consumers, co-ownership of FC United involves participating in the life of the club. If we are unhappy with the direction that the club is taking, then we have the power to change things – that's the beauty of fan ownership: it is they who determine its future. In the past we shook our fists at the likes of the Glazers and Martin Edwards but now we're the ones in charge. The transition from angry protester to responsible owner takes some getting used to as a review of the club's management structure by three of its co-owners in 2018 highlighted.

The report spoke of how FC's development has moved beyond our initial phase as a protest club focused largely on bringing the fun back to watching football again, through a second phase which saw us focused on building our own ground to the third post-2015 phase which demands we take collective responsibility for owning and running a £1.2m turnover business and a £6.5m stadium and community facility. And, arguably, six years on from this review we're now into a fourth phase where we map out a sustainable long-term future for the club rather than treading water. 'We, the owners, need to evolve, act like owners and take our share of responsibility,' the report concluded. Subtext: grow up.

It reckoned that around a quarter of office time is spent directly or indirectly responding to queries from members – one of the hidden costs of being a supporter-owned club – and highlighted the need for a maturer approach that recognises that our resources are scarce and that, as responsible owners of a semi-professional football club, we must make the best possible use of what we have and avoid placing unrealistic demands on precious staff and volunteer time.

Meanwhile, the role of the board in all this (something also considered in the structural review in 2018) is often misunderstood, possibly because historically, for various reasons, it's been difficult at times to discern where the management team ends and the board begins. FC United finished the 2023/24 year with seven board members, although Matthew Haley resigned soon after, and I spoke to the remaining six (and general manager Danny Davis) to gauge their thoughts on the year just gone and how they'd found life on the board.

In his resignation statement, Matthew described it as 'an honour and privilege to be elected to represent the co-owners of the football club we all love' but acknowledged that it had been difficult to meet the demands and expectations that come with being a board member with a busy full-time job. Nevertheless, he continued to play an important role as a communications volunteer, something he's been doing since the summer of 2005.

Interestingly, former board chairs Tim Worrall and Adrian Seddon both reckoned that the current board is operating at 'another level' from their times as chair and there was a feeling that the changes to the club's staffing structure and the introduction of the committees has enabled the board to become more strategic.

* * *

It's half past five on a Monday evening in late September when I meet up with FC's board chair Nick Boom at Broadhurst Park – he typically spends at least one day a week in the office as he feels it's important for the chair to be visible. It's a few days after the tragic death of Paul Hilton, the 43-year-old chair of Radcliffe FC, so there's a heightened awareness of the toll that being chair of a football club can take on your health and wellbeing. A few people have mentioned to me the amount of time that Nick devotes to the club and the need for us all to look after ourselves.

'I didn't want to stand for the board,' says Nick. He lives in Leeds and also has a school-age daughter so it wasn't going to be easy to find the time for board duties. But he was 'concerned about the trajectory the club was on' and felt that it's crucial to break the cycle – that predates the club's move to Broadhurst Park – of regularly running into cash flow problems.

Nick is retired now but spent over 30 years in senior leadership roles at big financial institutions like Lloyds Bank. 'It taught me a lot about strategy, people, money and good decision-making – the sorts of skills that we need to keep FC financially stable,' he says. He's also supported charities and community groups.

He's been a co-owner since the start and, prior to joining the board, had already been volunteering for several years, including as deputy chair of the stakeholder relationships committee (which preceded what is now known as the finance and risk committee) in which he played a crucial role in building positive working relationships with the club's main stakeholders including Manchester City Council. The council now considers the club's governance to be 'the strongest it's ever been'.

Nick said he was shocked by what he saw when he was elected to the board last November – in particular the lack of any long-term strategies for the club's football teams (where do we see ourselves in five to ten years' time and how do we get there?) and its commercial operation. He believes the board should drive the rest of the club with the ultimate aim of becoming an elite sports organisation rather than just another non-league football club. Other board members were keen for Nick to take on the chair role but he pointed out that there is no point becoming chair if all we do is keep muddling along. 'We need to set ourselves up for long-term success,' he stresses.

Hence the reason for setting out the club's five key missions for the next few years at January's board meeting – which include the need to grow attendances and develop a football strategy. 'We need to be obsessional about these missions,' urged Nick. And he added that without us all working together – board, staff, volunteers and co-owners – we won't achieve the success we all desire for this club. In addition, he felt that the staff team felt 'very siloed' and wasn't aligned to the club's vision, and the committees had 'become a play pen' with little direction and purpose.

Three quarters of the way through his first year as chair, Nick feels that 'there is more purpose to board and committee discussions now' and, importantly, the club's financial reporting has improved. He added that having Bhavna Mistry on board as a non-executive director has brought challenge and fresh thinking, particularly to the club's commercial outlook.

The committee structure, established in 2022, was Nick's idea and was designed to enable co-owners, with expertise in particular areas, to make a contribution to the running of the club – especially those who don't live close to Manchester, as many of the tasks required of a committee member can be performed remotely. 'I know it's a cliche,' he says, 'but our co-owners are our greatest asset and we should make it as easy as possible for them to contribute.'

Nick also feels that the reference to co-owners, rather than members – something that Jules Spencer, who was on the club's steering committee in 2005, introduced – is important as it conveys the sense that people play an active role in the life of their club rather than being a more passive 'member'.

Typically Nick spends at least 70 to 80 hours per week on club business and sometimes works through the night – it's not unusual to receive emails from him in the early hours. He adds that not all of this is necessarily board-related as he also line manages the club's general manager Danny Davis and oversees relationships with the likes of Moston Juniors. 'I try to be the quiet public face of FC United,' he says.

Nick would like to see the club bring in sufficient revenue to enable it to double its playing budget over the next few years. It's crucial that we do this, he says, if we are to remain competitive on the pitch given the extent to which semi-professional football has changed over the last few years.

'What happens on the pitch matters,' he says and it was important that we've been able to set out the club's football strategy this year. Up to now 'we've effectively been appointing managers and hoping for the best' he said but it clearly hasn't worked as the club has stagnated somewhat in the Northern Premier League and operates with a smaller playing budget than most clubs at the same level. 'If we don't address this, then there is a risk that we end up in a downward spiral and ultimately we might not have a club at all,' Nick adds.

He reckons that the worst aspect of being on the board is 'the cynicism of some supporters who feel they can have a free swing at you', especially online. And he recalls Warren Heppolette's comment about the worst moment of his week being when he logs on to the message board. Nick adds that while scrutiny and criticism is always welcome, it needs to be done in a constructive way – too often it feels like some supporters are searching for a 'gotcha' moment.

Nick feels that we're generally well received by other clubs. 'In the past we were often perceived to be arrogant,' he says, continuing, 'We're more humble now and more open to talking about the challenges we face, which tends to be welcomed by other directors.' He adds, 'We've matured from being a protest vehicle to become a more collaborative, campaigning club on key issues that affect supporter-owned clubs and non-league clubs in general. We've demonstrated that on several occasions over the last year.'

* * *

Amid the hubbub of post-work drinks in the Britons Protection pub in Manchester city centre, the club's deputy chair Warren Heppolette tells me that being on the board has heightened his enjoyment of games as he feels a sense of pride in knowing that he's played a key part in making it possible for those 11 players representing FC United to take to the field. When the board learns, that 'We're going to sign a new player but we need to find £1,500, it feels like we're at the sharp end of something vaguely glamorous,' he smiles.

And he adds, 'We shouldn't forget the simple pleasure of standing beside a patch of grass on a Saturday afternoon or midweek evening watching a game of football and finding a release from the stresses and strains of everyday life.' Music also provides a release for Warren and, in his X bio, he describes himself as 'a Fall fan and post-punk obsessive'.

In his day job Warren is the chief officer for strategy at NHS Greater Manchester, a demanding role in which he typically works at least 70 hours a week, and he was instrumental in the trailblazing 'Devo Manc' deal a decade ago that gave Greater Manchester greater control of a range of public services including health and social care. Aside from being a director of FC United, he is also a trustee of two charitable organisations.

Despite such a high-profile full-time job, Warren estimates that he spends, on average, up to 15 hours per week on FC-related tasks, which typically includes an hour each evening checking and replying to emails and a full day on Sunday. Despite this commitment he says he still often feels guilty that he isn't able to devote more time to FC, particularly when things aren't going well and we need all hands on deck. 'They are all things I believe in,' says Warren, 'so I don't begrudge putting the hours in.'

He's worked in the public sector for more than 25 years having been a neighbourhood housing officer prior to joining the NHS in 2006. On entering the health service, one of the first things he did was read Michael Foot's biography of the founder of the NHS, Nye Bevan, to understand what Bevan was thinking when he created it. It's shaped Warren's perspective on the NHS ever since and he reckons that there are similarities with being a director at FC United – there's the same need to marry the club's strategy, two decades on, with its original ideology. Warren adds that while it's important that we recruit board members with the right skills and capabilities, 'We mustn't lose sight of our original ideology.'

When it comes to recruiting new board members – something that we've tended to struggle with over the last five or six years – Warren feels that the introduction of committees has helped and he reckoned that there's probably a pool of around 20 possible future board members from the club's six committees at present. Although he acknowledged that there is a need to replenish the committees with co-owners who have expertise in some areas such as legal matters.

In the past Warren feels that co-owners might have been put off standing for the board through the fear of putting themselves in the firing line but he reckoned that now the board is operating more strategically and the club is more stable, the main factor deterring possible board candidates might be the time commitment.

A common theme of my conversation with Warren is the need for co-owners to be conscious of their responsibilities. He feels that too many of us still see ourselves as consumers, rather than participants in the running of the club, and often end up ranting about the board and management team like we would've done years ago about the likes of David Gill and Martin Edwards. 'Unlike most football supporters we don't have that luxury,' reckons Warren. For instance, one of the persistent worries for the board is the club's cash flow but he doesn't feel that this concern is necessarily matched by co-owners – 'consciousness needs to exist at a certain level for us to operate successfully'.

Warren feels that the fact that we are still able to exist as a 100 per cent fan-owned club, 20 years on, should be seen as a success: 'We're a unique, well-respected club with a multinational following – it's something to be proud of.' However, he's concerned about FC's debt and the fact that it may take another three or four decades to pay it off but, at the same time, he felt that the club's sound working relationship with Manchester City Council has given it a much better chance of it still being around in 50 years' time.

Warren played a key role, as a member of the club's stakeholder relationships committee (now known as the finance and risk committee), in helping the club to reach an agreement in December 2019 that committed it to working in partnership with the council and strengthened the club's long-term future by allowing it to refinance its debt and draw on a new loan of up to £250,000. The deal recognised the professional way in which the club was now being run and its finances managed.

As for the club's democratic health, Warren feels this again comes back to how conscious co-owners are of their responsibilities. He reckons that if this consciousness is high, then co-owners will read monthly board reports and vote at general meetings. But he acknowledged that we might have reached a point where we have a professionally run club overseen by a competent, strategically minded board that results in co-owners putting their trust in the board and disengaging, to some extent, from the club's democratic processes. Does he think that's a good thing?

'There's no point in being fan-owned if we're not also fan-influenced', he cautioned.

* * *

Paul Hurst is the supporter interviewed by the Sky reporter at Wimbledon in the opening paragraph to this book. Nearly two decades on he's not only acquired a big coat but was also elected to the board of FC United last November. In a coffee shop close to Piccadilly station he tells me that without being involved in the co-ownership committee beforehand he probably wouldn't have stood for the board.

Paul reckons, 'Being involved in a committee gives you a much better feel for the work of the board and whether being a board member would suit you or not.' It's not for everyone and it's important that supporters find a role which suits them – whether that's being a volunteer, committee member or board director. In the past we often saw people elected to the board who subsequently found, after a few meetings, that it wasn't for them.

Paul is a founder member of FC and has been a volunteer from the start, writing for the matchday programme and also selling it. FC has very much been a family thing for Paul – he went to games with his dad in the early days (both his parents had season tickets at Old Trafford but ended up following FC) and nowadays he brings his four-year-old daughter to games.

But he says that the variety of issues that the board has to deal with has surprised him. For example, only a few weeks after being elected he was involved in preparing a club statement to the Northern Premier League regarding the charge that we had fielded an ineligible player last November. Paul has some legal knowledge so offered to help out.

On joining the board last December he became the board's lead on the co-ownership committee and recently, following Matthew Haley's resignation, he also took on interim responsibility as the lead for communications. It's been a difficult period for the club's communications and Paul admits that he has found it frustrating at times – particularly with concerns from some communications volunteers that the board interferes too much.

Paul explains that we need to get better at not only announcing player departures but explaining the reasoning behind these moves – which is why he's recently begun penning a weekly squad update that is posted on the members' forum and has been well received by supporters so far. Paul has for several years ghostwritten the manager's column in the matchday programme so he's familiar with the manager's thoughts on his squad.

When FC was born in 2005 the communications landscape was very different to now – Twitter and Instagram weren't around, Facebook was in its infancy and Myspace was the first social media service to attract a global audience. Paul feels that the club's communications have struggled to keep up with the latest trends – if we're serious about attracting younger supporters, then sharing video content on the likes of YouTube and TikTok are the best ways to do that but we've barely got a presence on either. Paul is also keen for us to link up with local universities and get students involved in our communications.

There are always going to be situations where the board will have to offer direction to the communications team regarding specific communications – as was the case with the pre-season friendly at Southport where we had agreed a specific statement with the host club on what was an emotional day.

In terms of his time commitment, Paul reckons he spends, on average, a minimum of two hours per day on FC-related business, which isn't easy on top of a full-time job as a project manager and looking after a young daughter. He describes how, on a recent family holiday in Scotland, he sat outside in the car for nearly two hours attending an online meeting of the co-ownership committee as space where they were staying was limited and a local bar didn't have an internet connection. 'You need an understanding partner,' smiles Paul.

* * *

'I was ready to stand down at the 2022 AGM,' Dave Ashurst tells me, 'but when I phoned Viv [the club secretary at the time, Viv Ware] on the deadline day for board candidacies she said that no one else was standing.' Dave ended up standing for election again as, in his own words, 'I didn't want to leave other board members in the lurch.' Dave is the longest-serving member of the current board having been elected to the board in 2020 and he's now coming to the end of the second of his two-year terms.

Prior to being elected to the board Dave was one third of an interim management team that looked after the club following Damian Chadwick's departure as CEO in 2018. He focused on the commercial side while John Bentley managed the ground and facilities and Luc Zentar took care of the office.

He reckons that, on average, he spends around 40 hours per month on board-related business with a further four or five hours per month liaising with the Northern Premier League. Dave's retired now after a long career in IT consultancy which included spells at large multinational companies and also running his own business for a while.

Dave is the board's lead for liaising with the Northern Premier League and he's been on the league's board for over two years. It comprises a mixture of independent members and club representatives and Dave laughs, 'When I joined I was one of the board's younger members – and I was in my mid-60s.' His time on the NPL board has demonstrated how FC's structure and governance is pretty much unique in this league. 'We've got a pretty good relationship with other clubs and directors,' says Dave, 'but it's noticeable how the directors at some clubs are much more operational, which means that they are often busy on matchdays with only a limited amount of time to chat in the boardroom.'

Dave points out how we've tried to speak out more on important issues affecting supporter-owned and lower-league clubs over the last year or so. For many years after moving into Broadhurst Park we struggled to find the time to campaign. Following a recent meeting with Kevin Miles at the FSA, Dave said that he'd also spoken to Andy Walsh, FC United's original CEO and now the FSA's lead for community-owned clubs, and we'll be looking to work with two other fan-owned clubs – Exeter City and Bury – to campaign on key issues affecting us. 'We are still seen as a leading light in the supporter ownership movement,' says Dave.

Are we a good example of how supporters can run football clubs? 'Yes, I think so, but it depends on how we measure success,' he adds. The level of participation across the club whether in volunteering, working on one of the club's committees or voting at general meetings (where turnout has risen to around 30 per cent following the introduction of online voting) is impressive.

* * *

Bhavna Mistry is a rare example of a female British Asian on the board of a football club and, on a Teams call, she admits that she knew nothing about football when she first joined. So how on earth did she end up on the board of FC United? 'I found out about the role through my husband who had done some work for the club and had connected with then commercial manager Frances Fielding on LinkedIn. He saw that FC was looking for someone with a marketing and commercial background to join the board and told me about it.

'I was looking to establish my board career as I'd like to work full-time in board roles when I retire. Anyway, I sent in my CV and was interviewed and, in the end, they couldn't decide between Gemma [Avery] and myself so they offered us both a role.' Since joining FC United, Bhavna has also taken on another role as a trustee of an examining board.

Bhavna says she found it difficult when she first joined, not knowing what to expect, and she describes her first board meeting in July 2023 as 'chaotic'. 'There were no figures to make decisions on and the CEO struggled to answer the board's questions,' she says. Bhavna left her first board meeting wondering 'what have I let myself in for here'.

She says the last year has been a difficult period for the club with key members of staff departing and, as a result, board members have had to become involved in the operational side of the club at times. Bhavna had previously been the director of a multinational business and was used to taking difficult decisions so none of this fazed her.

'I'm used to working in family-run businesses so to be answerable to more than 2,000 football club owners has been very different,' she says, 'but ultimately the basics of running a business are still the same.' She feels that the current chair Nick Boom has been 'brilliant at running the club like a proper business. He understands the importance of process, procedures and good governance.'

Bhavna says that as someone who has come in from outside the club she can be more objective in her decision-making. 'My bottom line is always about what is best for the club and whether it makes sense commercially,' she says. 'That's what I was brought on to the board for.'

One of the things Bhavna noticed in her early days at FC was 'how passionate people are about their football club. I've been overwhelmed with how generous people are with their time and money to support something that they love and really believe in.'

On the commercial front she feels that while the club has the plans and strategy in place to grow – 'the foundations are there' she says – we struggle because we haven't got enough staff and so are very reliant on volunteers to get things done. But inevitably the amount of time volunteers can devote to the club is limited. And she adds that while she admires the club's stance on commercialism she feels, 'It does hinder us when it comes to bringing money in. It limits who we can go to for sponsorship.'

We identified a need to employ someone to manage the club shop in the review of the club's merchandise that Bhavna undertook earlier this year but haven't been able to do anything about this due to the perennial cash flow difficulties. This emphasises again the need to break out of this cycle of regular cash flow problems so that we can invest to move the club forward. 'The danger is it could become a vicious circle if we don't,' says Bhavna.

She also adds that we shouldn't forget how precarious the wider economy has been over the last few years and this impacts on other businesses too, 'They're feeling the pinch just like us, and some are having to make redundancies and be cautious when it comes to spending.' And that affects us too when it comes to seeking sponsorship.

One thing that has surprised Bhavna is the impact the club has on its wider community and the local economy. 'It's been a real eye-opener for me,' she says, 'how much impact we have on people's lives beyond just football – through the academy, our community programme and the use of our facilities.' We bring a lot of value to the local community. 'But many of our supporters probably don't necessarily realise this,' she adds, 'as we don't tend to publicise it.'

* * *

'It's addictive,' says Simon Preston as he tells me how he's enjoyed his time on the board since he was elected in November 2023. By being on the board he feels like he's at the heart of the running of the club and driving it forward. 'I've loved football ever since I was four or five years old, so to get this insight into the workings of a football club is great,' he says.

Nevertheless, Simon adds that it's been stressful at times. 'It often feels like you're carrying the weight of two and a half thousand people,' he says, 'and whenever we're faced with a decision I always think about what's in the best interests of the club.' But he feels, 'It can be demoralising at times reading some of the comments on the forums and social media.'

Simon works full-time in his day job as an account executive at a large car dealership so it can often be difficult finding the time to devote to board duties with evenings often taken up by FC-related tasks rather than relaxing with family. And, like Nick, he lives in Yorkshire so there's travelling time to factor in too.

As a board member, Simon reckons that he watches matches in a different way and victories don't just bring joy on the pitch and terraces but are important for boosting attendances in the future and help with bar and shop takings. 'I end up constantly looking at my phone during home games,' he says, 'checking on things like the attendance and thinking about what that means for our matchday revenue.'

'I'm a bit of a sponge at away games,' Simon continues, 'as I like to learn from the directors of other clubs about how they run their clubs and absorb as much information as I can.' He said it's been interesting to hear about how several other clubs have installed 3G pitches to reduce the impact of losing matches to the weather and also to host more fixtures.

Simon says that of all the clubs he's met over the last year or so he particularly admires Marine as they've invested the money they generated from their FA Cup run a few years ago wisely – installing a 3G pitch and upgrading their clubhouse which has become a valuable space for functions and events for the club's local community.

As the board's football lead, Simon speaks to Brian Richardson, the director of football, pretty much every day and he also spoke to Neil Reynolds regularly too. It's a challenging role. With the introduction of men's and women's development squads we've got more teams now. Hours of work went into developing the club's first football strategy.

And, as a member of the commercial committee, Simon reckons that we're still under-performing hugely on the commercial front. In the past we tended to be purely transactional when it came to bringing in commercial revenue but he feels that our new emphasis on forming partnerships with businesses and organisations should be the way forward.

Simon points out that we've had some success on the merchandise front, particularly with the home shirt with the names of hundreds of our co-owners on it, of which we sold around 1,000. In comparison, we've so far sold around 300 of the current home shirt. And he says that he really likes the fact that we have involved our junior members in designing the third kit for the 2025/26 season by running a competition for kids to submit their designs and then turning those initial ideas into four shirts for co-owners to vote on at the AGM.

These are the fans who are most likely to end up wearing a replica shirt so why shouldn't they be involved in designing it? Up to now we've tended to be pretty conservative in our shirt designs – too often striving to recreate a Jimmy Greenhoff in 1979 vibe for an ageing fanbase – but this will shake things up a bit and that's no bad thing.

Simon says that when he does eventually step down from the board he'd like to be able to look back and take pride in having played an important part in building a solid foundation from which the club can continue to flourish for generations to come.

* * *

'It's been a rollercoaster,' says Danny Davis of his first year at FC United. He joined as commercial manager in May 2023 having found out about the position from his predecessor Frances Fielding. Then within a matter of weeks the CEO Natalie Atkinson departed and Danny was appointed as general manager. It's a role he wanted to do although not quite so soon after joining the club. But he says he's had excellent support and mentoring from his line manager Nick Boom. Prior to joining FC, Danny had been a commercial manager for eight years at Blackburn Rovers (his local team) where he sold hundreds of thousands of pounds of advertising and sponsorship deals. He also spent ten years living and working in Tenerife, which he describes as his 'university of life'.

'The board has professionalised the way it works and I want to be able to deliver on the targets we've set,' says Danny, so, under Nick's tutelage, there's been a strong focus on his personal development and he's taking part in sessions run by the Greater Manchester Business Growth Hub that helps businesses across the conurbation 'unlock and develop their creative potential'. 'My wife thinks I'm going through a mid-life crisis,' he laughs.

A colleague at Blackburn once advised him that 'in football there'll always be someone who wants to have a pop at you' and these words perhaps apply even more so at FC United with more than 2,000 co-owners, many of whom reckon they are experts on how to run a football club.

Although we managed to generate a small operating profit on core activities in 2023/24, cash flow remains a problem, and Danny acknowledges that through the winter months there were times when we weren't sure whether we would have enough to pay staff wages at the end of the month. He adds that it's crucial that we begin to build cash reserves to fund capital projects in future.

Danny puts the improvement in our financial position in 2023/24 down to initiatives like the FA Cup Final screening and inviting Bury to play a home game at Broadhurst Park, which boosted our coffers towards the end of the season. But he feels that we need to get better at hosting functions and events. 'Most football clubs are in a locality where people have grown up close to the club,' he says, but that's not the case with FC. 'We need to become the go-to venue for events across north Manchester.'

One of the big differences to working at an EFL club is the large number of volunteers on which FC United is reliant and, while this is a tremendous asset, Danny feels that it occasionally presents problems as some volunteers prefer to do things their own way rather than what's best for the club.

One of the successes of the last year has been the introduction of the Fanbase ticketing system and Danny would like to see as many supporters as possible use it and buy their tickets for the match in advance 'to help us plan matchdays'. And while we'll always allow supporters to pay for their admission and everything else that goes with matchday by cash, Danny notes that there has been a significant increase in the number of card transactions across the club – during the nine-month period from September 2023 to June 2024, 72 per cent of transactions at FC United were paid for by card.

As well as being in the office during the working week, Danny also works on Saturdays when we're at home – typically arriving at Broadhurst Park at midday and leaving shortly after the final whistle – making sure that everything runs smoothly, which includes a host of tasks from fixing broken printers and blown fuses to making sure that the toilets are clean and the function room is ready for any post-match events. 'The "general" in general manager is very apt,' he laughs. He brings both of his daughters to home matches and both are junior members and part of the ball crew. 'They love it,' says Danny.

16

This is the club
I've grown up with

'BY FAR and away the driest, dullest, deadest members' meeting ever,' reckoned one of the 20 attendees at an online meeting at the end of August to discuss the ongoing work to update FC United's rules to reflect its status as a community benefit society. From the 2005 defiance of 'our club, our rules' – a slogan which, combined with a raised fist, adorned one of the club's most popular T-shirts down the years – to the administrative burden of having to update those rules (which probably won't inspire any new clothing ranges) provides a neat snapshot of the club's protester-to-responsible-owner evolution over the last two decades.

And we got another 2005 flashback in early November 2024 as FC's away match at Leek Town provided a trip down memory lane for many of us as the home side's Harrison Park ground was the venue for our inaugural league match, in August 2005, when a crowd of 2,590 saw us make our debut in the North West Counties Football League against Leek County School Old Boys who were ground sharing with Leek Town at the time.

There were no television cameras or reporters to greet us at the turnstiles this time but beneath a rooftop advert for a local supplier of 'specialist floor adhesives and floor preparation products' several hundred FC United fans roared their team on to a battling 2-1 win after going behind early, just as we had done 19 years earlier. The words to a wonderful new addition to the songbook, sung to the tune of 'Sweet Child O' Mine' by Guns N' Roses, hung in the damp Staffordshire air as a hymn to the last 19 years.

I always smile when I'm at FC
Reminds me of childhood memories
Before the Glazers
And Murdoch or Sky
With tears of joy running down my face
Because Broadhurst Park is a special place
This love for the club I have
Will never die

It was a shame, as manager Mark Beesley noted, that FC didn't manage to score at the end where most of the away support was located – the 'limbs', as the youngsters say, would've been a sight to behold. But it was a terrific day out that was neatly summed up in a post on The Soul is One that read: 'If you think FC United "isn't the same any more" you should have been at Leek Town away.'

Nineteen years earlier I'd watched Manchester United's lunchtime game in a pub in Leek town centre before heading to Harrison Park but nowadays, except occasional highlights on *Match of the Day*, I barely see any United matches and my knowledge of goings-on at Old Trafford is mostly gleaned from social media and the pages and podcasts of the *United We Stand* and *Red News* fanzines.

Even by the appalling standards of the last 20 years, the news, in the last week of November 2024, that Manchester United were raising the price of tickets for the remainder of the 2024/25 season to £66, even for kids, was grim. Even if it was

275

only for the three per cent of tickets that were still available for sale for this season, the optics were abysmal, particularly when the club was also making dozens of working-class Mancunians redundant. And it was exacerbated by Jim Ratcliffe attempting to justify the price increase by suggesting that 'it doesn't make sense for a Manchester United ticket to cost less than a ticket to see Fulham' in an interview with *United We Stand* editor Andy Mitten.

Manchester's booming city centre with its skyscrapers and luxury apartments may resemble London in some respects but it remains a proudly working-class city and the second-most deprived local authority in England – charging local kids £66 to attend a football match is borderline class war as Baz (Jonathan Cardoza) noted in his introduction to Course You Can Malcolm ahead of the match against Mickleover at the end of November.

FC United condemned the price rise as another example of 'fan exploitation' and called on United's owners 'to properly engage with fan groups and forums and to listen to the grave concerns of our fellow United fans already struggling to afford to go to Old Trafford'. And it reminded United supporters that they are 'always welcome to sample the club created by United fans and for United fans, in the image of what Manchester United should be'.

One match-going United fan who has sampled plenty of FC United fixtures down the years is Matt Ford, who is a regular contributor to *United We Stand* and a freelance football journalist based in Germany who's written for several publications and websites including *The Guardian* and BBC Sport.He also reported on FC's 'civil war' in 2016 for *Mancunian Matters* and, more recently, on the club's trailblazing in the Fenix Trophy for the French football magazine *So Foot*.

I spoke to Matt the week before the price rise at United was announced and he described the relationship between the two clubs as 'two equivalent expressions of the red, white and black football fan culture in Manchester' given that they share the same roots. He reckoned that 'anyone who shares this fan culture should be proud that both clubs exist', and also remarked on how the pair complement each other as, while Manchester United is an enormous global brand, FC United is community-focused and affordable. 'FC United provides an antidote to all the things we don't like about Manchester United,' says Matt.

Matt noted that among United's match-going support there's been a noticeable shift in how FC are perceived over the last decade, particularly as managers have come and gone and it's gradually dawned on many United fans that the club's problems are deep-rooted and sit with its owners. There's been a recognition that those fans who left the club in 2005 to form FC United might have had a point after all regarding the Glazers' ownership.

And to think that, as the Glazers appeared to be finally heading for the exit at Old Trafford in 2023, some people were even questioning FC United's right to exist. FC's statement on the price hike at Old Trafford reaffirmed the club's commitment to providing affordable football and doing everything in its power to ensure that prices remain as affordable as possible to as wide a constituency of supporters as possible.

Interestingly, FC United's co-owners voted in favour of raising the admission price for adults from £13 to £15 and for concessions from £9 to £10.50 for the 2025/26 season at the AGM in December 2024. Like all clubs, FC has faced a significant increase in its costs over the last few years and it also needs to provide a competitive playing budget and be able to meet its various financial obligations, in particular the need to repay the club's debts. The price of admission for 18-to-21-year-olds will, however, remain the same at £5, with the price for under-18s also remaining unchanged at £3.

Around this time, a television documentary by the legendary Dutch football presenter Tom Egbers was aired in the Netherlands that captured the spirit of the club wonderfully. Egbers had visited Broadhurst Park for a match in September and had interviewed current board member Paul Hurst and former board member George Baker and explored the relationship between the two Uniteds. He seemed to thoroughly embrace FC and what it stands for.

In December the club also featured in *Diario Sport*, a Spanish daily sports newspaper, after journalist Iker Lloveras had visited Broadhurst Park for the match against Mickleover at the end of November and had spoken to Chantal Adams, George Baker and Matthew Haley from the communications committee. A video accompanying Iker's article, which was shared by *Diario Sport* on social media, was viewed more than two million times, and Chantal, who manages FC's Instagram account, noted that the club attracted 13,000 new Instagram followers, mainly from Spain and other Spanish-speaking countries, in the space of three days after the article and video were published. The communications team quickly got to work in creating some Spanish language content to tell these new followers all about the club.

Both visits from abroad offered a reminder of how FC United's story resonates with football fans across Europe and beyond and Matt Ford told me, 'In Germany there is a lot of respect for FC United and what it stands for.' He continued, '[I] first met two long-standing German footballing friends at an FC United match at Stalybridge ten years ago – one supports FC Köln and the other is a Borussia Dortmund fan and they'd both travelled over to England to take in an FC match.'

With co-owners in 45 different countries including as far afield as China, USA, Japan, Australia and New Zealand, it's doubtful if any other football club has a more cosmopolitan ownership than FC United. And despite living thousands of miles from Broadhurst Park many of these co-owners are able to play an active role in the life of the club whether it's as a committee member, an observer at a board meeting or regularly contributing ideas on the members' forum.

A football club, like any organisation or business, evolves over time and the FC United of 2024 isn't the same as the club in 2005. Just as if you wound the clock back a further 20 years from the mid-2000s, then the Manchester United of 1985 is barely recognisable from the United of 2005. In an era of saturated television coverage of football it's easy to forget that United's record start to a league campaign in the autumn of 1985 – in which they won their first ten league games playing swashbuckling football – is largely recalled only by those who were at the matches as there was barely any live coverage on television at the time. English teams were also banned from European competition in 1985 – and didn't return until 1990 – yet four decades on, three teams from English football's seventh tier competed in a European tournament for non-league clubs in 2023/24.

Similarly the make-up of a club's support shifts over time and FC United is no different. There's been a noticeable shift, as we've seen, in how some fans perceive what is and isn't acceptable, when it comes to commercial activities for instance. The club has matured and we've become more responsible, and it feels like we can debate important topics, such as admission prices and the commercial strategy, without risking tearing the club apart. And we have also become more open and transparent since 2016 so, as a result, more participative. The club expects much more from its co-owners than in the early years and the level of participation in the running of the club – typified by the committees – is perhaps greater than it's ever been.

In recent years we've also become more collaborative – looking for like-minded clubs to work with on key issues – and less combative. Some view this as a loss of the 'punk football' spirit of 2005 but to label us as 'just another football club', as some have done, is well wide of the mark.

Back in 2005 I was convinced that other supporters might follow our example – particularly Liverpool fans, politicised by years of fighting for justice for victims of the Hillsborough disaster. So it wasn't a surprise when, three years later, a group of Liverpool supporters formed their own club, AFC Liverpool, offering football for a fiver to those who couldn't afford to go along to Anfield any more. But it was made clear at the time that the club had not been established in opposition to the ownership and running of Liverpool – instead it was hoped that it 'could become a little brother to Liverpool FC' – and Rick Parry, the then chief executive of the Anfield club, wrote to AFC to offer his backing. 'There is every reason to believe we can co-exist and co-operate,' he said and he wished the new fan-owned club 'the best of luck'. Quite a contrast to FC United's relationship with Manchester United.

A decade and a half on, however, AFC Liverpool are still in the North West Counties League, crowds have dwindled – in recent years attendances have typically been in the 100–150 range – and the club is yet to find a home of its own. It puts into perspective what FC United has achieved over the last two decades.

When Exeter City celebrated 20 years of being supporter-owned in 2023 their chair Nick Hawker told *The Guardian* that success 'doesn't have to be on the pitch. It can be good financial performance, what you do in the community, how you treat your supporters.' And he added, 'If all you're worried about is how you feel at five o'clock on a Saturday, then you're wasting a huge opportunity.'

There have been plenty of times when we've been miserable at 5pm on a Saturday over the last few seasons but when you own, as well as support, a football club, there's a bigger picture to see beyond simply what happens on the pitch.

On the pitch, while the men's and women's teams both had disappointing 2023/24 league campaigns, they nevertheless both won cup competitions and the academy side finished as league champions to complete an unlikely treble which, oddly, was mirrored across town by Manchester United's men's, women's and academy teams.

Off the pitch a return to profitability for the first time in five years (ignoring the Covid period when the club received external financial support) was encouraging and no mean feat given the dire financial position that many clubs found themselves in, with the likes of Marske United, Nuneaton Town, Coalville Town and Loughborough Dynamo all resigning from their leagues during the 2023/24 season. The improvement in FC's finances provides a foundation for being able to, finally, begin paying off the club's debt from 2024/25 onwards. But it's crucial that we break the cycle of regular cash flow problems.

The current board is perhaps the strongest we've ever had and, importantly, is thinking strategically rather than fighting fires. The club has a long-term vision and strategies for improving performance on the pitch and off it. But we've struggled again commercially and we've also endured a high turnover of key members of staff.

When more than 700 FC United co-owners participated in a survey in 2021 that asked where we'd like to see the club in five years' time, the majority, not surprisingly, said they'd like to see us promoted. But providing an affordable and sustainable alternative to big football, a vibrant matchday atmosphere and doing our bit for our local community were seen as important too.

And that community needs us. While in many respects Manchester is booming, the data on life expectancy across the city makes for grim reading. If you ranked the more than 300 local authorities in England from top to bottom based on average life expectancy, then Manchester, with an average life expectancy of 75 years, is firmly in the relegation zone. Only Blackpool has a lower average life expectancy, at 73, while Wokingham in Berkshire sits top of the table with an average life expectancy of 83.

And if we zoom in and look at healthy life expectancy – the average number of years a person would expect to live in good health – the gaps are similarly stark. Shockingly, men in Miles Platting, Newton Heath and Harpurhey have a healthy life expectancy of barely 50 – close to the worst of the nearly 7,000 electoral wards in England – while the average across England is 62.

You don't have to be an expert on health service policy to join the dots and understand why Greater Manchester currently has the largest financial deficit of any local health system in England. Poor housing, badly paid and insecure jobs, lack of education, pollution and lack of access to green space significantly shortens the amount of time that someone lives in good health and, as a result, means that they inevitably require the support of local NHS services for much longer than someone who resides in a more affluent area. And with that comes an increased financial cost to the health service. Meanwhile, evidence shows that after a decade and a half of austerity these health inequalities are getting worse.

If we're going to close the gap in healthy life expectancy between Manchester and the rest of the country, then FC United's Broadhurst Park home in Moston with its football pitches, on-site gym and academy that offer a source of recreation and learning for local people, young and old, and its function room and other spaces, which offer the opportunity for social connection, have a crucial role to play.

More than 30,000 people use the club's 3G pitch annually and it runs a multitude of activities that aim to improve people's health and wellbeing: twice weekly 'bootcamp' fitness sessions that combine cardiovascular and strength training; yoga sessions; disability football; walking football; Wildcats football sessions for girls; school holiday camps for children who receive free school meals; and a long-standing Sporting Memories Group that meets weekly and offers an important social connection for people aged 50 and over. The leader of Manchester City Council, Bev Craig, has urged FC to become the focal point for north Manchester.

The main challenge that the club faces to achieving its goals, like all fan-owned clubs, is money. A wealthy owner can cover losses and pump cash in when it's needed but at a fan-owned club it's less straightforward. While we generated a small operating profit on core activities in 2023/24, cash flow remains a cause of sleepless nights for the board and management team. And it holds the club back when it comes to investing in improving facilities and strengthening a lean staffing structure – investments that would pay for themselves over time but require cash to make them happen in the first place. Not to mention the need to begin paying our debts.

The board recognises this and in setting out its priorities for the next few years, growing attendances and improving commercial performance will be crucial to boosting cash flow and ultimately repaying debt. It makes no sense that in a football-mad city and at a time when attendances at non-league level are booming, as more people are priced out of big football, our attendances are declining.

Realistically, there's probably a limit to what fan-owned clubs can achieve in the current environment. Exeter City Supporters' Trust, for instance, declared in its 2021/22 annual report that for them this level now 'appears to be EFL League One'. But for clubs that are wholly owned by their supporters that ceiling is probably National League level right now.

And it's clear that FC United won't be troubling the upper tiers of English football anytime soon. How can we get anywhere near that level when the financial odds are so clearly stacked against supporter-owned clubs? Manchester United's 2023/24 accounts revealed that the club spent nearly £40m on legal fees and other costs relating to Jim Ratcliffe's acquisition of a minority stake, which is more than FC United have spent in our entire 19-year history even including the £6.5m cost of building our own ground.

The Football Governance Bill and the introduction of an independent football regulator offers hope that things might change. But, as was highlighted in a recent call with the chief executive of the Football Supporters' Association, Kevin Miles, we would need to see a fairer distribution of football's wealth across the entire football pyramid – not just down to the National League.

So, 20 years on, have we achieved our original aim of being a good example of how a club can be run in the interests of its members and be of benefit to its local communities? The fact that we're still here after two decades, providing a beacon for fan ownership as the largest football club in the country wholly owned by its supporters, is surely a positive.

FC's formation was about much more than the fight against the Glazers – it was about building a sustainable fan-owned club and showing that fans can own and run clubs that are at the heart of their communities – and disproving the old-fashioned notion that only fabulously wealthy individuals can own and run clubs. Supporter ownership is a modern phenomenon – at the turn of the century there weren't any fan-owned clubs in England – and we're striving to redefine modern football.

There are some important broader messages too in owning and running a club collectively. We've seen how a club with more than 2,000 co-owners has a vast array of skills, knowledge and experience to draw on, whether it's laying bricks, crunching numbers, designing websites, writing copy, fixing electrics or as a senior executive in a multinational corporation.

And with this collective ownership model comes empowerment. As co-owners, we're not treated as mere customers dictated to by a distant super-rich owner but instead are able to participate in the running of the club and exert a collective power that is often denied us in other areas of our lives. And the club also empowers its local community not only in its extensive community work but also through its academy, its role as a local employer (in 2014

FC United became the first football club in the country to become a Living Wage employer) and the countless volunteering opportunities it offers. We shouldn't consign people to the low-paid drudgery of working lives spent generating more wealth for the wealthy, packing boxes in warehouses, stacking shelves in supermarkets or answering phones in a call centre. We're better than that.

And as for the club's impact on its local community, let's finish, like we started, with a question from a journalist. During his visit to Broadhurst Park last September the Dutch television presenter Tom Egbers spoke to a young lad who had just been playing football on the 3G pitch adjacent to the stadium with his mates and asked him, if he ever got the chance to play for FC United or Manchester United in the future, 'Which one would you choose?'

'To be fair, honestly, FC United,' the boy smiled. 'I'd rather play for my home team than a big team and this is the club I've grown up with.'

I daresay that he may have been trying extra-hard to be polite in his reply but nevertheless it illustrates how far we've come as a club in the last two decades that there are now local youngsters who've grown up with FC United and see us as their local team. To 'encourage young and local participation' was one of our founding principles.

We've got a long way to go to realise this club's full potential but thanks to an extraordinary collective effort by staff, volunteers, board members, players, co-owners and supporters, it feels like we can look forward with renewed optimism that this club, just like the one formed down the road by railway workers in 1878, will be around as a source of recreation, learning and matchday thrills for generations to come. This thing of ours, 20 years on, is still something special.

Acknowledgements

THANKS TO everyone who very generously gave their time to talk to me about this book: Dave Ashurst, Nick Boom, Lynette Cawthra (who also very kindly helped out by proofreading an almost-final version of the text), Andy Davies, Danny Davis, Matt Ford, Paul Haworth, Warren Heppolette, Paul Hurst, Bhavna Mistry, Simon Preston, Adrian Seddon and Jake Worrall.

Thanks also to Lewis Mckenna, FC United's volunteer photographer, for supplying all the photos that appear in this book and also the image on the front cover.

And thanks to Nadim Hammad for crunching the numbers on FC United's membership in 2023/24 which was more complicated than it sounds as, for a while, he was unable to export data from the relevant database for analysis.

I'd also like to thank Jane Camillin at Pitch Publishing and Duncan Olner, Gareth Davis, Andrea Dunn and Graham Hales for their support, advice and graft in helping to turn this book into reality.

I would also like to thank the *Manchester Mill* for giving me permission to use the content of an article I wrote for them in 2023 about Course You Can Malcolm ('The best club night you've ever been to on a Saturday afternoon').

And, last but certainly not least, thanks to my partner Maeve Stevenson for her love and support, as ever, through the 18 months I've been working on this book.